# FLASH POINT NORTH KOREA

# FLASH POINT

# NORTH KOREA

The *Pueblo* and EC-121 Crises

Richard A. Mobley

NAVAL INSTITUTE PRESS

Annapolis, Maryland

Naval Institute Press
291 Wood Road
Annapolis, MD 21402

Library of Congress Cataloging-in-Publication Data

Mobley, Richard A., 1952–
    Flash Point North Korea : the Pueblo and EC-121 crises / Richard A. Mobley.
    p. cm.
    Includes bibliographical references and index.
    ISBN 1-55750-403-2 (alk. paper)
    1. Pueblo Incident, 1968. 2. Military intelligence—United States. 3. Military
surveillance—United States. 4. Korea (North)—Foreign relations—United States.
5. United States—Foreign relations—Korea (North) 6. Korea (North)—Military
policy. I. Title.
    VB231.U54M63 2003
    358.4'5—dc21

                                                        2003012358

Printed in the United States of America on acid-free paper ∞
10 09 08 07 06 05 04 03    9 8 7 6 5 4 3 2
First printing

# CONTENTS

# PREFACE AND ACKNOWLEDGMENTS

At first blush, the United States seemed blind and impotent in the late 1960s when it failed to either anticipate or retaliate for two related North Korean provocations. In 1968, the North seized USS *Pueblo* and held the crew for nearly a year of brutal mistreatment. The ship is still in North Korean hands. Less than four months after *Pueblo*'s crew returned to San Diego, thirty-one U.S. sailors and marines were killed when North Korean aircraft shot down an EC-121 reconnaissance aircraft some ninety miles off North Korea's east coast. Figuratively, lightning had struck twice; decision makers in Washington evidently had failed to learn anything from the first incident and seemed no better prepared for the second.

Yet, even contemporary press coverage and books published shortly after these events took place show that the United States was not as incompetent as it may have seemed. Contemporary statements suggest increasing concern at high levels about the growing threat. The United States was providing hundreds of millions of dollars of military assistance aid to help South Korea redress the military imbalance and was implementing a program to reduce North Korean infiltration. Moreover, within days of both incidents, the United States had marshaled sufficient striking power in the region to inflict major damage on the DPRK. It took high levels of professionalism, organizational ability, and planning to move, prepare, and sustain such forces—particularly at a time when the Vietnam War was raging.

During the subsequent decades, questions about the performance of the national intelligence community and military planners lingered. Why were they surprised? Why were they unprepared? Why did they not retaliate (at least in the case of the EC-121 incident, when there were no prisoners whose lives had to be protected)? Answers to these questions began appearing in the 1990s when the U.S. government began releasing formerly "top secret" documents about these incidents as part of a normal declassification schedule. Other documents became available through Freedom of Information Act requests.

The new material paints a richly detailed picture of two dramatic national crises. When assembled chronologically and combined with subsequent accounts, the extensive collection of documents provides context for North Korea's behavior in the late 1960s and associated U.S. intelligence collection efforts against that nation. The documents afford insights into *Pueblo*'s mission and chronicle U.S. national- and theater-level responses during the first few days of the crisis. They also reveal the unpublicized role played by the military during the prolonged negotiations to free the crew and offer insights into lessons the U.S. Navy might have learned during the *Pueblo* crisis.

The hundreds of documents reveal profound concerns about North Korea and a determination to respond by collecting more intelligence about the North. They betray deep U.S. apprehension about the vulnerability of U.S. and ROK forces to surprise attack. They show how intensive National Security Council deliberations hammered out strategies for potential U.S. responses. They reveal the details of a wide range of retaliatory plans. They reveal resource strains. And they reveal an extensive effort to learn lessons and change the procedures for sensitive intelligence collection operations following these incidents.

Most Americans alive today have either forgotten about or never heard of the *Pueblo* incident, and fewer still recall the bloodier EC-121 shootdown. Even had no new evidence become available in the three decades since these incidents, the facts as they were known in 1969 would be fascinating. The raft of books written about *Pueblo* in the few years after the seizure still make for a good read. Perhaps the most fascinating contemporary document is the report of the Special Subcommittee on the USS *Pueblo* of the House Armed Services Committee. Entitled *Inquiry into the USS* Pueblo *and EC-121 Incidents,* the report rightly compares the two related events; it is the only lengthy public study to do so. The report is painful to read. Rightly or wrongly, the subcommittee spared virtually no one involved in the incidents. In both open and closed sessions, its members reviewed all aspects of both incidents, and its criticism was sweeping. Although one might challenge some of the subcommittee's conclusions, individuals interested in studying or participating in complex, high-risk U.S. military contingency operations should scan the document. They will not find a dull page in it.

Even so many decades after the fact, the once highly restricted documents that have recently come to light conjure up the emotions of the crisis—the challenge of having to respond quickly when American lives were at stake.

The documents are intriguing in themselves, but I had additional reasons for choosing to investigate the twin incidents. During my assignment at U.S. Forces Korea headquarters in Seoul during the late 1990s, I had firsthand experience with attempts to anticipate North Korea's behavior. I developed an appreciation of the difficulty of fashioning a realistic model for "reasonable" North Korean behavior and for anticipating North Korean provocations. The challenges of anticipating a "surprise" attack—even a very limited one—were sharply apparent at the command headquarters (just as they had been in the late 1960s).

This book stems from two articles I recently wrote. The *Naval War College Review* published "*Pueblo:* A Retrospective" in spring 2001, and the *Naval Institute Proceedings* published "EC-121 Shootdown" in August 2001. While enjoyable, the task of researching these incidents was a formidable one. Some of the documents were readily accessible in on-line sources or in the appropriate volume of the *Foreign Relations of the United States;* however, the majority were buried in archives.

Editors at the *Naval War College Review* and the *Naval Institute Proceedings* encouraged me to use the articles noted above as resources for a book; for that, I thank them. I particularly want to thank Tom Cutler of the Naval Institute Press for approaching me to write the book after he had read the articles. I am grateful for the support of the Public Records Office in Great Britain and the U.S. National Archives, Naval Historical Center, and Lyndon B. Johnson Library in the United States. This book would have been impossible to write without the assistance of several archivists. I am particularly grateful to Mike Parrish (formerly of the LBJ Library in Austin, Texas); Kenneth Johnson, Richard Walker, and Mark Evans of the Naval Historical Center in Washington, D.C.; Pat Anderson of the National Archives and Records Administration in College Park, Maryland; and James O'Donnell and Karl Swanson of U.S. Forces Korea. I deeply appreciate the support of Defense Intelligence Agency Historian Deane Allen. I am also grateful to Chuck Hoing of DIA Public Affairs for facilitating the prepublication release paperwork at the DIA and CIA. Finally, I wish to thank my wife, Ann Marsh, for moral support and careful editing of each of the seventy-thousand-plus words that constitute this manuscript. However, I alone remain responsible for any residual errors of fact or omission.

# ABBREVIATIONS

| | |
|---|---|
| AAA | antiaircraft artillery |
| AGER | auxiliary general environmental research [vessel] |
| AGTR | auxiliary general technical research [vessel] |
| CAP | combat air patrol |
| CINCPAC | Commander in Chief, Pacific |
| CINCPACFLT | Commander in Chief, Pacific Fleet |
| CINCUNC | Commander in Chief, United Nations Command |
| CNO | Chief, Naval Operations |
| COMUSFK | Commander, U.S. Forces Korea |
| COMSEVENTHFLEET | Commander, Seventh Fleet |
| CTF 69 | Commander, Task Force 69 |
| CVA | attack aircraft carrier |
| DCI | director of central intelligence |
| DD | destroyer |
| DDI | deputy director of intelligence (CIA) |
| DEFCON | defense condition |
| DIA | Defense Intelligence Agency |
| DOD | Department of Defense |
| DPRK | Democratic People's Republic of Korea (North) |
| ELINT | electronic intelligence |
| GCI | ground-controlled intercept |
| HAWK | homing all the way killer (missile) |
| INR | State Department, Bureau of Intelligence and Research |
| JCS | Joint Chiefs of Staff |
| JRC | Joint Chiefs of Staff Joint Reconnaissance Center |
| KCNA | Korean Central News Agency |
| KPA | Korean People's Army |
| MAC | Military Armistice Commission (UN) |
| MDL | Military Demarcation Line |
| NCA | National Command Authorities |

| | |
|---|---|
| NKAF | North Korean Air Force |
| NSA | National Security Agency |
| NSC | National Security Council |
| NSF | National Security Files |
| PARPRO | Peacetime Aerial Reconnaissance Program |
| POL | petroleum, oil, and lubricants |
| ROK | Republic of Korea (South) |
| ROKAF | ROK Air Force |
| SAC | Strategic Air Command |
| SAR | search and rescue |
| SIGINT | signals intelligence |
| SNIE | Special National Intelligence Estimate |
| UN | United Nations |
| UNC | UN Command (in South Korea) |
| USFK | U.S. Forces Korea |

# FLASH POINT NORTH KOREA

# 1
# LIGHTNING STRIKES TWICE

In January 1968, North Korean patrol boats seized USS *Pueblo* (AGER-2) as it was operating off Wonsan, the primary east coast port of the Democratic People's Republic of Korea (DPRK). U.S. forces did nothing to prevent the capture and were unprepared to retaliate immediately. Instead, the U.S. Navy's Seventh Fleet assembled the multicarrier task force required to go to war with North Korea, and the U.S. Air Force flew hundreds of frontline aircraft into the western Pacific. This posturing apparently did little to influence North Korea; for a year, the *Pueblo*'s captive crew was humiliated, beaten, and even threatened with execution. Only a formal, written apology (orally recanted at the signing) freed *Pueblo*'s surviving eighty-two-man crew in December 1968. *Pueblo* itself remains in North Korea as a tourist attraction.

Only four months after *Pueblo*'s crew was released, North Korean Air Force (NKAF) MiG fighters shot down a U.S. Navy EC-121 surveillance aircraft on 15 April 1969, leader Kim Il Sung's birthday. The aircraft had been flying over the Sea of Japan some ninety miles off the North Korean coast when the fighters attacked it. All thirty-one crewmen aboard perished. The U.S. Navy (with Soviet Pacific Fleet assistance) recovered only two bodies and some wreckage. The U.S. intelligence community had been surprised a second time. It took even longer for the navy to move forces to the scene this time because the nearest available carriers were operating in the South China Sea.

Yet, only a few days after assembling another large task force in the Sea of Japan, the National Command Authorities (NCA; the president and secretary of defense or their duly deputized alternates or successors) released most of the ships to their previous duties. The United States again had done nothing to punish North Korea for its transgression.

North Korea had twice surprised the U.S. intelligence community, and both times the Seventh Fleet lacked immediately available forces to support sensitive and manifestly vulnerable intelligence collection operations. The coincidence tempts investigation. Recently declassified documents facilitate such an investigation. Among other things, the documents reveal that many of those making decisions at high levels during the two incidents were the same men. Gen. Earle G. Wheeler (chairman of the Joint Chiefs of Staff), Brig. Gen. Ralph Steakley (director of the JCS Joint Reconnaissance Center), Richard Helms (director of Central Intelligence), Lt. Gen. Joseph Carroll, USAF (director of the Defense Intelligence Agency), Adm. John McCain (commander in chief, Pacific), Gen. Charles Bonesteel III (commander in chief, U.S. Forces Korea), Ambassador William Porter (U.S. ambassador to Seoul), and James Leonard (U.S. Department of State's country officer for North Korea) played some role in both crises. Certainly, many of their subordinates and colleagues also participated in both crises because the two occurred so close together in time.

There was, however, at least one crucial difference in the chief actors: Richard M. Nixon was the president when the second incident occurred, having replaced Lyndon B. Johnson as president in January 1969. Nixon had criticized Johnson's handling of the *Pueblo* crisis, alleging that LBJ had not been sufficiently forceful and assertive in dealing with the North. Nixon, on the other hand, had a reputation as a decision maker who advocated force in the pursuit of Cold War objectives. Yet, to the surprise of many, President Nixon seemed relatively passive during this first crisis of his presidency.

A special subcommittee of the House Armed Services Committee investigated both incidents. The actions of all those involved at high levels came under intensive scrutiny, as did the U.S. intelligence-collecting program itself. The conclusions drawn by the subcommittee are instructive.

The subcommittee was skeptical of both the extent of sensitive surveillance programs and the intelligence community's contribution to national security:

The subcommittee is not convinced that the magnitude of this intelligence reconnaissance activity is completely justified, nor is it persuaded that the many millions of dollars which are expended annually to support the activities of our individual defense intelligence activities, that is, DIA [Defense Intelligence Agency] and NSA [National Security Agency], are fully and properly utilized.[1]

The subcommittee concluded that the risk assessment process and mission approval cycle for *Pueblo* were deeply flawed.

No level of authority in either the intelligence chain of command or the operating chain of command was sensitive to the abundant evidence indicating the development of a progressively more aggressive and hostile attitude by the North Koreans. . . . The risk assessment criteria established by the Joint Chiefs of Staff were not observed by responsible naval authorities and it is questionable whether the Defense Intelligence Agency observed these criteria when approving the minimal risk category for the *Pueblo* mission.[2]

The subcommittee claimed that raw intelligence collected about the DPRK and finished intelligence such as an NSA warning report were improperly disseminated:

Pertinent information on increased North Korean hostility toward intelligence gathering activities was not conveyed to appropriate authorities . . . a more explicit "warning" message sent by National Security Agency on December 29, 1967, which urged consideration of "ship protective measures" for the *Pueblo* mission never reached responsible authorities.[3]

The subcommittee devoted considerable effort to dissecting why the Seventh Fleet and Fifth Air Force did not attempt to rescue *Pueblo* during the several hours between its seizure and its mooring in Wonsan. Finally, it concluded: "The Navy had no contingency plans whatsoever to provide for going to the rescue of the USS *Pueblo* in an emergency."[4]

The communications systems were more satisfactory than many other aspects of the two incidents. Even here, however, there were some delays and mishandling of message traffic:

The technical ability of military units involved in the USS *Pueblo* and EC-121 incidents to transmit messages . . . appeared . . . satisfactory. However, the advantages of speedy, modern and sophisticated communications equipment

4 Flash Point North Korea

were often more than offset by the indecisive and inefficient handling of these communications by the various commands involved.[5]

Although there is no question that the United States was both surprised by and ill prepared to respond to both incidents, some of the subcommittee's conclusions might have been challenged even at the time they were made. Many of the participants in the crisis published memoirs, and Trevor Armbrister published a comprehensive study of *Pueblo* in 1970. Armbrister's *A Matter of Accountability* is informed by some three hundred interviews and sheds light on the problems cited by Congress.[6] However, Armbrister's investigation was doubtless hampered because he had to rely primarily on interviews. The official paper trail for both incidents remained classified for more than two decades after he wrote his book.

Many of these sensitive documents are now in the public domain. The newly available documents make plain the imperfection of the intelligence available to the operational commanders involved. Caught by surprise, they had to plan and move forces quickly to respond to a wide range of contingencies. These records also reveal the dynamics in Washington and establish the options the decision makers considered. Finally, they show how military forces were in fact employed once the national strategy for the crises was decided.[7]

Collectively, the documents reveal good as well as bad news. First, they show that no U.S. government organization was complacent about North Korea. U.S. analysts understood the broad outlines of its policies and had a refined understanding of Korean People's Army (KPA) capabilities. U.S. decision makers were worried about where both intentions and capabilities were trending, especially as the North's belligerence intensified during the so-called second Korean War, a three-year period characterized by exceptional transborder North Korean violence against the South.

The documents also reveal one of the paradoxes of intelligence collection. As North Korea appeared more threatening, U.S. policy makers demanded more information. At the national level, there were repeated references to filling intelligence gaps and doing a better job collecting information on Pyongyang. The commander in chief of the United Nations (UN) Command repeatedly demanded new national intelligence estimates. As the North became more bellicose, however, the threat to the intelligence collectors also grew.

Given the subsequent loss of life in the intelligence-collecting activities initiated to meet this demand, the documents reveal a second bit of good news. National decision makers were not as casual in approving collection missions as Congress appeared to believe. There were tensions in the approval process. The State Department disapproved some proposed collection missions, and the DIA raised the risk assessment for others.

Occasional doubts aside, U.S. intelligence collection efforts did increase, and some new methodologies were put to work. USS *Pueblo* was the first unarmed naval surface collector assigned to loiter off the North Korean coast. The documents reveal that Washington quickly approved the patrol, but not without reservations. At least one NSA analyst documented his concerns about the mission in a formal message. The CIA's deputy director for intelligence received written notification implying that the mission patrol might elicit an abnormal Korean response. Yet, the mission was approved nevertheless.

Declassified Special National Intelligence Estimates (SNIEs) show that the national intelligence community acknowledged North Korea's growing threat to U.S. and Republic of Korea (ROK) forces on the Korean peninsula. The North Korean Air Force had achieved frightening air superiority, and the number of trans-DMZ provocations had skyrocketed. North Korean agents' assiduous attempts to assassinate President Park Chung Hee of South Korea had been reported by the CIA months before the *Pueblo* incident. The national intelligence establishment thus presented the context for further North Korean misbehavior. However, other than asserting that the North did not really want an all-out war, analysts did not identify the upper limit for North Korean violence. They certainly seem to have delivered no warning that the North might take direct action against a ship sent to gather intelligence.

The North Korean media had become so hostile that they were not a useful gauge of the country's next move. The North Korean media had been making allegations against "spy ships" for years; those alone would not have been a tip-off that *Pueblo* was in danger. The KPA certainly did not telegraph its moves by deploying ships or raising its state of alertness before either incident.

The records (and General Bonesteel's oral history) do, however, refer to anomalous North Korean behavior before the EC-121 shootdown, including unpublicized, remarkably vitriolic comments made to U.S. personnel at UN Military Armistice Committee meetings in Panmunjom a few days before the shootdown. In any event, the United States was sufficiently concerned to restrict but not completely stop Peacetime Aerial Reconnaissance Program (PARPRO) reconnaissance missions off the DPRK's east coast a few days before the EC-121 was downed. (PARPRO was the overall program by which the United States managed sensitive airborne intelligence collection worldwide. It specified approval and operational procedures for reconnaissance aircraft flying in potentially hostile areas.)

The documents also show in remarkable detail the speed and complexity of the U.S. military's response to both incidents. Efforts were made to get at least some kind of air power to *Pueblo* before it was taken into territorial waters, and plans were developed to tow *Pueblo* out of Wonsan. The fleet operating schedule, disrupted by the crisis, disintegrated altogether when the Tet Offensive erupted in Vietnam a few days after the DPRK seized *Pueblo*. Simultaneously prosecuting the Vietnam air war and supporting contingency operations in the Sea of Japan put an enormous strain on U.S. resources in the Pacific.

The vulnerabilities of U.S. forces then in Korea are starkly apparent in the records. General Bonesteel quickly documented his concerns about his ability to prosecute a war, should one erupt. He was especially concerned about the vulnerability of six unhardened ROK airfields, surface-to-air missile sites, and nuclear weapons sites. There were in addition serious shortfalls in ordnance and fuel. However, the primary sources also reveal that the United States was quick to identify some of the most glaring shortfalls in the ROK-DPRK military balance and quickly moved to close the gap.

Critics of the government's actions may be surprised to learn that the declassified documents also reveal that a multilevel "lessons-learned" process followed both incidents. The military modified the way it planned, approved, and supported sensitive intelligence collection. However, the records also show that the military was well aware of its inability to forestall North Korean attacks on U.S. intelligence collectors.

The hundreds of assessments, memoranda, messages, command histories, and raw intelligence reports that constitute the historical record of the *Pueblo* and EC-121 incidents contribute enormously to the second half of this book. They provide insights into PARPRO missions in general and the nature of Fleet Air Reconnaissance Squadron One's (VQ-1's) explicit collection efforts (and successes) against the DPRK. They also provide more information about the shootdown. They certainly dispel any notion that the attack was accidental (North Korea never claimed that it was). Rather, they provide evidence that North Korean MiG-21s likely deployed to a staging base in extreme north-eastern North Korea in advance and then ambushed the EC-121 as it was approaching the northern limit of its elongated reconnaissance orbit off North Korea.

When the diaries and first-person accounts of by the participants in the crisis are interpolated with the newly declassified documents, the National Security Council's reluctance to retaliate becomes quickly apparent. Only as the administration started to identify courses of action—a process that did not start in earnest for more than twenty-four hours after the shootdown—did messages demanding contingency planning start to fly. It was a slow-motion response. However, the national command authorities' determination to retaliate for future incidents becomes emphatically apparent.

The documentary trail concludes with a second set of lessons learned and actions taken to prevent a recurrence—in particular, a second set of fighter escort requirements for sensitive reconnaissance missions, a review of the overall PARPRO program, and a revamping of contingency planning. For at least all of 1969, fighters had to be aloft whenever PARPRO missions were flown over the Sea of Japan. The United States evidently also sharply reduced the number of reconnaissance missions being flown worldwide. By the end of 1969, U.S. planners had prepared an elaborate collection of contingency plans to use against North Korea in retaliation for at least twenty-six different kinds of provocations.

Many aspects of the twin crises still resonate today. North Korea is still unpredictable. The United States and ROK still must counter unusual outbursts of North Korean activity, and UN Command planners still must compensate for military imbalances on the peninsula. A review of the challenges of intelligence collection and planning in the late 1960s encourages us to understand the vagaries inherent in assessing a nation that continues to be one of America's most profound foreign policy challenges.

# 2
# AN
# INTELLIGENCE
# BLANK

The *Pueblo* patrol and the ill-fated EC-121 mission occurred because U.S. decision makers profoundly distrusted North Korea's intentions. The North had amassed sufficient forces to conduct limited unassisted incursions into South Korea. It enjoyed superiority over the South in several military mission categories. Although few expected the power elite in Pyongyang to issue orders to overrun the entire Korean peninsula, the upper limits of their willingness to engage in violent incidents were uncomfortably murky. Between 1967 and 1969, a period sometimes called the "second Korean War," the North staged so many provocations that it became difficult to predict what form the next incident might take. Consequently, throughout that period, U.S. decision makers demanded more intelligence about the DPRK and sought to redress significant imbalances of power between North and South.

## The U.S. Role in Korea

The United States was bound to the Republic of Korea by treaty commitments, UN obligations, and the presence of some forty-eight thousand U.S. troops in-country, many astride the primary invasion corridors the North might use to reach Seoul. The command relations were, and are, complex, and they determined the theater commander's role in anticipating and responding to both the *Pueblo* and EC-121 incidents.

Gen. Charles H. Bonesteel III, the senior U.S. officer in Korea, wore several hats. As far as the U.S. chain of command was concerned, he was Commander, U.S. Forces Korea (COMUSFK), a subunified commander who reported to Adm. Ulysses S. Grant Sharp, Commander in Chief, Pacific (CINCPAC), in Hawaii, and through him to Gen. Earle G. Wheeler, Chairman, Joint Chiefs of Staff (JCS), in Washington, D.C. In peacetime, he controlled only the U.S. forces on the peninsula; he did not control the forces operating off Korean coasts, nor did he approve or control the intelligence collection missions flown off the coasts of Korea. The latter fell under the Strategic Air Command (SAC) or Commander in Chief, Pacific Fleet (CINCPACFLT). The U.S. forces sent into the waters off Korea after the *Pueblo* and EC-121 incidents also were not under General Bonesteel's control.

In 1968, U.S. Forces Korea was predominantly a U.S. Army force. The United States based few aircraft in the ROK before the *Pueblo* incident, and U.S. Navy assets that might support Bonesteel's force in the western Pacific fell under a separate navy chain of command going from Commander, Seventh Fleet (COMSEVENTHFLEET), on to CINCPACFLT in Hawaii.

The U.S. Army presence primarily took the form of two divisions: the Second Infantry Division (which remains in the ROK) and the Seventh Infantry Division plus the large logistic infrastructure required to support them. Although the ROK Army would have done most of the fighting had war broken out—it had more than ten times as many active-duty troops on the peninsula—the U.S. Army would have been in the midst of some of the bloodiest combat. ROK Army troops were responsible for defending the eastern two-thirds of the 150-mile-long Demilitarized Zone (DMZ) separating the two Koreas, and ROK marines defended roughly the western one-fifth. U.S. troops defended the area in between the two, a key sector centered on a line between Kaesong, North Korea, and Seoul. In other words, they would have to defend the invasion corridors that the KPA had used so successfully at the beginning the Korean War in June 1950.[1]

Bonesteel's real power and responsibility came with a second position: Commander in Chief, United Nations Command (CINCUNC).[2] On behalf of the UN, he commanded all ROK and U.S. forces on the Korean peninsula.

This responsibility gave him access to the South Korean leadership (then primarily of military origin). In return, Bonesteel was the primary target if the ROK Ministry of Defense (or President Park Chung Hee) was unhappy about some aspect of U.S. national security policy. Bonesteel also lobbied for those items on the ROK's military shopping list that would best enhance ROK combat readiness.

The latter was a major worry for Bonesteel, for despite its large army the ROK was far from ready for war. South Korea was rapidly modernizing and quickly making the jump from a Third World country to a developed, industrialized nation. However, the Korean War (and its associated devastation to the ROK) had ended only fifteen years earlier. Enhancing ROK defense readiness was a "work in progress." Numerous infrastructure and equipment problems would handicap Seoul's ability to fight an all-out war, even with the tremendous U.S. reinforcements then envisioned. These discrepancies would become glaringly apparent when the United States had to envision fighting such an all-out war after *Pueblo* was seized.

General Bonesteel faced a stiff challenge to his efforts to enhance ROK military readiness. He had to compete for goods and manpower with the major resource magnet of the time: the Vietnam War. The *Pueblo* incident coincided with one of the most difficult years of the Vietnam War. In fact, it preceded the Tet Offensive by just a few days. The year 1968 also represented the high-water mark for U.S. involvement in Southeast Asia—more than half a million troops were deployed there then. Vietnam riveted the attention of U.S. decision makers as well as commanding the lion's share of U.S. resources in the Pacific. Even the *Pueblo* and EC-121 incidents could not deflect the focus away from the Vietnam War. With this senior leadership focus, Bonesteel would have to fight hard for resources during both crises.

## The North Korean Context

In September 1967, the U.S. intelligence community became aware of a profound change in North Korean paramilitary tactics. Virtually every contemporary academic source and internal U.S. government document on Korea written in the late 1960s highlights the skyrocketing incidence of DPRK-initiated violence across the DMZ. The challenge for intelligence analysts was identifying the reasons for the increased belligerence and, most important to the *Pueblo* story, where it would lead.[3]

Given the substantial gaps in U.S. intelligence, answering the "why" and "what next" questions was a difficult assignment. In an internal State Department memorandum written after the *Pueblo* seizure, State's Bureau of Intelligence and Research (INR) summed up the problem: "North Korea is the most denied of denied areas and the most difficult of all intelligence targets. Estimates of North Korean strength, intentions and capabilities, therefore, cannot be made with a high degree of confidence."[4] The memorandum did suggest that analysts could discern broad outlines of North Korean policy. Additionally, the U.S. intelligence community was aware of patterns of North Korean international relations and key changes within the party hierarchy. Beyond that, unfortunately, there would be a lot of guesswork:

> While we know of North Korea's political objectives, we do not know its immediate intentions and plans. We do not know the details of Pyongyang's defense relationships with the Soviet Union and Communist China. While we know generally of purges within the party and government structure, we do not know the nature of the struggle or the implications.[5]

U.S. decision makers at the national level certainly expected more than that, and the September 1967 Special National Intelligence Estimate (SNIE) addressed the problem of North Korea's intentions and capabilities without betraying INR's subsequent tenor of hopelessness. Not surprisingly given the skyrocketing levels of violence on the peninsula, the community produced four SNIEs (documents written for the nation's senior leadership reflecting the considered opinion of all members of the intelligence community about a significant problem) on North Korea's intentions toward the South during the turbulent 1967–69 period.

The September 1967 SNIE—the last one written before *Pueblo* was seized —admitted that since October 1966, North Korean infiltrators had initiated far more violent activity against U.S. and ROK forces along the DMZ than at any time during the preceding ten relatively peaceful years. The U.S. intelligence community identified several motivations for this behavior:[6]

1. The North remained committed to reunifying the Koreas under communist rule. North Korean attempts to foment revolution in the South

had failed. The numerous infiltrators and political agitators Pyongyang sent south were generally rebuffed.

2.  Northern hopes for an internal ROK revolution had diminished. Between 1960 and 1965, Pyongyang had been encouraged by a student overthrow of Syngman Rhee, a year of "confused and tolerant parliamentary democracy," a coup by "disaffected nationalistic officers," and "a bitter military civilian political struggle" in the South. However, President Park Chung Hee (a former division commander along the DMZ) had gained a degree of popular acceptance after he seized power. Violent protests capable of overthrowing his government in favor of a more "progressive" regime did not appear imminent. The North had failed to exploit South Korean unrest merely through propaganda and political subversion.

3.  The South's economy had begun to boom while the North's appeared to be stagnating. With the loss of Soviet aid in the early 1960s and the high costs of North Korean military expenditures, the 1961–67 Seven-Year Plan was faltering and had to be extended. Although the North's per capita GNP remained higher than that of the South, the ROK was outstripping Northern rates of growth in at least most industrial sectors. The opportunity to inspire the South with North Korea's economic achievement was slipping away.

4.  The ROK's commitment to support the Vietnam War in mid-1965 ultimately led to more than fifty thousand ROK troops being sent to Vietnam. ROK elites felt that this move gained them domestic and international prestige. In contrast, North Korean public and private comments revealed embarrassment because Pyongyang had neither deterred nor matched the ROK's intervention in Vietnam. (Pyongyang had sent small arms, construction equipment, medical supplies, machinery, and tools. Approximately forty North Korean Air Force pilots were assigned to fly defensive patrols around Hanoi. One had even shot down a U.S. fighter in air-to-air combat over North Vietnam!) Northern military pressure on Seoul might force it to reconsider its military commitment to Saigon and recommit forces to fighting North Korean infiltrators.

5.  The U.S. commitment to South Korea was essential to the South's ability to withstand Northern political and military pressure. The North sought to foster conditions that would weaken the U.S. commitment and reduce the American presence in South Korea.

The SNIE portrayed North Korea as an independent actor in its game of increased violence toward the South. It concluded that the power elite in Pyongyang had sufficient motivation to renew violence along the DMZ, without the help of the Soviet Union or China. In fact, neither Beijing nor

Moscow sought conflict on the Korean peninsula. A subsequent SNIE opined: "We believe that North Korea is pursuing an independent policy. Pyongyang probably does not consult with Moscow and Peking on the tactical development of its policy against the ROK and the U.S."[7] Finally, the SNIE concluded that while Pyongyang wanted increased tensions, it did not want war on the peninsula.

Historian Dae-Sook Suh portrayed North Korea's buildup as an outgrowth from a sense of isolation stemming from the Sino-Soviet conflict. As it tried to straddle the growing divide between Beijing and Moscow, Pyongyang suffered poor relations with Moscow in the first part of the decade. These improved in 1965, and Soviet aid resumed, but then relations with China soured.[8] In other words, given potentially unreliable allies, Kim Il Sung made self-sufficiency a virtue. Suh commented:

> Kim's quarrels with his two neighbors undermined the security he had taken for granted so long. He was therefore forced to concentrate on a costly military buildup, and it came with the prominence of the generals. The generals were his old comrades from the plains of Manchuria and fellow partisans, but they began to arm all the people and fortify the entire nation.[9]

These "partisan generals" constituted the faction that now pushed for increased guerrilla and sabotage operations as North Korea sought to divert the ROK from Vietnam and to establish a "foothold in the South, utilizing the popular dissent over South Korea's normalization of relations with Japan."[10]

Kim Il Sung had announced the new approach in his address to the Fourteenth Party Plenum in October 1996. He argued that reunification would result from the revolution of "patriotic" forces in the South, which "in unison with" North Korea would eliminate the U.S. presence in South Korea, overthrow the ROK government, establish a "people's government," and "democratize" South Korean society. The speech emphasized the North's "active struggle" in the South Korean revolution.[11]

Fourteen months later, just before North Korea seized *Pueblo*, Kim Il Sung gave another revolutionary speech. Addressing the Supreme People's Assembly in December 1967, he said that the North would support Southern revolutionaries:

> The entire people in the northern half of the republic bear heavy responsibility for carrying the South Korean revolution to completion, keeping pace with

the exalted fighting spirit of the South Korean people and rendering active support for their struggle. . . . We must accomplish the South Korean revolution and unify the fatherland in our generation. . . . We must quickly ripen all conditions for the realization of the unification of the fatherland. . . . The accomplishment of the great cause of the liberation of South Korea and unification of the fatherland at the earliest possible date depends not only on how the revolutionary organizations and revolutionaries in South Korea expand and strengthen the revolutionary forces and how they fight the enemy, but in a large measure on how the people in the northern half of the republic prepare themselves to greet the great revolutionary event.[12]

As table 1 shows, the levels of violence along the DMZ escalated during this period. Infiltration rates of North Korean agents—both across the DMZ and by high-speed boats into the South Korean interior—had sharply increased since May 1967. In September 1967, there were two incidents of sabotage against South Korean trains—the first such incidents since the Korean War.[13] The jump in the number of incidents between 1966 and 1967 was most dramatic; there was a tenfold increase in incidents along the DMZ and a ninefold increase in firing incidents in the ROK interior. Casualty rates on both sides reflected the heightened belligerence.[14]

**Table 1. Incidence of Violence in the DMZ, 1964–1968**

|                              | 1964 | 1965 | 1966 | 1967 | 1968 |
|------------------------------|------|------|------|------|------|
| Violent incidents            | 32   | 42   | 37   | 435  | 542  |
| North Koreans killed         | —    | —    | 45   | 228  | —    |
| North Koreans captured       | —    | —    | 19   | 57   | —    |
| UN Command forces killed     | —    | —    | 39   | 121  | —    |
| UN Command forces wounded    | —    | —    | 26   | 294  | —    |
| ROK police/civilians killed  | —    | —    | 4    | 22   | —    |
| ROK wounded                  | —    | —    | 5    | 53   | —    |

*Sources:* United DIA point paper, Lt. Comdr. J. Clay, 7 June 1968, folder "Korea 1 May 1968–30 April 1969 091," Records of the U.S. JCS, Records of Chairman (Gen.) Earle Wheeler 1967–1970, box 29, RG 218, NARA; Director of Central Intelligence, "North Korean Intentions and Capabilities with Respect to South Korea," SNIE 14.2-67, 21 September 1967, folder "SNIE 14.2-67," NSF Country File, NIEs, box 5, LBJ; letter from Kim Sung Eun (ROK minister of national defense) to Denis Healey (British defense minister), 22 February 1968, FCO 21/347, PRO.

With this background, the last SNIE written on North Korea's intentions before the *Pueblo* seizure predicted increasing levels of trans-DMZ violence and sabotage. The SNIE also predicted that Pyongyang would avoid acts likely to provoke an all-out war. (The subsequent three SNIEs also maintained that Pyongyang did not want war.) Beyond avoiding the tripwire that would provoke war, the potential upper limit of North Korean violence remained ill defined in U.S. analyses:

> North Korea will almost certainly continue its campaign of military harassment in the DMZ area at current or even increased levels. . . . Just as we consider it unlikely that North Korea intends to start another Korean war, we believe it unlikely that it plans at present to escalate its DMZ attacks to a point at which open warfare might result. The North might miscalculate, however, and raise the ante along the DMZ until the ROK resolves to strike back in force. . . . Rear area infiltration of guerrilla type teams could become a more serious problem in 1968.[15]

The CIA did suggest that the DPRK was preparing to employ assassination as a tool. A separate CIA memo prepared to support Vice President Hubert Humphrey's visit to the ROK in July 1967 raised the issue. The CIA was aware not only that the North had threatened President Park's life but also that it had dispatched teams of agents to assassinate him. Since Park was the "only real cement for whatever degree of political stability" existed in the South, he made a tempting target. In fact, a large North Korean team of assassins nearly succeeded only two days before *Pueblo* was seized.[16]

The thirty-one-member team left Pyongyang on 16 January 1968. They encountered, but did not kill, villagers just south of the DMZ. The team reached Seoul on 21 January and got within about five hundred yards of the Blue House (Park's presidential residence) before they encountered now-alerted police. In the ensuing firefight, twenty-seven guerrillas were killed, three escaped, and one was captured.[17]

Thus, evidence on the ground as well as predictive analysis suggested that North Korea was willing to take extreme measures against the ROK. Its willingness to do the same against U.S. intelligence collectors operating near its borders was not considered.

## A Shifting Balance of Power

While "will the North attack?" was an important question to U.S. and ROK commanders, "can the North attack?" was more important given uncertainty about the North's intentions. To put the North Korean threat into a 1960s perspective, it is important to understand the North Korean–UN Command (UNC) balance of power at that time. As was noted above, North Korea's economy was stronger than that of the ROK. Even in the late 1960s, the North had a higher per capita gross national product. In fact, it had enjoyed higher rates of industrial and agricultural growth earlier that decade. Militarily, the balance of power in key categories was the opposite of what it is today: In 1967, the UNC had a much larger army than the KPA and a much smaller (and more vulnerable) air force (see table 2, which summarizes a CIA table comparing the orders of battle for the two countries as of early 1968). In contrast, current publications and testimony indicate a numerically larger North Korean Army (supported by vastly expanded armor, artillery, and surface-to-surface missile battalions) and a relatively less capable air force.[18]

**Table 2. Comparative Orders of Battle**

| Military Forces | North Korea | South Korea |
|---|---|---|
| Army | 345,000 | 534,000 (plus 50,000 in South Vietnam) |
| Marines | — | 31,000 |
| Air | 18,500 | 25,500 |
|   Modern fighters | 27 MiG-21s<br>7 MiG-19s<br>34 MiG-19/21s | 57 F-5 A/bs |
|   Older fighters | 62 MiG-17s<br>358 MiG-17/17s | 30 F-86Ds<br>105 F-86Fs |
|   Light bombers | 80 IL-28s | — |
| Navy | 10,000 | 18,000 |
|   Submarines | 4 W class | — |
|   Guided missile boats | 8 Komar class | — |
|   Fast patrol boats | 2 Sherchen class | — |
|   Torpedo boats | 40 | — |
|   Sub chasers | 9 | — |
|   Patrol boats | 7 | 32 |
|   Minesweepers | 5 | 11 |
|   Amphibious craft | — | 133 |

*Source:* CIA Directorate of Intelligence, "Intelligence Memo: North Korea's Military Forces," February 1968, file "Korea Codeword vol. 1, 1966, 1968," NSF Country Files, Asia and Pacific, box 256, LBJ.

*Ground Forces*

In 1968, KPA ground forces comprised 345,000 men organized into nineteen infantry divisions, a tank division, and five infantry brigades. The KPA had also recently organized a parachute battalion. These units were manned at or near full strength, and most were deployed along the DMZ. The KPA had 430 tanks and 450 assault guns, and more than 1,400 120-mm and 160-mm mortars. Its military stockpiles appeared sufficient to sustain combat for at least a month. However, North Korea was also experiencing a severe manpower shortage. Although U.S. intelligence detected a twentieth infantry division by the end of 1969, the North could not create more divisions without either mobilizing some of its reserves or debilitating the civilian economy. The U.S. intelligence community concluded that the KPA's combat effectiveness was "good." It certainly could mount "limited offensive" operations as well as defend the North. U.S. Forces Korea was particularly concerned about the North's artillery superiority. Although the ROK Army was larger, the KPA outgunned ROK/U.S. forces by a factor of 1.5 to 1 in terms of numbers, weight as reflected by calibers, and range. The KPA's 168 122-mm guns outranged all UN Command forces cannon artillery except one U.S. 175-mm gun battalion.[19]

In contrast, the South's ground forces included the 534,000-man ROK Army in Korea, another 50,000 ROK troops in South Vietnam, some 31,000 ROK marines, and 48,000 U.S. troops (the current figure is roughly 37,000 U.S. military personnel). The ROK Army also had proportionally fewer personnel in combat units than did the North. The ROK Army was "well trained," but most of its equipment was old. Its indigenous logistics support was probably less developed than that of North Korea. However, the CIA also assessed that neither side could conduct a campaign extending beyond six months or "achieve a decisive advantage" without outside logistical support.[20]

As suggested above, the North was substantially improving its unconventional warfare capability in the late 1960s. During the winter of 1965–66, the DPRK modified its plans to subvert the ROK using unconventional warfare forces. The KPA's seven-thousand-person Reconnaissance Bureau established new training bases. The Communist Party's Liaison Bureau enlarged its agent training facilities.[21] According to South Korean estimates, the North had assigned fifteen thousand troops to special operations forces units: the

Seventeenth Foot Reconnaissance Brigade, the 283d Guerrilla Unit, and the 124th Guerrilla Unit. (The latter was responsible for conducting the ill-starred Blue House raid mentioned above.)[22]

## Air and Air Defense Forces

Of all categories of military strength, the North Koreans enjoyed the greatest lead in the air, and this lead appeared to be growing during the *Pueblo* and EC-121 incidents. The North Korean Air Force (NKAF) had quantitative superiority over the ROK Air Force (ROKAF). By May 1968 the North had about 450 jet fighters, compared with nearly 200 F-86 Sabers and F-5 Freedom Fighters in the South.[23]

In 1966, the NKAF had also started to surge toward qualitative superiority over the ROKAF. Although the number of light bombers and older MiG fighters remained unchanged, the North Korean MiG-21 Fishbed inventory was rapidly growing. The Fishbed was the most capable fighter in either country's arsenal. Introduced in 1965, the Fishbed fleet had jumped to more than sixty by 1968 and exceeded ninety by the end of 1969. Additionally, some eighty IL-28 Beagle light bombers provided a limited offensive capability against the South.[24]

The NKAF had trained extensively since Soviet aid resumed in 1965, concentrating on mobility exercises, the development of intercept techniques against aircraft intruding from offshore, and the firing of probable Atoll infrared air-to-air missiles. U.S. radars had tracked numerous air-to-air and air-to-ground exercises. An expanding inventory of early warning, ground-controlled intercept, and height-finding radars was also sharply improving its ground-controlled intercept capability—that is, its ability to direct the MiGs to intercept intruding aircraft.[25]

The ROK fighters were not only outnumbered, they were also more concentrated and vulnerable to surprise attack than their Northern counterparts. The ROKAF relied on six air bases, none of which had protective shelters for fighters. In contrast, the NKAF had thirteen primary operational air bases, and most of these had shelters or underground hangars. Additionally, the ROKAF was hampered by an inadequate aircraft control and warning radar system.[26]

The North also was deploying clusters of surface-to-air missiles around vital installations. Relying solely on the SA-2 Guideline surface-to-air missile (then with a seventeen-mile threat radius), the North had rapidly built missile sites on both coasts, going from only two SA-2 sites in 1965 to twenty (a majority of which were occupied) by 1968. In other words, the intelligence community concluded that the NKAF could mount "a strong defense" against an air attack.[27]

*Naval Forces*

Despite its high visibility in seizing USS *Pueblo,* North Korea's navy would have played a secondary role in a 1960s war on the peninsula. It was a coastal defense force equipped primarily with patrol craft incapable of long-range operations, especially in heavy seas. The North's four Whisky-class diesel submarines and eight Komar missile boats provided limited offensive capability. The navy operated from four main bases and eight subsidiary stations divided between the two coasts. In conjunction with its recent receipt of Komar missile boats, the North had opened up a base near Wonsan on the east coast. The base had a missile support facility and a sea-level tunnel likely leading to an underground dock for the Komar boats. North Korea also had relatively short range antishipping missile batteries.[28]

The ROK Navy was then also a coastal defense force, but it lacked the offensive power afforded by submarines and missile boats. Interestingly, it did retain a substantial amphibious lift capability (the ability to transport troops by sea to conduct an assault against a land target).[29]

## Warning of Attack

In view of the military balance described above (and the substantial gaps in U.S. knowledge about the KPA) in mid-1968, the INR painted a dismal picture of the intelligence community's ability to warn of a limited North Korean attack. North Korea's ground forces were said to be "fully mobilized" and in place along the DMZ and in rear areas, and troops in the rear could move forward undetected in a few days. The INR estimated that the North had stockpiled sufficient food, medicine, arms, and ammunition to last a month. If the North were confident that an incursion would not widen to an all-out war, it could launch a brief attack into the ROK or on limited objectives—islands on the coast near the DMZ, for example, or ROK territory north of the Imjin River—without warning.[30]

If the North sought to wage the all-out campaign required to overrun the entire peninsula or expected to fight the United States, however, then it might have to make more extensive, and discernible, preparations. The INR suggested some preparations to watch for:

- creation of stockpiles of tanks and artillery
- seizures of reserves of railroad rolling stock and motor vehicles
- redirection of construction materials
- acceleration of militia training
- approaches to Moscow and probably Beijing for support
- movement of additional Soviet troops into maritime provinces and Chinese troops into Manchuria
- greatly increased shipments of petroleum, oil, and lubricants (POL) into North Korea
- dramatic increase in shipping into North Korea[31]

However, INR analysts also suggested that the United States might misinterpret (or miss completely) some of these indicators even should they occur. A North determined to mask its war preparations might spread the imports out gradually so there would be no telltale spike. Many of the additional supplies could be stored underground or in caves. And any Chinese and Soviet troop movements might be erroneously attributed to the ongoing Sino-Soviet conflict.[32]

Information derived from political intelligence and foreign media was not reliable either. In a memorandum written months after *Pueblo* was seized, the INR discounted the value of "political intelligence" and the North Korean media as sources for indications that war or attack was imminent, noting:

> Pyongyang has been making intensely belligerent statements for years and has left little room for measurable increases in that direction. In addition, past events of major importance, such as the 1950 attack and the 1968 Blue House raid and seizure of the *Pueblo,* were not heralded by anything that could be interpreted as a warning.[33]

Indeed, after *Pueblo* was seized, North Korean rhetoric was so strident that analysts found it difficult to assess what the country might do next. The February 1968 SNIE update commented, "The North Korean attitude is more openly truculent than at any time since 1953. . . . The possibilities for miscalculation were even greater than in the previous fall."[34]

U.S. decision makers had a wide range of concerns in 1968. North Korea had suddenly begun behaving belligerently, and how far it might go was anybody's guess. Its capability to wage war—especially in the air—was growing qualitatively as well as quantitatively. The ability of U.S. intelligence analysts to discern its next (violent) moves was obscured by the secrecy that pervaded the remote regime, and outsiders' ability to detect many of its preparations for limited war was questionable. The United States clearly needed more intelligence about the DPRK. The U.S. Navy prepared to respond to that need both at sea and in the air.

# 3

# A RISKY
# PATROL?

As North Korea grew more belligerent in 1966, a new intelligence collector became available to monitor its activity: the auxiliary general environmental research vessel (AGER). These inconspicuous ships could be positioned in international waters off the coast of North Korea to obtain potentially new signals intelligence (SIGINT) information for periods of several days or even weeks. Faced with the urgent demands of the United States and ROK for intelligence on North Korea's intentions, the navy offered its AGER *Pueblo* as a potential solution.

Almost immediately, planners (and risk assessors) encountered the collections paradox. The more bellicose Pyongyang became, the greater the danger to intelligence collectors. To make this connection explicitly—that is, to assess whether or not the North posed an immediate threat to U.S. offshore intelligence collectors—would require new intellectual constructs regarding North Korean behavior. Such constructs would be very difficult to develop because there was no precedent on which to base them. Moreover, to assert in writing that a collection mission faced more than "minimal risk" might endanger the mission's approval. Thus, any command proposing a sensitive intelligence collection mission against the DPRK would be naturally biased toward stating that the mission entailed only minimal risk to get that mission approved.

## A New Collection Platform

The idea of a surface auxiliary intelligence collector was not new. Indeed, the Soviets had made an art form of employing these ships (designated "AGIs") against the United States for decades. The Soviet Navy had approximately forty AGIs in service when *Pueblo* was seized. Starting in the 1960s, the United States had started to follow suit by deploying its own collection fleet, reasoning that dedicating auxiliaries to intelligence collection would free warships for missions more suited to their capabilities and would be less provocative than assigning combatants to collect intelligence in sensitive areas. Moreover, an auxiliary could allot more space for an intelligence collection suite than could the typical destroyer.[1]

Under this philosophy, the navy converted former Liberty and Victory ships for national intelligence collection missions. The conversions started in 1961 and resulted in seven auxiliary general technical research ships (AGTRs) by 1968.[2] They were kept busy. At the time *Pueblo* was seized, for example, one was operating off Cuba, one was off Africa, two were in Southeast Asia, and one was in the Mediterranean Sea.[3]

These vessels were generally assigned at the national level. Seeking a second class of ship that could be responsive to *fleet* SIGINT requirements, the navy proposed the AGER program. The AGERs would be smaller than the AGTRs: 950 tons compared with 11,365 tons, and 83 personnel compared with the AGTR's complement of approximately 250. The navy planned to acquire between twelve and fifteen AGERs in three phases. In the end, only three would actually be converted: USS *Banner* (AGER-1), USS *Pueblo* (AGER-2), and USS *Palm Beach* (AGER-3).[4]

The first phase of the navy's new intelligence-gathering operation entailed placing *Banner* in the western Pacific in an effort to determine the Soviet Union's reaction to a U.S. intelligence collector in a Soviet naval operating area. *Banner*'s operations were to supplement—not duplicate—the overall SIGINT collection effort in the region; indeed, *Banner* was to collect hydrographic, acoustic, and photographic intelligence as well. The second phase would bring more ships on line in the western Pacific and test the Soviets' reaction to a *continuous* AGER presence in Soviet Pacific Fleet operating areas. Collection managers would integrate this permanent presence into the overall collection strategy for the western Pacific. The program's third phase was supposed to plug gaps in U.S. maritime intelligence collection and to expand coverage of the growing Soviet Navy.[5]

Phase 1 began when *Banner* arrived in Japan in October 1965. As would *Pueblo, Banner* operated under Commander, Naval Forces Japan, in his capacity as Commander, Task Force 69 (CTF 69). *Banner* completed fifteen collection patrols before *Pueblo* finally arrived on station in December 1967. As envisioned in the plan, these patrols monitored the USSR and the People's Republic of China. *Banner* collected against the DPRK three times (14–16 March 1966, 5–7 February 1967, and 15–16 May 1967), but only because the DPRK represented a target of opportunity while AGER-1 steamed to/from more lucrative collection targets. During the February 1967 transit, *Banner* had approached to within twenty miles of Wonsan. The crew had watched as high-speed patrol boats raced by within four to six thousand yards. They had shown no interest in *Banner;* the AGER's two other transits also elicited no reactions. However, *Banner* was harassed by Chinese trawlers on two patrols and was routinely and aggressively challenged by Soviet units.[6]

The Fifth Air Force had contingency plans to support AGER collection missions. However, COMNAVFORJAPAN requested such support only on an ad hoc basis—such as, for example, when it assessed that Chinese trawlers might harass *Banner* during an East China Sea patrol scheduled for late 1966. Responding to the request, the 313th Air Division in Okinawa alerted F-102s armed with 2.75-inch rockets and air-to-air missiles.[7]

*Banner*'s tenth mission was to include brief surveillance off North Korea. Concerned about the possible risk the DPRK might pose to *Banner,* Lt. Gen. Seth McKee, Commanding General, Fifth Air Force, requested the 314th Air Division commander in Osan, South Korea, to place U.S. and ROK fighters on alert. General Bonesteel, however, was reluctant to alert ROK aircraft to support a U.S. ship. Only a few months earlier, North Korea had attacked an ROK patrol boat and U.S. aircraft had not come to its aid. Bonesteel canceled the ROK alert and asked U.S. Naval Forces Korea to explain to COMNAVFORJAPAN the reason for his reluctance. After this incident, COMNAVFORJAPAN was hesitant to call on Fifth Air Force support unless convinced that an impending patrol was sufficiently dangerous to warrant an alert. (Interestingly, even when such support was arranged, the overall risk assessment remained "minimal.")[8]

Once *Pueblo* arrived in the theater, COMNAVFORJAPAN planned to alternate *Pueblo* and *Banner* on month-long patrols in sensitive areas such as Petropavlovsk, the Sea of Japan, and the East China Sea. COMNAVFORJAPAN proposed North Korea as the primary target for *Pueblo*'s first patrol. Its planners believed that the collection environment would be less demanding (presumably less dense and with much lower risk of harassment) than those off China or the USSR. In other words, sending the newly arrived unit on a "milk run" would be a good way to break it into an active theater. On its first mission, *Pueblo* was to sample the electronic environment of the east coast of North Korea, determine the nature and extent of North Korean naval activity, conduct surveillance of Soviet naval units in the Tsushima Strait, determine Soviet and North Korean reactions to an overt intelligence collector, report the deployment of North Korean and Soviet units, and evaluate its own capabilities.[9]

*Pueblo*'s initial patrol off Korea in January 1968 would differ significantly from *Banner*'s earlier transits in one crucial respect. *Pueblo* was to remain off the North Korean coast for seventeen days and in some cases to operate within patrol boxes that allowed it to approach to just outside of thirteen miles from DPRK territory. Moreover, *Pueblo* would loiter off Wonsan, the DPRK's primary east coast port and an area known to be very sensitive to the approaches of U.S. reconnaissance aircraft.[10]

The State Department later justified *Pueblo*'s relatively close approaches to the DPRK to Congress. Not only were they entirely legal under international law, State contended, they were essential to receive the relatively short (line-of-sight) range or relatively low powered signals that the AGER was expected to intercept.

> Radio and radar transmissions in the UHF and VHF ranges do not conform to the curvature of the earth and collection must be accomplished within range of the transmitter. Such "line-of-sight" transmission is directly comparable to reception of television. In addition, some transmissions in the regular HF ranges (which conform to the earth's curvature) are so low in power that close-in collection is required. Many transmissions tend to be directional because of antenna configuration and can be collected only in a small area. For these reasons it would have been useful from the intelligence point of view to have the *Pueblo* approach quite close to land; yet, even though the U.S. does not recognize the validity of a North Korean claim to a 12 mile territorial sea, the *Pueblo* was instructed to remain at least 13 nautical miles from North Korean territory.

Experience has shown that our ships are operating about on the fringes in many respects when they are 12–15 miles from land and that to require them to maintain 20 miles, 25 miles or any larger stand-off distance would substantially degrade the effectiveness of their operations. Soviet ships engaged in such intelligence gathering routinely transit within five miles of U.S. territory.[11]

In other words, *Pueblo* was placed in a potentially more provocative operating area to collect unique intelligence.

## Mission Validation and Risk Assessment

In the search for scapegoats following *Pueblo*'s capture, Congress singled out those involved in the multilayered risk assessment process. After all, these people had assigned the mission the lowest risk assessment possible. Had *Pueblo*'s proposed January 1968 patrol received a higher risk assessment, it might have been either disapproved or better supported by on-call contingency forces. Thus, the methodology for risk assessment of sensitive intelligence collection missions was a central issue in the *Pueblo* debacle (as it would be in the subsequent EC-121 shootdown).

The assessment process was cumbersome because it involved numerous players who had to validate hundreds of impending surveillance missions under a tight monthly deadline. Furthermore, the different commands evaluating the proposals used different standards for evaluating risk. At the highest level, two competing demands complicated risk assessment: A growing national-level demand for intelligence on the DPRK encouraged an increase in collection while a desire to avoid further incidents with Pyongyang militated against it. When General Bonesteel visited Washington, D.C., in the fall of 1967, he followed up his earlier messages warning that North Korea was up to something with a personal briefing. Citing captured agent reports, he argued that the North might have concluded that the Vietnam War had hamstrung the United States. Pyongyang might have concluded, that is, that America's focus and resources were so diverted by the war that U.S. Forces Korea might be unable to contain further provocations, let alone stop an all-out ground offensive.[12]

Bonesteel pushed for more analysis and intelligence collection, and urged the intelligence community to draft a new SNIE on the North Korean threat.[13] The State Department had also noted an "alarming" increase in North Korean activities and subversion across the Military Demarcation Line (MDL). State concluded that the United States had "serious gaps in our intelligence picture of military developments and resources north of the MDL."[14] On 25 October 1967, the U.S. Intelligence Board agreed that intelligence efforts regarding the political, economic, and military situation in North Korea should be increased given the North's "incipient campaign of terror and sabotage in rear areas of South Korea." In response, the Defense Intelligence Agency briefed the Critical Collection Problems Committee about intelligence gaps regarding Korea. In particular, the intelligence community increased the priority for electronic intelligence collection against the North.[15]

Tempering this desire for more intelligence was the desire to avoid an incident. The North Koreans had attempted to down an RB-47 reconnaissance aircraft operating well offshore in 1965.[16] NKAF fighters were known to be sensitive to reconnaissance operations approaching Wonsan. General Bonesteel, for example, later commented: "We knew the North Koreans . . . were very sensitive to any reconnaissance in that area. They had chased planes off from there before, and had made it very plain that this was an area they didn't want bothered."[17] The DPRK had trained its pilots to shoot down aircraft flying at the high altitudes used by Black Shield aircraft (presumably the A-12/SR-71).[18] With this background, State had balked at approving more Black Shield missions over North Korea. In fact, Black Shield would fly no missions over the DPRK during the several weeks preceding the *Pueblo* seizure.[19] Additionally, after USS *Banner* had encountered aggressive Chinese trawlers near Shanghai, INR had been skittish about approving AGER surveillance missions off the Chinese coast. The bureau had even forced the cancellation of a proposed *Banner* patrol into the Yellow Sea.[20]

Risk assessment for missions against North Korea was thus not a rubber-stamp process. *Pueblo*'s mission proposal was not lost in the shuffle. In fact, recently declassified documents show that *Pueblo*'s proposed January 1968 mission stood out among the others proposed for that period—a surprising fact considering that more than eight hundred sensitive military intelligence collection missions were reviewed that month.[21] Nevertheless, the fear of disapproval probably biased the assessment process toward reducing the risk assessment. This bias would have been particularly influential in a situation in which a mission could easily be given one of two risk assessments, one slightly higher than the other. The Naval Court of Inquiry that investigated the *Pueblo* incident concluded that the "only acceptable risk [for mission approval] for an AGER mission was 'minimal.' Consequently, it is considered that this factor unduly influenced the assessment of risk for *Pueblo*."[22] No operational command wanted to be denied the use of its assets for collecting useful intelligence, especially against an emerging threat like North Korea.

Risk assessment for *Pueblo*'s proposed January 1968 mission was a cumbersome process involving four echelons in the chain of command and at least six national organizations. The process was complicated by the short time allotted for the review. From start to finish, the approval took only twelve workdays—a significant feat considering that hundreds of other proposals were included in the monthly reconnaissance schedule. And it occurred in the middle of the Christmas holiday stand-down in Washington.

The overriding assumption justifying approval for *Pueblo*'s mission at all levels of the military chain of command was a simple one: North Korea would comply with international maritime law and recognize the right of a warship operating outside its claimed twelve-mile territorial limit to pass unmolested. Although the actual risk methodologies used by various elements in the approval chain differed, each command would return to this assumption in justifying its assessment of "minimal risk"—the lowest kind of risk in anybody's book.

COMNAVFORJAPAN, for example, estimated the risk as "minimal, since *Pueblo* will be operating in international waters for entire deployment."[23] In addressing Congress during the postincident investigation, Rear Adm. Frank L. Johnson (COMNAVFORJAPAN) ticked off the criteria Naval Forces Japan had used in its initial risk assessment (a one-line comment buried in its 14 December 1967 mission proposal to CINCPACFLT):[24]

- political climate
- sensitivity of target country
- material condition of the ship
- state of training of the ship's personnel
- climatological condition in the area of the patrol
- nature and sensitivity of the operation
- possibility of hostile reactions

- forces available for the mission
- previous experiences in the proposed area of operation
- difficulties of navigation in the proposed area of operation
- encounters with ships and aircraft (mutual interference to be expected)
- anticipated intelligence take
- support forces available
- opposing forces

Admiral Johnson had concurred with the "minimal risk" evaluation. "I was aware of the increase of incidents along the DMZ," he testified, "and I was aware over the past year of certain actions taken by the North Koreans. . . . Nevertheless, I did agree that the risk was minimal, and I personally made the final decision."[25]

It is interesting that USFK evidently did not participate in the assessment process, although it was an information addressee on the relevant message traffic. General Bonesteel was aware of the patrol and had voiced reservations:

> We had absolutely nothing to do with the *Pueblo*. I tried in a low key way to warn them about the sensitivity of Wonsan with regard to earlier expeditions of a similar nature. . . . I should have been more acutely interested. I knew vaguely what was there and I knew that my previous warnings, which were entirely at too low and informal a level, had apparently not clicked. But, hell, I had had this near assassination of the President and the ROKs screaming to march North, so I was slightly distracted from that Navy operation. . . . I think it was a case of failing to adequately evaluate the risks. The sensitivities of this area were known . . . the people who were responsible were totally out of touch with what the situation was in North Korea. The essential decisions on risks were made in Washington without reference to us in the area.[26]

The Hawaii links in the approval chain, CINCPACFLT and CINCPAC, concurred with the proposal and the risk assessment on 17 and 23 December 1967, respectively.[27] At CINCPACFLT, Capt. John Marocchi, the assistant chief of staff for intelligence, quickly endorsed the mission:

> The North Koreans were pushing bodies across the DMZ. They continued to seize South Korean ships and accuse them of being spy boats. What we saw and heard didn't seem any different from what we had been seeing and hearing for the past ten years. The Koreans, up to that point, had done nothing to

our ships, while the Russians had harassed them. The mission looked like it would be quite safe. The logic was in the message. It took me about as long to approve it as it did to read it.[28]

Meanwhile, the Joint Chiefs of Staff Joint Reconnaissance Center (JRC) had received a copy of the mission proposal message. The JRC began the Washington-level review while the approval process continued in parallel in Hawaii. In doing this, JRC played the role of ringmaster in securing the concurrence of disparate organizations.[29] The JRC prepared the monthly reconnaissance schedule book on 26 December and distributed it to the military services, the DIA, and other Washington agencies.

Within the DIA, the schedule was to have been forwarded to the Current Operations Office of the assistant director for intelligence production. (In fact, the DIA's internal postmortem revealed that key personnel within that office were unaware of *Pueblo*'s impending mission, let alone given an opportunity to comment on the proposal.)[30] The director later explained that the DIA's role in this process was threefold: to provide current intelligence support to the JRC, to validate the intelligence requirements for a given mission, and to assess the degree of risk associated with the mission. The DIA's Special Reconnaissance Branch was to provide this support. To validate a mission, it would compare the mission's intelligence collection potential with the standing intelligence requirements. Particularly, it would seek to avoid duplication in collection efforts.[31] The DIA was supposed to warn of any developments that might affect ongoing collection efforts, including reconsidering and reissuing risk assessments "when warranted by changing intelligence considerations" outside the monthly approval cycle. The DIA reevaluated the risk to airborne reconnaissance missions being flown against the North in 1967 but evidently did not issue such a risk assessment reevaluation in the short time between North Korea's attack on the Blue House on 21 January 1968 and its seizure of *Pueblo* two days later.[32]

Testimony by Lt. Gen. Joseph Carroll, the director of the DIA, implied that the DIA's Special Reconnaissance Branch was supposed to brief several senior DIA officials (including the assistant director for intelligence production) using color-coded charts displaying the track of the reconnaissance platform. The color used corresponded to the color associated with the appropriate risk assessment (see below). The Special Reconnaissance Branch was also supposed to monitor the reaction to ongoing reconnaissance operations. It was expected to provide daily updates to the chiefs of the Current Operations Office and the Intelligence Support and Indications Division on ongoing missions and significant reactions. Branch members were supposed to prepare DIA officials for JCS meetings.[33]

The DIA assessed risk at one of four levels, combining an assessment of anticipated enemy reaction with an assessment of the collection effort's sensitivity. (Anticipated reactions reflected the nature of the defense penetrated, the provocative nature of missions, the mission vehicle type and capabilities, the sensitivity of the area, and the history of reactions in the area. Sensitivity included the effect of compromise, environmental considerations, political considerations, etc.)[34] Using methodology that the Department of Defense (DOD) adopted in 1963, each of the four levels of risk corresponded to a color code—the color of the paper (and transparency) on which the proposal was presented:[35]

Level 4 (buff): hostile intent remote; intercept actions unlikely; defensive patrols possible

Level 3 (blue): hostile intent unlikely; intercept actions likely; defensive patrols almost certain

Level 2 (salmon): hostile intent possible; intercept actions almost certain

Level 1 (red): hostile intent almost certain

"Defensive patrols" likely refers to fighter reaction to U.S. reconnaissance aircraft. Responding to the mission aircraft, the fighters would take off and fly patrols that would allow them to intercept the mission aircraft should it approach or enter their airspace. Had the assessors wanted to apply the term to a North Korean *naval* reaction to *Pueblo*, they would probably have concluded that naval patrols in that situation were at most "possible." The North had not reacted to *Banner*, and the patrol boats of the North Korean navy normally remained close to shore—and, moreover, their operational tempo dropped sharply in winter.[36]

On 26 December, the *Pueblo* mission proposal was shotgunned to other Washington agencies as part of the monthly reconnaissance schedule proposed for January 1968. The next day, the deputy director for reconnaissance convened the final planners' meeting, which consisted of representatives from the services, DIA, JRC, NSA, CIA, and INR. The meeting was to consider the entire reconnaissance schedule for January before the schedule was presented to the JCS for consideration and approval. By the time the planners met, they would have been aware of *Pueblo*'s proposed mission, areas of operation, and evaluated risk category for at least ten days. When four of the attendees were polled about the meeting some fifteen months later, it became apparent that *Pueblo* had not played a prominent role in the discussions. One individual said that the review covered airborne platforms only. The other three said that *Pueblo* was mentioned only briefly. Nevertheless, testimony prepared for the director of the DIA to present to Congress stated that the proposed *Pueblo* operation was presented on buff-colored paper representing a minimal risk assigned mission. His testimony noted that "there was nothing in these considerations to cause us in DIA or the JRC to alter the risk assessment which had been tentatively assigned to the proposed mission."[37]

The JRC, its review completed, then submitted the proposed schedule for approval by the JCS, DOD, and State Department. In response, on Friday, 29 December, the members of the Joint Chiefs of Staff (or their operations deputies) approved the entire schedule, as did the Office of the Secretary of Defense and, ultimately, the 303 Committee. The 303 Committee oversaw highly sensitive intelligence collection worldwide. On 29 December, the committee, which evidently included Director of Central Intelligence Richard Helms, Deputy Secretary of Defense Paul Nitze, and Undersecretary of State Nicholas Katzenbach, concurred via telephone with the JRC mission forecast for January. (Interestingly, the 303 Committee did not then include a senior military member, although it oversaw sensitive military intelligence collection as well. This would change after the *Pueblo* incident.)[38]

It is tempting to conclude that the *Pueblo* patrol proposal was inconspicuous among the other 808 sensitive collection missions proposed for January 1968; but that seems not to have been the case. *Pueblo* was to make its first patrol off Korea and would be the first naval ship to loiter off the North Korean coast in a long time. Thus, the patrol proposal elicited additional comments from the CIA and NSA, both of which indirectly made the case that the patrol might encounter conditions more threatening than those specified for "minimal risk." However, the CIA and NSA documents appeared *after* the patrol had been approved.[39]

After the deliberations were completed on 29 December, the NSA sent an analytic message highlighting North Korea's sensitivity to reconnaissance operations. The JRC was the sole addressee. (The JCS's servicing communications center readdressed the message to CINCPAC and Director, Naval Security Group, Pacific, as well.) According to Trevor Armbrister, who published a book analyzing the *Pueblo* incident shortly after it ended, a retired navy chief working at the NSA did not agree with the "minimal risk" assessment. He persuaded his boss, the deputy to the assistant director of NSA's Office of Production, to draft a message voicing his doubts. Although it revealed no new information, the message summarized patterns observed over a period of years. Because it illustrates some of what U.S. analysts knew prior to *Pueblo*'s mission, the advisory (DIRNSA 292228Z December 67) is quoted at length below:

> Reference (CINCPAC 230239Z December 1967) states, "Risk to *Pueblo* is estimated to be minimal since operations will be conducted in international waters."
>
> The following information is forwarded to aid in your assessment of CINCPAC's estimate of risk.
>
> The North Korean Air Force has been extremely sensitive to peripheral reconnaissance flights in this area since early 1965. (This sensitivity was emphasized on April 28, 1965, when a U.S. Air Force RB-47 was fired on and severely damaged 35 to 40 nautical miles from the coast.)
>
> The North Korean Air Force has assumed an additional role of naval support since 1966.
>
> The North Korean Navy reacts to any Republic of Korea Navy vessel or Republic of Korea fishing vessel near the North Korean coastline. (This was emphasized on January 19, 1967, when a Republic of Korea naval vessel was sunk by coast artillery.)
>
> Internationally recognized boundaries as they relate to airborne activities are generally not honored by North Korea on the east coast of Korea. But there is no [deleted] evidence of provocative harassing activities by North Korean vessels beyond 12 nautical miles from the coast.
>
> ... The above is provided to aid in evaluating the requirement for ship protective measures and is not intended to reflect adversely on CINCPACFLT deployment proposal.[40]

The message did not persuade the few intelligence analysts who saw it to raise the risk assessment. CINCPAC analysts concluded that it offered nothing new and that no further action was required. In its explanation to the JCS after the seizure, CINCPAC noted that the information the NSA had provided "was reviewed at staff level and it was considered to contain no new information pertaining to the North Koreans' attitude. Accordingly, no further action was deemed necessary."[41] Nevertheless the subsequent Navy Court of Inquiry averred that had the message been readdressed to CINCPACFLT and COMNAVFORJAPAN, "it would have caused these commands to have reviewed the risk assessment and might have resulted in a re-evaluation."[42]

Doubts about the wisdom of the mission popped up in other places as well. After the 303 Committee approved the schedule, R. J. Smith, the deputy director of intelligence (DDI) at the CIA, addressed a 2 January 1968 memo to Rufus Taylor, the deputy director for central intelligence. The memo forwarded the JRC monthly schedule for that month and recommended that Taylor approve it. However, Smith also highlighted a few proposed missions that were "somewhat different from the norm." The declassified paragraph addresses operations of two ships off the North Korean coast but does not identify the second ship. The DDI noted that *Pueblo* would be operating off North Korea, "a new area for SIGINT ship operations." He opined, "in view of the current hostile attitudes and activities of the North Koreans along the DMZ and against South Korean vessels off its coast, it is possible that they might choose to take some sort of action against these ships." The last paragraph of the document concludes that with the "possible exception" of the SIGINT ship's operations off North Korea, "we are not aware of any significant political situations which might cause abnormal reactions or countermeasures against missions as planned." The logic in this wording implies that *Pueblo* *might* cause "abnormal restrictions or countermeasures."[43] Smith's phraseology could readily have justified raising the risk assessment a notch or two.

With the benefit of hindsight, several organizations roundly condemned the risk assessment process. Congress treated it as a key culprit in the *Pueblo* seizure, concluding that "no level of authority in either the intelligence chain of command or the operating chain of command was sensitive to the abundant evidence indicating the development of a progressively more aggressive and hostile attitude by the North Koreans."[44] The Court of Inquiry called to review the risk assessment process at all levels of the chain of command likewise faulted the process:[45]

As borne out, COMNAVFORJAPAN, CINCPACFLT, CINCPAC, and State all underestimated the risk. It appears that no level of authority in the intelligence chain was sensitive to a possible change in attitude on the part of the North Koreans, evidenced by the increased border incidents with South Korea, the attempt to assassinate the South Korean president, and the North Korea broadcasts with respect to U.S. ships off her claimed territorial waters. Previous North Korean pride, warnings, conduct, and hostility were not properly appreciated, especially when a "quid pro quo" situation did not exist.

"Quid pro quo" refers to the availability of North Korean surveillance vessels that the United States might seize in retaliation. The North Korean Navy remained focused on coastal patrols.

A January 1968 editorial in the *New York Times* also accused the U.S. government of failing to heed North Korean press warnings. The *Times* claimed that "the evidence that at least twice this month, after seizing South Korean vessels, North Korea had warned that it might also take countermeasures against American 'spy boats,' raised serious questions about the American command and control system that permitted the *Pueblo* to be captured."[46] This assertion raised the tempting theory that a more astute interpretation of the North Korean media might have prevented the incident. In the end, the several internal reviews prompted by the accusation showed that the *Times* was following a false lead.[47]

Responding to the movements of the ROK fishing fleet and escort naval vessels, the DPRK had been making "spy boat" accusations for years. Any boat that operated in areas the North viewed as contested could earn that epithet. Notably, these accusations did not correlate to *Banner*'s transits past the DPRK. The North made no spy boat accusations during *Pueblo*'s patrol. When, in April 1969, President Nixon claimed that the North Korean press had provided adequate warning, his national security adviser, Henry Kissinger, tried to correct the record by providing him with a copy of Richard Helms's testimony before Congress. In closed hearings, Helms had stated that the Foreign Broadcast Information Service had reviewed potentially relevant North Korean statements between November 1966 and January 1968, and had found only statements that applied "broadly to South Korean naval and fishing boats." The content analysis of the North Korean media was complicated because the North Korean press treated South Korea as a surrogate of the United States. Consequently, DPRK media routinely described incursions by South Korean ships—whether fishing boats, naval ships, or actual agent infiltrations—as "provocations by U.S. imperialism" or by "the U.S. aggressor."[48] Kissinger concluded his memo by advising President Nixon that if he were asked about the so-called warnings again, he might characterize them as only "generalized in nature."[49] Other reviews of the North Korean press—some going back to the early 1960s—arrived at a similar conclusion. In other words, the anti–U.S. content in the North Korean media had reached such a crescendo that it failed to serve as a useful warning indicator, at least as far as *Pueblo* was concerned.[50]

Another potential indicator of increasingly hostile activity might have been associated with recent personnel changes among the top DPRK leadership. The period from 1966 to 1970 was characterized by enormous turbulence at the upper levels of the government and the Korean Workers' Party. Several organizations watched and tried to interpret these developments. Unfortunately, at the time it was virtually impossible to correlate the leadership changes with particular incidents. In a detailed study of North Korean leadership changes between 1966 and 1970, the British Foreign Office concluded: "It is reasonable to suppose that the changes in policy are related to the changes in top leadership. It should be emphasized, however, there is *no* evidence available to support speculation linking particular policies with any of the personalities involved in, or apparently unaffected by, the reshuffles."[51] In fact, the most extreme proponents of violence had been removed from their jobs before the EC-121 shootdown occurred.

## Risk Assessment Reevaluated

If the North Korean media were unhelpful, what evidence *should* the assessors have seized on to place the proposed *Pueblo* mission in a more appropriate risk category? While no single piece of information would have made the risk factor clear, there are several flaws in the way the data were arrayed and the finished analysis disseminated. Any "lessons-learned" committee should have recognized the following failures in the risk assessment process.

The *need to link* attacks against U.S. forces on the ground and in the air

(RB-47 shootdown attempt in 1965) with the assessed threat to a naval unit loitering off North Korea's coast. Since 1966, North Korea had shown itself to be quite willing to kill American military personnel. More than one hundred South Koreans and Americans died in 1967–68. The attacks had been deliberate, and the rising tide of trans-DMZ violence was not directed against ROK Army units alone. On 22 May 1967, North Korean infiltrators had destroyed two American barracks and killed or wounded twenty-one U.S. personnel.[52] Yet, somehow, risk assessors throughout the chain of command ascribed to a small, virtually unarmed U.S. naval ship a special protected status not enjoyed by a well-armed U.S. military facility in a sovereign country.

The need to *beware of false analogies* when comparing potential North Korean, Chinese, and Soviet reactions to U.S. surveillance missions. The risk assessors noted that both China and the USSR had harassed *Banner*. In reviewing these incidents, the analysts trying to anticipate a North Korean reaction felt reassured because China and the USSR had limited their responses to vigorous harassment. However, no state of even limited hostilities existed between the United States and either Moscow or Beijing. Moreover, the Soviets seemed very comfortable with the concept of close and prolonged maritime surveillance—at least as practiced by their AGIs. The reassurance gained from the relative ease of collection efforts against neighboring countries should have played little role in assessing a reaction by the DPRK.

The need to *consider that the DPRK was sensitive* to any kind of maritime activity in its waters, and to aircraft approaching Wonsan in particular. Although *Banner* inspired no North Korean media warnings about "spy boats," risk assessors should have given more credence to the other warnings than they did. Even the most casual reading of the North Korean media should have led an analyst to conclude that the North was highly sensitive about its maritime boundaries. The fact that North Korean fighters had reacted to U.S. reconnaissance planes approaching Wonsan should have made planners reconsider when they were drawing up patrol boxes that would authorize *Pueblo* to approach within nearly thirteen miles of that particularly sensitive area. Finally, the assessors drew a second false analogy: North Korea's reaction to a vessel lingering off its coast would be the same as its response to a ship in transit. In other words, they erroneously concluded that the North would not react to an AGER on patrol off Wonsan because it had not reacted to three AGER transits by *Banner* along its coasts.

The need to *consult the supported command.* Although these sensitive air and maritime surveillance missions were conducted to support CINCPAC, the more immediate beneficiaries of the intelligence "take" were U.S. Forces Korea and some fifty thousand U.S. personnel who were at risk from North Korean attack. Although an addressee on some of the message traffic planning the *Pueblo* mission, USFK evidently did not contribute formal evaluations to the risk assessment process. Had there been a more formal and established mechanism for USFK to weigh into the process, General Bonesteel's doubts might have had a better hearing than they received. Ambassador William Porter in Seoul was not informed about *Pueblo* until after the mission went awry; that is, the country team that would have to resolve the crisis was not even given an opportunity to comment on the mission. (After *Pueblo,* USFK would be authorized to provide the ambassador with monthly updates on planned reconnaissance activity against North Korea.)[53]

The need to justify the risk assessment with *a more detailed written discussion.* The written risk assessments submitted up the chain of command were perfunctory. However, the Court of Inquiry's conclusion that better dissemination of the NSA analyst's summary might have caused the risk to be reevaluated gets closer to the heart of the problem. Had COMNAVFORJAPAN provided a detailed written explanation justifying its risk assessment—the one that was included in the proposal that started the whole approval process—its logic could have been more readily challenged (or endorsed) as the proposal rocketed up the chain of command. Likewise, the conscientious NSA analyst might also have taken one or two further steps. First, had he felt strongly that the risk assessment was too low, his message should have stated that. In addition to sending the message to the JRC, he might also have repackaged the information slightly and then transmitted it as a standard—but widely disseminated—analytic product. This would have ensured that everyone was on the same page.

Should *Pueblo* have been sent on its initial patrol off North Korea at all? Going by the knowledge then available, a case could be made that *Pueblo* should have undertaken the mission but with a higher risk assessment (and the appropriate support that would have implied). After all, there was a growing demand for intelligence about North Korea, and *Pueblo* would be in a position to collect unique information. An analyst could have made a persuasive argument for undertaking the patrol even if the risk assessment were bumped up from risk category 4 to category 3. The assessors would merely have admitted that hostile intent was unlikely (versus remote) and that intercept actions (in this case, a naval surface reaction) were likely (versus unlikely).

A higher risk assessment might have jeopardized—and certainly would have complicated—approval for *Pueblo*'s patrol. However, the unusual nature of such a determination would also likely have raised the issue of on-call support from the Fifth Air Force (or even from a scarce Seventh Fleet surface unit). Instead, COMNAVFORJAPAN assessors stuck to their guns. They continued to treat *Pueblo* as a minimal-risk affair even after the vessel was on station. There is no record that the Blue House raid caused anyone at any level of the chain of command to reevaluate the risk to *Pueblo* or to suggest modifying the proposed patrol boxes. Members of the COMNAVFORJAPAN staff, the immediate operational commander, reasoned that the patrol was nearly over, that there was no evidence that the DPRK had reacted to *Pueblo*, and therefore there was no need to pull *Pueblo* off station. They even elected not to send a special advisory message to *Pueblo* on the Blue House event. Instead, they assumed that *Pueblo*'s commander would retrieve the information from the fleet intelligence broadcast being sent to all Seventh Fleet ships and take appropriate precautions. *Pueblo*'s commanding officer, Comdr. Lloyd Bucher, stated that he never got the word on the Blue House raid. Had he been advised of the event, he would have moved *Pueblo* from harm's way.[54]

# 4
# PLAYING
# CATCH-UP

*Pueblo* began its patrol in the Sea of Japan on 10 January 1968. On 23 January 1968 that patrol was abruptly interrupted by the North Korean Navy. *Pueblo* was in port in Wonsan, North Korea, within six hours of being boarded. All levels of the U.S. chain of command responded frantically during the first few hours after the seizure. Although no command was prepared for the incident, Herculean efforts were made at crisis management, contingency planning, and force deployment. But the United States could send no ships and few aircraft to *Pueblo*'s aid in the few hours between its seizure and nightfall. The handful of fighters that might have arrived would have been overmatched in a "come as you are war." Indeed, General Wheeler, the chairman of the JCS, said, "We would have been in a fine fix if we had sent planes up there. We probably would have been in a war."[1]

The U.S. military responses on 23–25 January were successful in the sense that they rapidly increased U.S. readiness to retaliate for the seizure and to defend the ROK against a surprise attack. In more ways than were then publicly apparent, the U.S. military handled a daunting array of planning, deployment, and logistical tasks smoothly and within a remarkably short period. Although the incident remains painful to recall, even so long after the fact, the material now available reveals a successful response on the part of military commanders and national decision makers to an unprecedented and challenging situation.

## Seizure

The JCS had advised CINCPAC on 2 January 1968 that the *Pueblo* mission was approved. As the approval worked its way down the chain, *Pueblo*'s crew completed preparations for a patrol that ultimately commenced from Sasebo, Japan, on 10 January. *Pueblo* would first steam to the far north of the DPRK and then work its way south toward Wonsan through a series of patrol boxes named Pluto, Venus, and Mars. The vessel had been on patrol off the Korean coast for thirteen days when it was seized.[2]

When the National Command Authorities approved *Pueblo*'s mission, the U.S. intelligence community likely was advised to be alert for potential North Korean reactions to the patrol. Nevertheless, there was no explicit evidence that *Pueblo* itself would be threatened. After the seizure, COMNAVFORJAPAN reportedly received a report from a Japanese merchant ship captain that there was extraordinary naval activity going on in Wonsan. The captain had visited Wonsan many times and reported the unusual activity on his return from there on 19 January 1968. The hiatus on U.S. manned reconnaissance flights over the North for several weeks before the seizure, however, prevented this activity from being noted. Even had U.S. intelligence analysts detected abnormally high levels of activity in Wonsan, this activity would not necessarily have been seen as threatening to *Pueblo*. After all, Pyongyang would have likely increased its state of alertness to prepare for potential ROK retaliation for the 21 January Blue House raid.[3]

The crew of *Pueblo* itself reported that North Korea was a very quiet collection environment for most of the patrol. On 21 January, *Pueblo* observed a probable SO-1 sub chaser that slowed and approached to within three hundred yards. Not absolutely certain it had been detected, the AGER did not break radio silence to report the contact. However, the North certainly detected *Pueblo* the next day. Two North Korean trawlers, *Rice Paddy* and *Rice Paddy One*, circled and approached to within thirty yards of *Pueblo* as it operated approximately twenty miles northeast of Wonsan. North Korea must have been sorely tempted to harass the vessel, at the very least.[4] The CIA later assessed that the "report which the trawlers probably made would have been enough to justify making plans to deal with the *Pueblo* and sending a naval vessel out on patrol."[5]

Neither the United States nor the ROK provoked North Korea into seizing *Pueblo*. The AGER remained outside North Korea's territorial waters. It had been loitering off Wonsan with a claimed closest point of approach more than 15.8 miles from the nearest North Korean territory. Postseizure reviews conducted by U.S. Forces Korea revealed that no ROK air or navy units had operated off the east coast of North Korea during the two days preceding the *Pueblo* incident. Moreover, ROK ground activity had been confined to intensified counterinfiltration operations.

The seizure of *Pueblo* was the first of two surprises. The second occurred when the COMNAVFORJAPAN staff discovered that no aircraft were standing by to come to *Pueblo*'s assistance. For reasons described earlier, COMNAV-FORJAPAN had not requested the Fifth Air Force to alert aircraft to provide "on-call" support for *Pueblo*.[6]

As several first-person accounts and published sources discuss the seizure in great detail, only a short summary follows here. At midday on the twenty-third, one SO-1 sub chaser and three P-4 patrol boats approached *Pueblo*. At 1300, the North Korean vessels directed *Pueblo* to follow them to port. (All times are local Korea/Japan times. To convert to Eastern Standard Time, subtract fourteen hours. Thus, the patrol boats asked *Pueblo* to follow them at 2300 EST on 22 January.) The Koreans attempted to board the AGER at 1315, but *Pueblo* responded by steaming away at one-third speed. At 1327, the North Korean vessels fired on *Pueblo* in an attempt to stop it. *Pueblo* was boarded at 1345 while two MiGs circled overhead. It reached the North Korean claimed twelve-mile territorial limit at 1530 and the internationally recognized three-mile limit at 1645. Local sunset was at 1737.[7]

During the events described above, *Pueblo* provided a steady stream of updates via radio operator chatter and, ultimately, OPREP-3 messages. Based on this flow of information, COMNAVFORJAPAN requested assistance from the Fifth Air Force at 1335. The Fifth Air Force, however, was unprepared to provide immediate support because no request had been made to put support aircraft on alert. In fact, no unit anywhere in the western Pacific was standing by to come to *Pueblo*'s assistance. CINCPAC, Adm. U. S. Grant Sharp, summarized the mess: "The United States was not in very good shape in Korea. We were not ready for any kind of a hassle up there, neither from the point of view of air defense or ground defense or air offense. There were many things that would have to be done before we could have said that Korea was ready to do something."[8]

Table 3 lists the aircraft potentially available to help *Pueblo*. In each case, however, hours would have been required to prepare the aircraft and their crews for the mission and to fly them the long distances to Wonsan—if a commander was willing to risk war by responding before the National Command Authorities gave permission.[9]

**Table 3. Aircraft Dispositions in the Western Pacific on 23 January 1968**

| Type | Number | Disposition |
|---|---|---|
| F-4C | 6 | Republic of Korea |
| F-105 | 8 | Japan |
| F-4C (USAF) | 32 | Japan |
| A-4 (USMC) | 20 | Japan |
| USS *Enterprise* air wing | | 470 nautical miles southeast of Wonsan |
| A-6 | 12 | |
| F-4B | 24 | |
| A-4 | 23 | |

Additionally, the ROK Air Force had forty-four F-5As, twenty-three F-86Ds, and sixty-one F-86Fs ready for combat. Many of these aircraft were already on alert in response to the Blue House incident two days earlier. Washington had not informed the ROK about *Pueblo*'s impending mission, however, and it would have been awkward to ask for their assistance. General Bonesteel mentioned that he initially considered requesting ROK assistance but ruled it out because details on *Pueblo* were for Americans' eyes only, because tensions between the two Koreas were already high, and because doing so might have "UN command complications."[10]

The F-4s already at Osan Air Base in Korea were the closest U.S. aircraft. However, they were on nuclear alert, and it would have taken hours to plan the mission, download the special weapons they carried, and replace them with three-thousand-pound bombs. In addition, their bomb racks would not accommodate the smaller ordnance appropriate to antiship attack. Those bomb racks would have had to be flown in from outside the country if the F-4s were to be really useful.[11]

Despite the difficulties in coming to *Pueblo*'s aid from a cold start, the commander of the Fifth Air Force, General McKee, tried to get *something* airborne en route to Korea. COMNAVFORJAPAN had requested Fifth Air Force assistance at 1335. The F-105 Thunderchiefs the Fifth had available to send had been involved in training and were armed only with guns. Furthermore, they would need to refuel in Korea: the distances were too great to allow any loiter time near Wonsan without additional fuel. Determined to respond somehow, the Fifth Air Force started launching pairs of aircraft for Osan at 1611, one hour and twenty-three minutes after McKee ordered them to launch from a nonalert status. Unfortunately, the refueling stop at Osan guaranteed that the Thunderchiefs would not reach Wonsan before nightfall. Ultimately, the Fifth Air Force ordered all available F-105s from Okinawa to Kunsan and Osan. By the next day, twelve had deployed to Osan and all Fifth Air Force fighters and reconnaissance aircraft were on alert. Additionally, the air force command had begun planning for a massive augmentation.[12]

The American fighter planes based in Japan could offer little assistance. Under a diplomatic agreement, U.S. fighters based in Japan could not fly directly into combat from Japanese bases. They would have to fly to Korea first.[13]

Finally, the *Enterprise* air wing had sustained heavy damage from a storm. In any event, those aircraft that could fly would have encountered the same approval, planning, and loading delays encountered by other U.S. squadrons in the western Pacific. General Wheeler estimated that it would have taken them approximately three hours to arrive over *Pueblo*.[14]

General Wheeler took all of these factors into account when he explained to the president why no aircraft had come to *Pueblo*'s rescue. Wheeler explained that "their use could have been more harmful than helpful" and made several additional points.[15]

- The North Korean air defense environment was decidedly unfavorable for a successful U.S. response. Approximately seventy-five MiGs were based in Wonsan, and North Korea was maintaining a prolonged airborne alert during the seizure. The "rescuer" aircraft would be flying well within the North Korean air defense control net; NKAF radar coverage and ground-control intercept capabilities would have been effective against U.S. fighters even at low levels.

- The weather was poor. Cloud cover was at six thousand feet, with broken, occasional overcast and lower scattered clouds at three thousand feet. There were occasional snow showers. Even finding *Pueblo* might be impossible.
- The handful of U.S. fighters attempting to warn away the North Korean patrol boats would have been vastly outnumbered by NKAF fighters. The United States would have needed other aircraft to "pin down" the MiGs that might take off as well as those already airborne.
- There was reasonable doubt that the U.S. aircraft would have been able to drive off the North Korean boats without sinking one or more of them, and perhaps also sinking *Pueblo* in the process. It was also unlikely that the mere presence of U.S. aircraft would have caused the North Korean boats to free *Pueblo,* since the MiGs would certainly have engaged the U.S. aircraft fighters.

In other words, the JCS chairman felt that the small contingent of U.S. fighters that might have flown to *Pueblo*'s aid would have been in serious jeopardy.

## Initial Responses in the Theater

The documentary record shows that as the National Command Authorities began in the first twenty-four hours to formulate a strategy for dealing with the seizure of *Pueblo,* forces in the theater were already preparing to carry out any of several retaliatory contingencies. COMNAVFORJAPAN notified CINC-PACFLT of the seizure at 1420 Korean time, within an hour of the event. For the commanders and staffs of the Pacific Fleet and its subordinate Seventh Fleet, preparations entailed rapid planning and unit redeployment. The U.S. Air Force also began planning to move the first of several hundred aircraft toward or into the Republic of Korea. General Bonesteel heightened his forces' alert and surveillance status and considered increasing readiness from the normal Defense Readiness Condition (DEFCON) 4 to DEFCON 3.[16]

During the first day of the crisis, the Pacific Fleet staff considered many options, some of which anticipated the more deliberate assessment process that would occur in Washington over the next six days. These options included requesting permission to conduct land-based or naval air strikes against "a suitable target"; steaming a carrier task group into the Sea of Japan and conducting photo reconnaissance; seizing a North Korean ship on the high seas; positioning USS *Banner* off Wonsan; disposing naval forces in such a way that the U.S. government could credibly demand compensation, apologies, and guarantees from North Korea; and blockading Wonsan.[17]

Navy messages flew across the theater. At 1506 on the afternoon of the seizure, the commander of the Seventh Fleet directed the nuclear-powered aircraft carrier USS *Enterprise* (CVN-65), the nuclear-powered guided missile cruiser *Truxton* (CGN-35), and three destroyers to proceed "at best speed" to the southern end of the Tsushima Strait. Between 1800 and 1900 that evening, Pacific Command ordered its forces to prepare for photo reconnaissance of Wonsan to determine *Pueblo*'s position; at about the same time, the commander in chief of the Pacific Command asked the Joint Chiefs to authorize this reconnaissance if North Korea remained silent as to the ship's location. As a precaution, USS *Banner* was ordered to discontinue surveillance operations off the east coast of Honshu and return to Yokosuka.[18]

At 1921, the commander of the Pacific Fleet directed the commander of the Seventh Fleet to

> take steps to place and support [a] destroyer ASAP [as soon as possible] off Wonsan immediately outside 12-mile limit. Be prepared to engage in operations that may include towing *Pueblo* and or retrieval of *Pueblo* crew/provide air cover as appropriate. Make sitreps [situation reports] as appropriate and at least hourly.[19]

The Seventh Fleet staff amplified this order seventy-five minutes later, directing *Enterprise* into the Sea of Japan and sending the destroyer USS *Higbee* (DD-806) toward Wonsan. A second destroyer would follow.[20] At about the same time, the Pacific Fleet commander also directed the Seventh Fleet commander to conduct photo reconnaissance missions over Wonsan.[21] The commander of the Seventh Fleet relayed this order at 2334 but advised his subordinates that since *Pueblo* was believed to be inside North Korean territorial waters, any offensive military action had to be authorized by higher authority.[22] Shortly after midnight, the task group commander on board *Enterprise* responded that he planned flight operations during daylight from a position east of Pusan to rearrange the air wing for future operations.[23]

Evidently, the National Command Authorities suddenly put the brakes on this planning, preparation, and northward surging of naval forces. At 0138 in the morning of 24 January, the Pacific Fleet commander directed all U.S. naval forces to remain south of 36 degrees north latitude and to make no show of force in the area of the incident. No destroyer would be positioned off Wonsan.[24] By 0700 the Pacific Fleet commander had also directed the cessation of signals intelligence flights over the Sea of Japan and Yellow Sea. Further, no antisubmarine warfare flights were allowed near the incident site with the exception of a two-plane barrier near the battle group.[25]

At 0730, the commander in chief of the Pacific Command confirmed that the Joint Staff had prohibited shows of force. He explicitly directed the commander of the Pacific Fleet not to position *Higbee* off Wonsan; other fleet units repositioned as a result of the incident were to steam no farther north than their present locations.[26] *Enterprise* had advanced as far as the northeast end of the Korea Strait, south of Pusan; by noon, the carrier had withdrawn southwest into the East China Sea to gain sea room. *Higbee* and three other destroyers—*Osbourn* (DD-846), *Collett* (DD-730), and *O'Bannon* (DD-450) —were to rendezvous with *Enterprise* there between 24 and 26 January.[27]

By midday on 24 January, CINCPAC took further steps to reduce the risk of war, ordering his subordinate commanders to

> initiate no show of force along the Korean demilitarized zone or elsewhere adjacent to North Korea. . . . U.S. naval and air forces will remain outside repeat outside of the area within 80 NM [nautical miles] of the coast of North Korea north of a line extending east from the DMZ. This instruction does not alter your existing authorities and responsibilities for the security of your forces.[28]

In Seoul, General Bonesteel notified his forces of the *Pueblo* seizure on the afternoon of 23 January and directed I Corps to bring its command posts to operating strength. He instructed subordinate commands to heighten their alertness state, to ensure that key personnel were available in command posts, and to review the checklist for steps required to assume DEFCON 3 (U.S. Forces Korea would have been at DEFCON 4 at the time). Although Bonesteel advised CINCPAC late that afternoon that he was considering going to DEFCON 3 "shortly," he ultimately decided to remain at the lower alert status.[29] Between 1960 and the present, USFK has raised the DEFCON status only once in response to conditions on the peninsula itself, and that was after North

Korean provocations in the Joint Security Area at Panmunjom in 1976. A shift to DEFCON 3 would have sent a serious signal of preparations for war.

Why did General Bonesteel decide not to raise the DEFCON after *Pueblo* was seized? As mentioned earlier, he had devoted considerable effort to dissuading the enraged South Korean leadership from retaliating after the attempt on President Park's life. To approach the ROK to ask for assistance after an *American* asset had been seized would have seemed hypocritical. Moreover, Bonesteel was also the commander of the UN Command forces. If he raised the U.S. defense readiness condition, ROK commanders might take it as the signal and blessing they needed to raise their own readiness levels and then retaliate. The benefits that might have been gained by increased U.S. readiness might have been lost in a war of retaliation initiated by the ROK.

Nevertheless, Bonesteel did contact the ROK defense minister later on the twenty-third to inform him (post facto) of the *Pueblo* seizure and explain the U.S. responses. (Initially, the message traffic on the increased U.S. readiness was for U.S. eyes only, but Bonesteel secured permission to brief the ROK leadership.) When he was told that the United States was reviewing the checklists required to raise the alert status to DEFCON 3, the minister asked if Bonesteel had evidence that the North was actually preparing for war. When advised that the United States lacked such proof, the minister said that U.S. moves to increase readiness even to the point of reviewing DEFCON 3 checklists were an overreaction.[30]

In the event, USFK did not change the DEFCON. However, major elements of American and South Korean forces remained engaged in counter-infiltration operations, which had accelerated after North Korean agents had attempted to assassinate President Park on the twenty-first.[31] Bonesteel also raised other issues. On the twenty-fourth, he again warned the National Command Authorities that he feared Pyongyang might be making a serious miscalculation. In a "personal for" message to General Wheeler and Admiral Sharp, he wrote:

> Continuing evidence crop [*sic*] up in both North Korean actions and statements that Kim Il Sung may be suffering from serious miscalculation as to U.S. capacity to react in Korea at the same time the war continues in Vietnam. This contains seeds of real danger if credibility of U.S. deterrent against overt action remains in doubt. . . . My concern . . . is that while some of our predic-

tions have seemed "far out," the North Koreans have exceeded them and at higher tempo.[32]

Bonesteel was particularly concerned about the active threat North Korean infiltrators posed to the security of surface-to-air missile and nuclear weapons sites. He concurred with some of the U.S. Air Force commander's proposed steps to enhance air defense readiness. (Likely anticipating the ROK Air Force's desire to retaliate, Bonesteel directed the air component commander not to break out weapons for offensive strike aircraft.) On the twenty-fourth, he reported that he was considering deploying another battalion from the U.S. Seventh Division to reinforce local defenses at these sites. Bonesteel also recommended an "expeditious decision" to augment the Eighth Army, particularly for local security. Concerned with the maritime borders, he indicated that he might soon recommend that two U.S. destroyers and maritime patrol aircraft reinforce the South Korean naval and air force units then conducting maritime patrol and interdiction. The command staff was also concerned about protecting the capabilities of the headquarters element. Fearing that the North might cut the communications lines from the headquarters tactical operations center to the "advance camp," the commander ordered staff elements to arrange for communications backups for this link. Moreover, a few days later the staff directed its subordinate logistics command to develop plans to allow the headquarters to relocate to its alternate command post if necessary.[33]

## National-Level Deliberations

The seizure of *Pueblo* spawned a series of meetings among the national leadership. Initially the pace was frenetic—in some cases four such meetings per day—and the topics discussed wide ranging. The courses of action the United States would eventually pursue were mentioned in the very first meeting, but they were buried among other, more belligerent suggestions. By the end of the first week of meetings, President Johnson and his National Security Council advisers had identified diplomacy as their primary strategy for dealing with the crisis. The discussions became much less frequent and more focused as direct negotiations with the DPRK began. However, national decision makers also retained an array of "pressure tactics" to use if talks with the DPRK stalled, and punitive measures should the crew be harmed.

The *Pueblo* story broke in the very early morning hours of 23 January, Washington time. (All times in this section are Eastern Standard Time. Add fourteen hours to convert this time to Korea/Japan time.) National Security Adviser Walt Rostow informed President Johnson at 0225 after talking with the NSA and CINCPAC staffs and several DOD officials.[34] Rostow worked throughout the night to assemble more information in time for the weekly national security luncheon between LBJ and his advisers. In an inconclusive meeting, they discussed *Pueblo* only in the broadest terms: what had happened and what options were available to the United States. The meeting was probably one of generalities because the leadership still lacked solid information about really had happened and why—let alone how to respond to it. Nevertheless, even in this first meeting, Secretary of Defense Robert McNamara mentioned the course of action the United States would rapidly pursue—a buildup of U.S. assets in and around the Koreas. The luncheon concluded with LBJ directing his top decision makers to identify more options.[35]

The next day was far more productive. The senior leadership met four times on 24 January to consider information assembled the previous day. The day entailed a huddle by the top advisers without the president, a more formal meeting with LBJ, another senior advisory meeting, and then finally a second meeting with LBJ. At the end of the day they had addressed issues falling under three broad themes: (1) what had happened and why, (2) what the DPRK was likely to do next, and (3) what steps the United States should take. Although they discussed military courses of action, the group felt it was too early to pursue hostilities. The danger to the crew and the risk of distraction from the ongoing Vietnam War were too great. First, the group sought more information. The DCI was asked to prepare a reconnaissance plan for them by day's end. Second, State recommended a wide array of diplomatic initiatives, placing greatest hopes in a discussion in the United Nations Security Council, an approach to the USSR, and approaches to any country that might have influence in Pyongyang. The diplomatic approaches would also allow LBJ to buy the time required to increase U.S. readiness for conflict by building up air assets in Korea and selectively mobilizing reserves. LBJ concluded that they would flesh out the Security Council option the next morning and directed McNamara to proceed with plans to send more than three hundred aircraft to the ROK and associated selective reserve mobilization.[36]

On the morning of 25 January, President Johnson breakfasted with the U.S. ambassador to the UN, Arthur Goldberg, and his key advisers to refine plans for a presentation to the UN. LBJ hoped that diplomacy would work: "Our primary objective is to gain time," he told the group, "to give all concerned an opportunity for reasoning together. It will give the Soviets time to bring influence to bear on North Korea, if they will."[37]

Meanwhile, McNamara argued that the United States should increase its air power on the peninsula in case North Korea attacked. He reminded his audience that the North had "substantial" air superiority over the South. Transferring several aircraft units from frontline USAF combat units to the Far East would redress the difference. He would compensate the U.S. strategic reserve by selectively activating air force and navy air reserve units. With this argument McNamara submitted a proposed executive order selectively activating air reservists and bringing 332 aircraft into the active inventory.[38]

During these deliberations, Secretary of State Dean Rusk made a side comment that revealed the general uncertainty about North Korea at that high level. Earlier Special National Intelligence Estimates had predicted that the North would not attack: sustained infiltration and sabotage were its likeliest options. A CIA assessment produced the first night of the crisis reiterated that opinion, but no one could be sure. Rusk had been closely involved in Far Eastern affairs throughout his career. His comments revealed a profound distrust of the North (and healthy skepticism about U.S. intelligence analysis): "The North Koreans may have decided to make a try at South Korea," he said. "We must jar the North Koreans loose from the idea of taking South Korea. This call up may do just that." He repeated this theme in his subsequent luncheon with the president. When secretary of defense designate Clark Clifford questioned the wisdom of the impending large military buildup, Rusk observed that without it, "if North Korea goes crazy and launches an attack we couldn't do very much."[39]

The same day, McNamara, in a meeting with the top military and DOD leadership, explained that securing the return of the crew was the primary objective; getting the ship back was secondary. He also advised the top leadership that "excessive" military pressure could backfire.[40]

The group also addressed tactical concerns that might be translated into action within the week. The navy was to start moving USS *Kitty Hawk* toward Korea. USS *Oriskany*'s western Pacific deployment might be extended. (Chief of Naval Operations Adm. Thomas Moorer advised that the Seventh Fleet could position two carriers off Korea for up to six weeks without endangering the Vietnam War effort.) Additionally, the Joint Chiefs recommended that nine submarines be sent to Korea to support surveillance and potential attack missions. The attack boats could be deployed covertly within a week. Although the commander of the Pacific submarine force thought that the resultant number of submarines off North Korea might be excessive, he immediately canceled the departure of two diesels from the Seventh Fleet and dispatched four submarines to the western Pacific. The seventeen submarines in the theater would allow the Seventh Fleet to man nine patrol stations off North Korea for at least three months, albeit at the cost of abandoning nearly every other theater patrol commitment. In the meantime, USS *Ronquil* was immediately authorized to conduct covert and potential search-and-rescue operations in the Sea of Japan.[41]

The JCS also recommended moving another twenty-six B-52s to the western Pacific. The U.S. Air Force chief of staff advised that the ROK base infrastructure could accommodate 352 aircraft in support of the impending deployment. He also warned that if the United States planned to fight, it should plan to first take out *all* North Korean air capability.[42] (This view would also appear in subsequent planning documents prepared for LBJ.)

Addressing the ground situation, the leadership was concerned about ammunition shortfalls. The DOD intended to divert between ten and fifteen thousand tons of aircraft ordnance from Vietnam to Korea. The air force needed a full array of air-to-air and air-to-surface missiles moved to the Korean peninsula. The DOD was also concerned that U.S. Forces Korea was undermanned with only 79 percent of its authorized personnel on board; the Joint Chiefs felt that figure should be 90 percent. In other words, USFK should have the additional 8,500 people that its billet structure authorized. McNamara thought this number was high, however, and directed further review of the request. (The USFK manning issue remained unresolved throughout the *Pueblo* crisis.) The Joint Chiefs also wanted to consider sending Bonesteel two HAWK surface-to-air missile units from Fort Bliss, Texas.[43]

By day's end, LBJ had approved the approach to the UN, some limited reserve call-ups, and some of the aircraft deployments to Korea. McNamara evidently had argued persuasively that any appearance of weakness in Korea would embolden the Soviets and North Vietnamese and might significantly prolong the war in Vietnam. He also argued that a "measured show of force" would support U.S. diplomatic efforts in Korea. General Wheeler showed LBJ a movement schedule that would get the preponderance of aircraft to the Far East in about nine days. Although earlier in the day he had wanted more justification for the aircraft deployment, that night LBJ directed that twenty-eight fighters and fourteen reconnaissance planes be dispatched immediately. He agreed that a "spaced out" flow of aircraft to Korea was appropriate. Despite Clark Clifford's repeatedly expressed misgivings about a massive military buildup in the Far East, the air surge had begun.[44]

The military proposals became even more specific in a 26 January meeting with the president. McNamara urged LBJ to make a final decision on the details of the aircraft deployment package: B-52s, carrier air, and land-based air. As LBJ prepared to take the issue to Congress, McNamara also pushed for the authority to extend military tours of duty, call up individual reservists, and expand the ROK military assistance program by another $100 million. Although LBJ ultimately approved the requests, his focus on the twenty-seventh was to develop a strategy to sell them to key congressional leaders. LBJ would make his case to them on 30 January.[45]

## Intelligence Responses

As the president and his cabinet debated their options, the intelligence community sharply increased collection and analysis to support them. Although it had failed to anticipate the seizure, the community compensated with a full-court press in support of operational- and national-level decision makers. In fact, photo reconnaissance had been a common topic in many of the meetings discussed above. Collectively, the meetings revealed some of the steps taken to enhance collection in the early days of the crisis:

- U.S. satellites were programmed to enhance coverage of Wonsan.[46] However, the resolution of images taken by aircraft was more detailed than that available from KH-4 Corona satellites; accordingly, national decision makers would push for "air-breather" imagery.

- The United States scheduled an A-12 Oxcart flight over North Korea the night of 25 January (Washington time). (The CIA's single-seat, Mach 3–capable Oxcart was a predecessor of the dual-seat SR-71s that the Air Force deployed to Okinawa. Both seem to have been associated with the term *Black Shield*. The last A-12 mission over the DPRK was flown on 8 May 1968. Subsequent flights would be flown by SR-71s.) The first A-12 flight against the DPRK had been scheduled for 25 January but had been postponed when a technical malfunction forced the pilot to abort. Although there was slight risk from North Korean surface-to-air missiles, the Oxcart evidently was to make three high-speed passes over North Korea on its first *Pueblo* crisis mission. Each pass would last seventeen minutes. Overall, planners calculated that the risk to Black Shield would be less than 1 percent, even against experienced surface-to-air missile crews. National leaders were a little concerned that the North would try to shoot it down, and the CIA was ordered to prepare responses in case Pyongyang publicly protested about the mission. In the event, North Korean and Soviet radars detected the aircraft but the North did not try to intercept it. The imagery itself was read out in Japan and was also flown to Washington by 28 January.[47]

- The national leadership did see that high-speed A-12/SR-71 missions were potentially provocative. Indeed, certain missions were postponed at crucial diplomatic junctures. At other times, some planners recommended flying these missions primarily as a means to pressure North Korea. The idea of flying reconnaissance missions to exert pressure stayed in the planning folders for some time, primarily because it was low cost/low risk.[48]

- The United States also continued to fly Bumble Bug drone reconnaissance missions against the North. The drone, launched from a C-130 aircraft, covered a smaller area than the Oxcart/Black Shield flights. Two of the last ten drones had either malfunctioned or been shot down. National decision makers discussed flying a drone mission over Wonsan, but the record does not show if the mission occurred. The next drone flight was scheduled for 29 January.[49]

- DOD wanted to maintain a SIGINT collection aircraft on station south of the DMZ. For the first three days of the crisis, State had managed to block this initiative. The documentary record does not reveal whether DOD ever got its wish.[50]

With collection efforts in gear, the intelligence community soon answered many of the questions that originated on the first day of the crisis, as summarized below.

*Was the North preparing to invade?* The answer, corroborated by extensive imagery coverage, was *no*. Following *Pueblo*'s seizure, North Korean military units assumed a heightened state of alert and maintained it throughout the early days of the crisis. Analysts believed that the alert was defensive; there were "no signs of significant preparations for offensive action."[51] For example, the CIA reported that North Korean naval patrol activity remained heavy, particularly off Wonsan, where it extended thirty miles out to sea.[52]

The most reassuring information came from the images collected by the Black Shield reconnaissance mission flown over the DPRK on 26 January.[53] Although it provided coverage of both coasts and much of the country's southern half, the readout disclosed no evidence of a KPA buildup near or in the DMZ. (However, the interpreters warned that a large number of tunnels, caves, and underground facilities complicated determination of North Korean force levels.) The CIA interpreters concluded that the aircraft complement at eight important airfields was within previous estimates. In some cases, the number of aircraft observed was lower than expected, but interpreters concluded that many aircraft were likely concealed in the extensive system of underground hangers. Naval inventories also appeared normal, with the exception of two Shershen-class patrol boats that had appeared in Wonsan. (However, the DPRK's four Whiskey-class diesel submarines were not observed.) There was no unusual road or rail activity near the DMZ; activity to the north of there could be ascribed to normal economic activity. Industrial activity was within seasonal norms.

The only unusual activity that the photo interpreters observed was defensive. They reported equipment at thirteen of the fourteen known surface-to-air missile sites that the mission covered. At all but one of the sites, one to three missiles were on launchers. Additionally, disruptive painting had been used to camouflage one of the buildings at one of the Samlet cruise missile coastal defense sites. Unfortunately, the mission did not obtain adequate coverage of seven NKAF airfields or the east coast submarine base at Mayang-do. Additionally, analysts wanted an update on KPA ground positions covered in the first Black Shield mission as well as those in the northeast and along North Korea's border with China. CINCPAC and DIA quickly requested a second Black Shield flight.[54]

Black Shield also spotted *Pueblo* at an offshore anchorage in a small, isolated bay north of Wonsan. No damage was discernible. Two patrol boats were alongside; otherwise, there was no evidence of activity around the ship. (The U.S. intelligence community would monitor the location of the ship throughout the crisis. For example, on 12 February, the CIA forwarded a human intelligence report indicating that the North Koreans had moved *Pueblo* from Changjahwan-man [Chojikan] to the nearby naval facility at Munp'yong-ni [Wonsan].[55] On 29 April, the DIA reported that *Pueblo* had been moved from Munp'yong-ni to Najin, an east coast port nineteen miles from the Soviet border.)[56]

*What was Pyongyang's objective?* The CIA, DIA, and State Department rapidly concluded that North Korea had acted independently.[57] *Pueblo*'s seizure had grown out of the regime's desire for unification. Pyongyang's public statements had become more militant since October 1966. On top of this, the CIA noted, North Korea had been "uniformly hostile" toward all vessels in nearby waters since the Korean War. In fact, few South Korean or U.S. ships ever approached North Korea's coast; the exceptions were ROK Navy patrol boats escorting fishing vessels. The North had sunk one of these patrol boats in 1967, and in November 1967 had resumed accusations about "spy boats" that had begun in 1964.[58] The CIA concluded that *Pueblo*

> was almost certainly taken as a result of a decision at the highest levels of the North Korean government. . . . It seems likely . . . that the North Koreans had identified the ship and her mission at least a day in advance. It is possible that the original intent was only to harass and drive off the *Pueblo;* the final decision to take the ship into Wonsan may have only been taken when it eventually appeared that U.S. forces were not coming to assist the *Pueblo.*[59]

In any event, the CIA quickly warned senior U.S. officials that the North Korean regime was prepared for a "period of sharply heightened tensions." In its assessment, Pyongyang would seek to extract propaganda value from the crisis "for some days at least." Interestingly, the initial CIA assessment implied a role for U.S. military pressure, arguing that the North Koreans would release neither ship nor crew "unless they judge the U.S. will resort to retaliatory action, such as an air attack against the patrol craft that seized the *Pueblo.*"[60]

*What would happen if the United States attacked North Korea?* By 26 January the intelligence community had begun to assess likely North Korean responses to several possible U.S. actions. The State Department judged that there was "a fair chance" that the communist regime would release at least some of the crew in response to a combination of warnings, visible military preparations, and a U.S. show of force. Pyongyang would probably see little to be gained from holding the entire crew after the incident's propaganda value had been exhausted. But this outcome could not be guaranteed. Moreover, the assessment observed, shows of force and the like could be "damaging" to South Korea. Further, the Communists might regard some low-level military action (such as a blockade, attacks against a limited set of North Korean targets, etc.) as meant only to assuage American public opinion and might doubt U.S. determination to go further. In such a case, the North Koreans would probably "punish" the crew immediately. They might retaliate by launching air strikes against South Korean airfields or even U.S. aircraft carriers, although such acts seemed unlikely because of the high risk of escalation and ground war. In fact, a State Department memorandum suggested that if the United States should strike North Korea, the Soviets would probably go "quite far in private pressures" on Pyongyang to end the crisis—regardless of their public stance. Nevertheless, no foreseeable scenario guaranteed the crew's release, let alone that of the ship.[61]

*What were North Korea's economic and political vulnerabilities?* North Korea's predominantly overland trade patterns and communist trading partners were not susceptible to naval action or diplomacy. The CIA quickly reported that approximately 87 percent of North Korea's trade in 1966 was with the communist world, 75 percent with the Soviet Union and China. With the exception of bulk commodities, almost all of this trade with its two bordering neighbors was overland. Japan accounted for nearly half of Pyongyang's noncommunist trade. Therefore, a maritime blockade could reduce North Korea's trade by no more than 25 percent. Japanese- and Soviet-flag ships would be the ones primarily affected; they represented roughly two-thirds of all merchant ships entering North Korean ports. The remainder were Polish and British (8 percent each), Greek (5 percent), and an assortment of other ships flying free-world and communist flags.[62]

North Korea had only five merchant ships of its own (a sixth was being fitted out in Nampo) that could be seized in retaliation; the locations of those not believed to be in port were unknown. Four were attached to the fishing fleet. All were less than 2,000 gross registered tons except *Paektu-San* (7,218 tons). The status of three Polish-flag dry-cargo ships operated by the Joint Korean-Polish Ship Broker's Company was continually monitored.[63]

The U.S. leadership quickly looked at economic warfare as a means to force North Korea to release the crew. However, a study produced on 28 January concluded that the North was nearly impervious to free-world economic pressure. The effect of loss of trade with the free world would be small. The loss of access to free-world shipping would be insignificant.

The picture of North Korea painted by the CIA analysts showed a nation with similarly few political vulnerabilities. All communist states would wish the affair to "inflict the maximum feasible damage on the U.S. position, particularly with reference to Vietnam." Nevertheless, the CIA believed that while these allies would want to hinder U.S. efforts in Vietnam, none sought hostilities on the Korean peninsula. Moscow, accordingly, would seek propaganda points but would counsel Pyongyang to avoid further provocations that might trigger U.S. retaliation. The agency warned, however, that Moscow might not be able to restrain Pyongyang should the latter pursue a more belligerent course. China would probably offer ambiguous advice but counsel against "any course of undue risk." Both states were aware that South Korea could also take actions, with or without U.S. concurrence, that could "balloon the crisis out of control." This factor, the CIA believed, gave Moscow and Beijing additional incentive to moderate their advice to Pyongyang.[64]

*What were the Soviets doing?* State's Bureau of Intelligence and Research concluded that the USSR appeared "to have been caught unawares by the *Pueblo* incident." The INR analysts argued that there was little evidence that "Moscow instigated the North Korean seizures of the *Pueblo* or . . . even knew in advance that the incident would take place." In fact, Moscow probably wanted to remain aloof from the North Korea–U.S. imbroglio.[65]

Moscow did, however, act quickly to harvest the intelligence windfall that had been brought into Wonsan Harbor. On 25 January, Rostow advised the president that a North Korean aircraft was flying to Moscow with two men and 792 pounds of cargo that could be *Pueblo* gear. General Wheeler commented that North Korean vessels were attempting to salvage equipment from the area where the *Pueblo* crew might have jettisoned it. Subsequent Black Shield imagery did not confirm this. However, on 28 January, the CIA reported that a Soviet Pacific Fleet aircraft had made a highly unusual flight into North Korea. The agency believed that the aircraft might have carried Soviet personnel sent to examine *Pueblo* and its surviving equipment.[66]

## Reviewing the Military Options

As gaps in the intelligence picture filled in, diplomacy was becoming the paramount and preferred U.S. strategy. Nevertheless, the president wanted a more refined understanding of his military options. On Friday, 26 January, the State Department established an interagency Korea Working Group comprising representatives from the State and Defense Departments, the Central Intelligence Agency, the Agency for International Development, the White House, and the U.S. Information Agency. The group was to flesh out ten options in "think papers" addressing purpose, feasibility, risk, and anticipated North Korean response. A high-level advisory group met on Monday, 29 January, to weigh these possible courses of action and the working group's evaluations of them. The options and their evaluations are summarized below.[67]

### Selected Air Strikes on North Korea

In retaliation for *Pueblo*'s seizure, ninety-two U.S. Navy, U.S. Air Force, and ROK Air Force aircraft could strike the Wonsan air base and the naval base at Munp'yong-ni.[68] The Korea Working Group cautioned that the strikes would not free the crew or substantially reduce—let alone disrupt—North Korea's military capabilities. The attacks would be difficult to defend legally; they would put the United States on the diplomatic defensive; and they would risk escalation. In its report, the working group noted that the Joint Chiefs preferred to attack all North Korean military airfields and neutralize the entire North Korean Air Force in this course of action. Otherwise, losses of strike aircraft would be high because the North Korean air defense system could concentrate on defending one or two targets.

### Naval Blockade of Wonsan

With sufficient air cover, U.S. and possibly South Korean naval units could impose a blockade within Wonsan's twelve-mile limit. To achieve air superiority, strikes against North Korean Air Force fields would "quite possibly" be required. However, the Korea Working Group assessed that a blockade would pose only a minor inconvenience to the DPRK. Moreover, if the North Korean regime did not respond in the desired way, the United States might be committed to an "indefinite, inconclusive, and politically awkward" military option. World reaction would be adverse. Nevertheless, the working group concluded that a blockade might eventually be useful.

## Mine Wonsan Harbor

*Enterprise*-based A-6 attack aircraft could, by flying seventeen sorties, drop eighty-three mines in one night; thereafter they could "reseed" the minefield as necessary. The working group projected the aircraft loss rate at less than 2 percent. On the other hand, it argued, mining would pose only a "minor inconvenience" given the availability of other North Korean ports and the possibility of Soviet mine countermeasures assistance.

## Seize North Korean Vessels

The purpose would be to retaliate in kind and then trade the seized craft, either a merchant vessel or a warship, for *Pueblo* and its crew. This option, the Korea Working Group believed, would be difficult to implement because the North's five primary merchant ships and most of its naval units were unlikely to be accessible. While not deemed risky, this option seemed to have little chance of securing the release of *Pueblo* and, more important, its crew; it might, though, be "advantageous" as a step in a "sequence of events."

## Sail USS Banner *into the Area Where* Pueblo *Had Been Seized*

This complex operation would demonstrate U.S. determination to exercise freedom of the seas. The idea was to position *Banner* a minimum of thirteen miles from the North Korean coast for eight days. Two destroyers, a cruiser, and possibly a South Korean unit would escort the AGER, and carrier aircraft would fly cover overhead. U.S. Air Force aircraft in South Korea would assume "strip alert" (immediate readiness to take off). The working group felt that the action would involve low risk but would also reduce the likelihood that *Pueblo* and its crew would be released. Nonetheless, the group recommended that a plan be prepared for this option in case Washington decided to carry out a "relatively unprovocative" operation.

## Recover Cryptographic Material Jettisoned by Pueblo

An attempt would be made to recover highly sensitive gear while exercising freedom of the seas. The recovery would require a tugboat and mine warfare vessels from Sasebo, Japan, along with special detection gear from the United States and probably a midget submarine (to be flown from Nassau). *Enterprise* and U.S. Air Force aircraft would provide air cover. The salvage unit would operate during daylight only and would terminate the attempt after ten days. The working group offered no opinion on the prospects of success but in general concluded that a recovery effort would constitute "a legitimate display of U.S. activity and concern for U.S. rights with little risk of provocation." Supporting the course of action was a draft operation order. However, the letter from the CNO, Adm. Thomas Moorer, forwarding the draft plan commented that its "disadvantages far outweigh its advantages" and recommended against it unless the recovery units were assured of adequate air cover.[69]

## Conduct Airborne Reconnaissance

This proposal entailed flying reconnaissance missions in an attempt to convince Pyongyang that the United States was preparing for military operations. High-performance tactical aircraft or drones would cross the DMZ and North Korean coasts and penetrate up to fifty miles inland. Electronic warfare aircraft would jam North Korea's air defense and surveillance radars. North Korea would likely down several drones, but the risk to Black Shield missions was quite low. The working group concluded that reconnaissance had some value as a pressure tactic.

## Inform the Soviets of Actual or Possible Military Moves

Officially, the Soviets would be advised that ongoing military movements were meant to deter further North Korean provocations; in addition, however, the United States "might pointedly warn the Soviets of actions we may be compelled to take." In this scenario, Washington would use an unofficial channel to warn Moscow of the "gravity of the situation" and the need for "some action by the North Koreans to avoid further deterioration."[70] The State Department would develop this option in greater detail as the crisis progressed.

## Raid across the Demilitarized Zone

A punitive raid across the DMZ could be staged against a significant installation, such as the North Korean Sixth Division command post. Relying on surprise, an armor-heavy combined U.S.–South Korean force would seize and destroy the facility. The working group, however, warned that the raiders would sustain high casualties and that the North Korean military should be expected to mount rapid "counter activities." Moreover, if the operation went poorly, it could result in escalation to major ground action; even if successful, it would be merely punitive.

## Economic Pressure on North Korea

This proposal entailed a total embargo on trade imposed by the United States and its allies, particularly blocking Japanese imports from North Korea and eliminating wheat exports to it. (Japan was the largest free-world importer of goods from North Korea, and wheat accounted for half of the free world's exports to that nation.) The Korea Working Group saw little prospect for success: communist shipping lines and overland routes would compensate for the loss of free-world vessels; and in any case, key U.S. allies trading with Pyongyang were unlikely to cooperate.

On 29 January, a senior advisory group including Dean Rusk and several high-ranking State Department officials, Richard Helms, Walt Rostow, and Gen. Maxwell Taylor (then acting as a special military consultant to the president) met to review the operational alternatives offered by the Korea Working Group. The advisory group rapidly and "universally" agreed that the United States should make no further military or diplomatic moves until it could ascertain whether U.S.–North Korean contacts at Panmunjom might be fruitful. The panel quickly eliminated several possible courses of action: in its view, selective air strikes were solely retaliatory and would diminish prospects for early release of *Pueblo*, blockade was inconclusive and potentially escalatory, and mining risked air combat and escalation. The panel further ruled out putting *Banner* on station, at least in the manner proposed, and concluded that recovery of *Pueblo*'s cryptographic material was "almost an impossible task" and could lead to "unsought sustained hostilities." The group found free-world economic pressure unattractive because of its limited impact and the difficulties of implementing it, especially since opposition from France, the United Kingdom, Japan, and West Germany was likely.[71]

The other options were received more favorably. In particular, if the crew and the ship—or even just the ship—were not returned, seizure of a North Korean vessel seemed to be a "punishment that fitted the crime." The panel recommended further staff work to locate North Korean vessels that might be susceptible to seizure in international waters. The senior advisory group recommended suspending reconnaissance flights for several days. If these flights were to be resumed, the panel recommended they be Black Shield missions. The group also recommended that the United States consider bombing exercises in South Korea for their demonstration value.[72]

After its deliberations, the panel met with President Johnson. The men advised him that "[we] should keep our eyes on the major objectives in this crisis: get the men of the *Pueblo* and, if possible, the ship returned; keep the confidence of the South Koreans and, especially, their willingness to provide an increment of force in South Vietnam; and avoid a second front in Asia."[73] Meeting privately with Democratic congressional leaders the following week, President Johnson echoed the theme: "We are trying to keep them [the North Koreans] talking. The Joint Chiefs have shown me twenty military plans, but none of them would get our men back alive."[74]

The National Command Authorities thus at least temporarily ruled out most of the options that used force, although they had already taken steps to prepare for a wide range of military contingencies. Some measures were visible immediately. On 25 January, some reserve units had been called up, terms of military service had been extended, and 361 aircraft had been ordered into the western Pacific. The White House had approved moving additional carriers into the Sea of Japan, stationing more aircraft in South Korea, and alerting B-52s for movement to Okinawa and Guam. The Joint Staff had taken unpublicized steps to enhance readiness for war on the Korean peninsula. The impact within CINCPAC's area of operational responsibility would be enormous.

# 5

# STAND DOWN

By early February the Johnson administration had chosen a course of prolonged negotiations with North Korea to free *Pueblo*'s crew. Although diplomacy assumed primacy, U.S. military forces were never far in the background. They would reassure the South while deterring the North from further provocations. If deterrence failed, the military might ultimately have retaliated with air strikes ranging throughout the DPRK. Consequently, the U.S. air and naval forces surged to the Far East in early February. Only reluctantly would U.S. diplomats concur with releasing them in March for the more urgent commitments of the war in Vietnam.

## Planning for the Worst

North Korea was proving to be astonishingly unpredictable. Although the intelligence community introduced careful constructs portraying North Korea as a rational actor, national and theater commanders recognized the need to guard against that nation's irrationality. What if the North really did make a run on the South, as Dean Rusk had suggested it might? What if the North

Koreans executed a few crew members as a demonstration of resolve? With this in mind, the United States prepared detailed contingency plans should retaliation—not deterrence—be the order of the day. As national-level planners looked for military means that might pressure the North to release the crew, the United States deployed sufficient assets forward to fight a war.

For the worst-case scenario, CINCPAC continued preparatory planning for sequential or selective employment of nuclear weapons against the North. Below this level, the command generated a raft of plans using combinations of land-based and carrier aircraft to attack a wide range of North Korean targets, including all key air bases.[1]

The ongoing assemblage of three carrier battle groups would have supported Formation Star, CINCPAC's three-option plan for quick-reaction strikes on at least one military target. Aircraft from two carriers would conduct strikes in support of option 1. Option 2 had fighters flying from the ROK or Okinawa to strike two unspecified targets in the North. The third option would entail both carrier- and land-based air strikes.[2]

In Fresh Storm—an option not shared with the South Koreans—CINCPAC would destroy "without delay" North Korea's entire inventory of military aircraft by striking all North Korean airfields. That option could include combinations of U.S.–only land- and sea-based aircraft, a combination of U.S. and ROK Air Force tactical air, and intensive B-52 strikes. A subplan, Port Bow, would use the twenty-six B-52 bombers that were deploying to the Far East. The B-52s previously dedicated to bombing North Vietnam would augment this force.[3]

Mining North Korea's coastal waters remained an option. CINCPAC had plans to drop sea mines in the North's nine most important ports. CINCPAC assured the Joint Chiefs that it had sufficient assets to conduct that operation without endangering its ability to mine key North Vietnamese ports as well. Four of the North Korean ports could be mined only by air; aircraft or submarines could mine the other five ports.[4]

These plans required quite a few aircraft. Joint Staff planners calculated that to negate an NKAF air attack on ROK air bases, the United States and Republic of Korea would need a number of air defense aircraft equal to the number of NKAF attackers. The NKAF attack force might comprise as many as 574 strike aircraft. The defenders would thus require more than 500 aircraft;

roughly 40 percent would belong to the ROKAF and the rest would be U.S. planes. In contrast, for the United States to neutralize the NKAF by attacking fifteen NKAF airfields, air operations control centers, and SAM sites, the United States and South Korea would have to generate eight hundred strike sorties. If the force (including more than one hundred B-52s) attacked in two waves, it would succeed. The force would rely on relatively few ROKAF aircraft —some seventy-three F-5s; the other 460 aircraft would be U.S. fighters and bombers.[5] The theater command had begun moving some of the required forces on the day *Pueblo* was seized. However, generating the forces needed to execute any of the plans effectively would take a wrenching effort. Dozens of ships and squadrons would have to move toward Korea.

## Force Buildup

On 25 January, after receiving Washington's commitment to augment the U.S. presence in the Sea of Japan, the Seventh Fleet implemented Formation Star. The operation order directed the USS *Enterprise* task group to prepare for several operations: assuming custody of and towing *Pueblo*, receiving returned U.S. personnel, conducting photo reconnaissance of Wonsan, and executing retaliatory air strikes or "other offensive actions as directed." The task group was to remain—and to conduct its flight operations—south of the thirty-eighth parallel; however, immediate ("hot") pursuit was author-ized north of that line, and ships and aircraft could operate north of it to pro-tect friendly forces. U.S. units were not authorized to penetrate North Korea's territorial sea or air space. Shows of force were prohibited; if attacked, how-ever, the task group was to take "immediate and aggressive protective meas-ures." In addition to the Seventh Fleet measures, the ROK Navy had placed nineteen ships and two fast patrol boats in sixteen patrol sectors around the Republic of Korea (see map 1).[6]

By 1 February, the task groups of the carriers USS *Enterprise*, USS *Ranger* (CV-61), and USS *Yorktown* (CVS-10) had arrived in the Sea of Japan and formed a task force. The Joint Chiefs on 27 January had also directed the Pacific Command to deploy up to nine diesel and nuclear attack submarines to Korea for surveillance and patrol "as soon as practicable."[7] Commander, Seventh Fleet, broke the key surface combatants down into four key units:

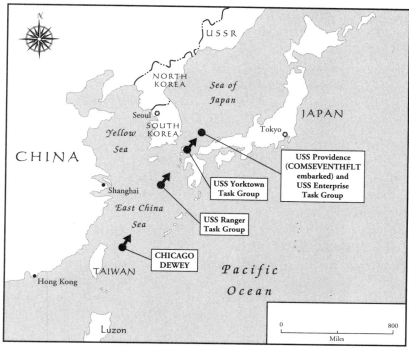

**Formation Star–Initial Seventh Fleet Response to Pueblo Seizure**

two attack carrier strike units, a surface/subsurface antisubmarine warfare unit centered on *Yorktown,* and a surface action unit.[8]

*Banner* was to augment the force; Pacific Command directed the Seventh Fleet to get the intelligence collector under way to join the task force as soon as feasible. The move was symbolic: "Technical collection capability is secondary to this mission and should not repeat not delay sailing." *Banner* rendezvoused with the force on 31 January but remained outside North Korea's claimed territorial waters.[9]

This large task force required extensive antisubmarine warfare support. Navy P-2 Neptunes and P-3 Orions flew more than 50 antisubmarine barrier patrols in the Sea of Japan in the eight days after the incident and would fly another 238 missions in February. The operational tempo was so intense that the Seventh Fleet had to augment its Japan-based patrol forces with several aircraft from the Philippines and Okinawa.[10]

Not unexpectedly, the Soviet Pacific Fleet reacted quickly to this large naval force appearing in what the Soviets considered an exceptionally sensitive area. The fleet commander committed more than half of the estimated Vladivostok-based cruiser/destroyer force to surveillance reactions/operations. Ultimately he deployed a reaction force of six combatants, a surveillance force of three combatants and two AGI intelligence collection ships, and a logistic support force of four tankers and a water tender.[11]

As the *Enterprise* group entered the Sea of Japan on 25 January, a Soviet Riga-class destroyer escort and Uda-class oiler greeted it. Additionally, a Kildin guided missile destroyer made a high-speed run south from Vladivostok and joined *Enterprise* on the same day.[12] Ultimately, the Riga and the Uda resumed gate guard duties in the Tsushima Strait. A Kotlin destroyer joined the Kildin, and together they monitored U.S. units throughout the crisis. To block potential approaches to the north, six major surface units deployed south from Vladivostok and formed a barrier north of the thirty-eighth parallel on 5 February. The force included several antishipping missile shooters: two Kynda-class cruisers, a Krupynyy guided missile destroyer, and a Kashin guided missile destroyer. There were also indications that one or two Soviet submarines were nearby.[13]

Soviet naval aviation bombers also joined in the surveillance. Several flights a day were not unusual. For example, on 7 February, ten Badger bombers approached the U.S. task force at altitudes between one hundred feet and thirty thousand feet. All were intercepted and escorted.[14] Rear Adm. Horace Epes, the task force commander, recounted the strong reaction.

> At first they'd [the Badgers] just fly down to take a look. We'd intercept them, and they'd turn back. Then they started going through our formation toward the Tsushima Straits. One day, they conducted thirty "raids" at all altitudes, a few as low as thirty-five or forty feet off the deck. That gave us a rather full schedule of flight operations ourselves.[15]

As might be expected, the proximity of U.S. and Soviet forces led to several incidents, especially in these days before the Incidents at Sea Agreement made Soviet–U.S. naval encounters more predictable. Between 23 January and 21 February, the U.S. Seventh Fleet reported fourteen cases of harassment by Soviet ships during the Formation Star operation.[16] The fleet commander concluded that many or all "were deliberately intended" and presented a "grave danger to life and property." Some included maneuvering against the rules of the road to force the U.S. ship to either back down or collide. For example, on 6 February, ASR *Gidrolog* maneuvered so as to become a burdened ship in a crossing situation with USS *Yorktown*. *Gidrolog* closed to within 900 yards of the carrier before turning to clear. In another instance, a Riga-class destroyer escort spotted USS *Banner* on the night of 29 January. Perhaps surprised that the United States had deployed a second intelligence collector so soon after *Pueblo* was seized, the Riga came in for a closer look. It approached to within 450 yards of *Banner* and then pinpointed the vessel with a searchlight for several minutes. Finally, the Riga's skipper decided simply to trail *Banner* at 5,000 yards.[17]

Such maritime encounters could be dangerous. On 1 February, USS *Rowan* (DD-782) collided with the Soviet merchant ship *Kapitan Vislobokov* (10,000 tons displacement) about a hundred miles south of Pohang, South Korea. The accident occurred in a crossing situation in which *Rowan* should have had the right of way under the rules of the road. Although none of *Rowan*'s crew was injured, the ship sustained a three-foot hole above the water-line on the port bow. *Kapitan Vislobokov* suffered minor damage to its stern.[18]

While U.S. and Soviet fleets were jockeying for position in the Sea of Japan, the U.S. Air Force was rapidly building up its military capabilities. On 26 January there were only 214 U.S. and South Korean aircraft in Korea, of which 187 were on alert.[19] USAF Operation Combat Fox called for massing hundreds of bombers, fighters, and support aircraft in Korea and nearby points by 6 February. On 27 January, the chief of staff of the U.S. Air Force released a flash precedence operation order for the rapid deployment of ele-ments of nine fighter and interceptor squadrons, along with B-52s and sup-port aircraft (see Table 4). Supported by sixty-six KC-135 tankers, the tactical units were to arrive in Korea within five days of receiving the execute order. Most of the aircraft were to move to one of five Korean bases: Kimpo (just northwest of Seoul), Osan, Kunsan, Suwon (south of Seoul), or Kwanju. Twenty-six B-52Ds would also deploy to Guam.[20] By 7 February, 395 Ameri-can and South Korean aircraft were in Korea, and 308 of them were combat ready. The deployment of 225 aircraft to Korea and Okinawa would cost $57 million.[21]

Table 4. U.S. Air Force Aircraft Deployed for Operation Combat Fox

| Type | Number |
| --- | --- |
| F-105 | 34 |
| F-102 | 38 |
| F-4 | 90 |
| RF-4C | 14 |
| F-100 | 18 |
| B-52 | 26 |
| EB-66 | 6 |

*Source:* "Movement of Combat Aircraft to Korea following *Pueblo* Incident," table in NSF—Walt Rostow memo to president, 25–31 January 1968, box 28, LBJ.

The United States had marshaled enormous striking power in a short time. CINCPAC commented that deployments had "enabled CINCPAC to assume a readiness position which will permit an early and rapid response in the event of North Korean aggression against South Korea or against U.S. or ROK forces or to carry out policy decisions."[22] The British ambassador reported that even by 31 January American air and naval forces had become strong enough to "take out" Wonsan (the option local U.S. military commanders seemed to think Washington had decided on). He added that this "may be no more than saber rattling, but here it sounds very loud."[23]

In a frank "personal for" message to General Wheeler, however, CINCPAC, Adm. U. S. Grant Sharp, stated:

> Our chances to get the crew back seem greatest if we do not make a show of force off Wonsan. . . . I have told CINCPACFLT and CINCPACAF [the commanders in chief of the Pacific Fleet and Pacific Air Forces] to caution their people that we want no belligerent statements from anyone at this juncture and that they should caution their people to remain quiet. . . . I don't believe there is any military move that we can make that will assist us in getting the *Pueblo* crew returned. . . . If diplomatic efforts for return of the *Pueblo* crew are not successful then we should consider moving *Banner* and escorts off Wonsan in accordance with the plan I have submitted. We could easily stir up a hornet's nest with this move and we must be prepared to take such steps as necessary to come out on top. The conventional weapons strike plan we have submitted gives various options for this contingency. We must also be prepared for retaliatory strikes against North Korea. Mining of Wonsan and/or

Hungnam and the harbor on the west coast can be accomplished without great difficulty. It should have a salutary effect on North Korea if a move of this severity is required. We also will be ready with various nuclear options. . . . I am not sure any of these military moves will assist in getting the *Pueblo* crew back but they would teach North Korea a lesson.[24]

## U.S. Forces Korea Responds

As the crisis developed, U.S. Forces Korea, the command that might well have received the brunt of North Korean retaliation for any U.S. military action, attempted to enhance its readiness for war. General Bonesteel, the force commander, took some steps immediately. For example, he enhanced rear area security and prepared to receive emergency shipments of munitions. Initiatives to enhance the military and logistics infrastructure in the ROK would take much longer. Attempts to substantially increase U.S. Army manpower—that scarcest of assets during the Vietnam War—in the theater would be fruitless despite quick and strong endorsements up the chain of command.

The vulnerability of sensitive installations proved worrisome both immediately and in the long term. U.S. planners were particularly concerned about the security of the unhardened South Korean airfields, Nike Hercules surface-to-air missile sites, and nuclear weapons facilities.[25] General Bonesteel had a profound respect for the threat posed by North Korean special operations forces. In another "personal for" message, he warned Admiral Sharp and the Joint Chiefs that the DPRK had between twenty and thirty thousand trained infiltrators "with far greater capabilities than the guerrillas of the Korean War days." He warned that the DPRK would try to infiltrate large numbers of saboteurs just prior to the opening of hostilities. They would target command and control, early warning, air defense, and immediate logistic movements occurring in the first days of hostilities.[26]

Bonesteel took several steps to protect the most vulnerable sites. To counter an air attack, the commander on 27 January urgently requested the movement of two additional HAWK surface-to-air missile battalions to the ROK. Bonesteel's request for the two battalions was in response to a JCS offer of 25 January. One battalion was to be ready in a week; the second would be available in two weeks. By 30 January, the ROK First Army had been directed to provide two infantry battalions for airfield protection—one for Osan Air Base and the other for Kunsan Air Base.[27] By 7 February, construction of semipermanent shelters and other forms of physical protection for the Nike Hercules sites and their missiles was under way.[28] The Joint Staff recommended that the Defense Department assign additional personnel to provide more security for nuclear weapons sites and initiated a longer-term study on physical security improvements to these facilities.[29]

Logistically, South Korea's air bases were ill prepared to support a prolonged intensive air war. The day after *Pueblo* was seized, the air force staff warned that there were "serious limitations on availability of POL [petroleum, oil, and lubricants], air munitions, and ground support equipment to fight this force beyond a very few days."[30] The Joint Staff assessed that Pacific Command's air force component (which had only 4,000 tons of ammunition stockpiled in Korea) would immediately require 12,700 additional tons of munitions, and Pacific Fleet naval aviation (which had 2,800 tons of munitions in Sasebo) needed 11,400 tons. More than 12,000 tons of ammunition were already en route and would be available to both by 10 February.[31] The Military Sea Transportation Service quickly diverted two ships. *Clearwater Victory* was diverted to Sasebo, Japan, with naval air munitions. *Ruth Lykes,* which had been transporting air force munitions to Guam, was diverted to Suyong, Pusan's ammunition loading port.[32] To accommodate the ordnance, USFK was also expediting an engineering survey of five alternative ammunition storage sites near selected airfields.[33]

U.S. Forces Korea warned CINCPAC that the ROK ground forces had significant war reserve ammunition shortfalls and urged CINCPAC to take "urgently needed" steps to secure $70 million worth of additional munitions.[34] Even by late February, however, ammunition was available for only forty-five combat days for the two U.S. divisions, and eighteen combat days for the South Korean units.[35] The U.S. Eighth Army had on hand only 23,300 tons of its war-reserve requirement of 39,400 tons. General Wheeler urged the DOD to order more munitions forward, hoping to build sufficient war reserves to allow the eighteen ROK divisions to fight for a month without borrowing from in-country stocks reserved for U.S. forces' use.[36]

Jet fuel also might be in short supply. CINCPACAF estimated that the air force would require four times as much JP-4 as currently programmed under OPLAN 27, USFK's plan to counter North Korean invasion. The South's relatively weak infrastructure would also complicate internal delivery of the fuel. USFK reminded the chain of command of the ROK's general shortage of tank cars, the limited port capacities at Kunsan and Gazan, and the limited availability of T-1 tankers in which to store the fuel.[37]

As for U.S. ground forces in Korea, the planners were immediately concerned about personnel and logistical shortfalls. As was mentioned earlier, the demands of the Vietnam War had left the two U.S. divisions in Korea at approximately 70 percent of their authorized strength.[38] General Bonesteel and Admiral Sharp urged their superiors to send another 8,500 troops to bring the force up to about 90 percent of its authorized levels.[39] Bonesteel made a compelling argument in a message that General Wheeler forwarded to the service chiefs and the national security adviser. In an urgent (flash precedence) message transmitted on 10 February, Bonesteel argued that "immediate and substantive action" to solve the manpower problem would "reestablish the credibility of our deterrent posture in minds of Kim Il Sung and other militant leaders" and would provide "vitally needed reassurance to President Park and his deeply troubled advisors as to firmness of U.S. intentions." Such moves would "do most to head off increasing likelihood of war by NK or ROK miscalculation."[40] Bonesteel would lose this fight.

## The Next Step

Starting on 2 February, the United States began a series of twenty-nine painstaking "private" meetings with North Korea using the representatives of the UN Command Military Armistice Commission. During February and March, Maj. Gen. Pak Chung Ku of the DPRK met thirteen times with Rear Adm. John Smith, the chief U.S. negotiator. They made little progress, although by mid-February the North's demand that the United States admit culpability and issue an apology had emerged as the major obstacle to resolving the crisis.[41] The North did provide a list of *Pueblo*'s dead and wounded.[42] On 16 March, the State Department country director for Korea told the British ambassador that State was "in fact very near the end of the line at Panmunjom." The United States did not see any options if the North simply stopped the private talks.[43]

North Korea remained unpredictable and at times even threatened to put *Pueblo*'s crew on trial. Accordingly, the United States issued several low-key (but high-level) warnings to protect the crew (and South Korea). When Prime Minister Harold Wilson of Great Britain met with President Johnson on 9 February, he received a worrisome warning: if North Korea maintained its present attitude and took further action against either *Pueblo* or the ROK, a "situation might be created which would bring us all in—you, the Russians, the rest of us." Perhaps the Russians, who had expressed interest in resolving the dispute, could use their influence to prevent the situation from getting out of hand. Wilson subsequently relayed LBJ's warning to Premier Alexei Kosygin.[44] On 18 February, State warned of "grave consequences" to any move to punish *Pueblo*'s crew as criminals.[45] When the North Korean chargé in Moscow indicated on 24 February that the crew might be tried and punished, the United States warned the Soviets that such action would seriously aggravate the already tense situation.[46] Rear Admiral Smith replied in the same vein on 9 March when General Pak made another veiled threat about a trial. Any trial, punishment, or threat of punishment would "only aggravate an already serious situation," he warned.[47]

With such a capricious negotiating partner, the U.S. leadership devoted considerable effort to evaluating additional military "pressure moves" against the North, even though they were skeptical of their efficacy. On 4 March, the director of the State Department's Korea Task Force concluded that "available military action would be mere pin-pricks unlikely to move North Koreans, and would probably prejudice chances of getting men back."[48]

The interagency Korea Working Group subsequently completed a rigorous review of four general courses of action: (1) stay the course and rely on diplomatic pressure, (2) increase political and military pressure to heighten North Korea's apprehension, (3) reduce the pressure (and reduce resource costs to the United States), and (4) pursue decisive military action such as neutralizing the entire NKAF. The group weighed the options against a range of U.S. objectives, particularly freeing the crew and the ship, and concluded that Washington should continue the current course of action while building up South Korea's capabilities and retaining the U.S. air augmentation force that had been sent to the ROK. Additionally, they suggested that the United States should avoid small-scale military actions and pressure tactics because they would degrade the U.S.–ROK legal position and encourage Northern retaliation (or at least gradual escalation).[49]

The task force members were skeptical of the usefulness of military pressure tactics even if the DPRK tried the crew. Evaluating possible actions if the North announced a trial, on 15 March the task force's chief expressed

> doubt that these reactions would be found appropriate or useful. Thus, we do not see how trial of the *Pueblo* crew would alter our judgment concerning the undesirability of various military actions, such as aerial strikes, aerial feints, sailing of USS *Banner* along the North Korean coast, blockading the North Korean Navy, etc. We also doubt that a threatening deployment of additional U.S. forces to the Korean area would serve any useful purpose. Calling up additional reserve units might improve our general posture, but could not be expected to have any significant impact on the North Korean decision to try the crew.[50]

## And Then There Were None

Thus the United States prepared for war while seeking to avoid it. The buildup was costly because it diverted assets needed in Vietnam. Naturally, the DPRK urged the United States to end the military pressure. In the second U.S.–DPRK private meeting, on 4 February, General Pak told the U.S. representative to "eliminate the atmosphere of compulsion" it had created by sending the Seventh Fleet (specifically *Enterprise*) into the Sea of Japan, introducing "numerous fighters and bombers into the ROK," and placing U.S. and ROK troops in South Korea on alert.[51]

In response, Samuel Berger, the director of the Korea Task Force, enumerated several actions that the United States could take to provide "evidence [of] our desire to get things moving." Moving the "Big E" south would be the "simplest and safest gesture," one that could be easily made without "placing our forces too far away to be useful or threatening." The move also would be less visible (and worrisome) to the ROK than removing aircraft or lowering the state of alert on the peninsula.[52]

Soviet pressure was also a factor in the decision to move *Enterprise* south. Responding to U.S. requests for its "good offices," Moscow argued that the naval and air buildup was counterproductive. Premier Kosygin warned President Johnson on 3 February that the buildup raised tensions and had no chance of resolving the crisis. Johnson responded on 5 February that "on the assumption that . . . we [Washington and Moscow] want peace in that area and that we will both work to that end," there would be no further air and naval buildup; in addition, he would order one carrier task group to move "somewhat southward."[53]

Accordingly, the *Enterprise* group prepared to leave the Sea of Japan. As it was preparing to move south, a five-ship Soviet surface action group entered the Sea of Japan. CINCPAC recommended that the *Enterprise* group be allowed to remain in the Sea of Japan in view of the sudden increase in Soviet presence, but General Wheeler overruled him. *Enterprise* accordingly transited the Tsushima Strait to a point approximately twelve hours' steaming time from its original position in the Sea of Japan.[54]

*Enterprise*'s repositioning angered South Korea, the second major audience for U.S. force posturing. On 8 February, in a two-and-a-half-hour meeting with Ambassador Porter, President Park angrily denounced the move, insisting that the *Enterprise* should have gone *north*, toward Wonsan, not south. The United States should have closed Wonsan Harbor until Pyongyang returned both ship and crew, he exclaimed, and if that act brought no action, the United States should have gone in to take the ship by force; neither the USSR nor the People's Republic of China (PRC) would have interfered.[55]

By this point, U.S.–ROK relations were severely strained. The ROK leadership was appalled that the United States had not retaliated for the Blue House raid and the *Pueblo* seizure. The South Koreans were so furious, in fact, that General Bonesteel feared that they might initiate an attack on the North: "I believe they are persuaded as to its [retaliation's] unwisdom as a unilateral, uncoordinated, rash action," he warned Admiral Sharp, " . . . but I do not feel entirely assured that the emotional reaction from top ROKs can entirely be controlled." To reduce tensions, LBJ sent Cyrus Vance to Seoul to meet with the top ROK leadership between 12 and 15 February. The meetings included a mixture of entreaties and warnings. Some of the ROK cabinet members warned Vance that the situation resembled that between the two Koreas just before the outbreak of the Korean War. The ROK leadership revealed deep concern about South Korea's ability to contain North Korean infiltrators. They also confirmed their desire to retaliate. In a meeting with the ROK military chiefs, General Bonesteel warned that the United States would not allow itself to be dragged into a war sparked by ROK retaliatory action. He even suggested that he might recommend that U.S. forces be withdrawn to prevent this from happening. Despite the tensions, the Vance mission secured Park's agreement not to retaliate for the Blue House raid or impede the Panmunjom talks, providing they did not drag on for months.[56]

Diplomacy was not the only pressure on aircraft carrier deployments. The diplomatic and resource demands of the war in Vietnam weighed heavily on the minds of the *Pueblo* decision makers. In his 3 February update on contingency plans, Admiral Sharp had warned that the *Pueblo* crisis was using resources needed for the war. He advised that he could not maintain five carriers on the line indefinitely, and that it was undesirable to reduce the carrier presence off Vietnam.[57] On 16 February, the *Enterprise* group was directed to detach and steam toward Subic Bay in the Philippines.[58]

In late February, General Bonesteel advised Ambassador Porter that he might soon lose more ships. In a subsequent report to the State Department, Porter warned that "we should not overlook or ignore the reaction of Park and the Korean people to any such military redeployments, or its probable meaning to the North Koreans before settlement of the *Pueblo* affair and just prior to expected commencement of agent infiltration season."[59] Perhaps in response, State advised Ambassador Porter on 9 March that the presence of the remaining two carriers in the Sea of Japan was in jeopardy. State explained that keeping three carriers on Yankee Station off Vietnam would require keeping four to five carriers in the western Pacific; of these, one or two would be in port for maintenance at any given time. The remaining nine Pacific Fleet carriers were either in transit or undergoing maintenance, training, and so on. To forgo maintenance would jeopardize the fleet's ability to respond to crises while still maintaining three carriers on the line off Vietnam. Accordingly, the JCS intended to withdraw the remaining two carriers from the Sea of Japan and the one carrier in Sasebo.[60] But Washington did intend to keep some naval pressure on Pyongyang. All carriers going to or from the western Pacific would stop at Yokosuka, Japan. Additionally, when Yankee Station carriers were released for mid-deployment repairs in Japanese ports, they could be diverted into the Sea of Japan for a few days at a time. State reassured the ambassador that even if ships were not in or near Japan, one to two carriers could be deployed north to Korea within four to six days.[61]

Ambassador Porter was unenthusiastic, and he thought the ROK's response would be even less so. In fact, Porter's answer characterized him as one of sea power's biggest fans. In an urgent, lengthy message, Porter warned that "withdrawal [of] CVA's will not advance matters at Panmunjom and might probably retard progress there." The CVAs (attack carriers) would provide "greater force" to deal with the North until the United States had more insight into North Korea's intentions. Further, the ROK would be reassured if the United States kept both land-based air and a residual naval presence in the Sea of Japan. In particular, Porter wanted to increase the extent and frequency of P-3 patrols. This would reassure President Park because it would improve South Korea's ability to interdict maritime infiltrators. A proposal to upgrade ROK jet-capable airfields would further reassure the South.[62]

Despite the ambassador's protest, the carriers soon steamed south. On 22 March, the USS *Coral Sea* and USS *Ticonderoga* battle groups were released from USS *Pueblo* contingency operations. No carriers remained in the Sea of Japan, although they and other U.S. ships entered the Sea of Japan intermittently as an outgrowth of exercises and port calls in Japan.[63] But State did not forget about the carriers. It would later seek to move one north of the CINC-PAC-imposed thirty-eighth-parallel limit line during a crucial juncture in the *Pueblo* negotiations.[64]

The first nine weeks of the *Pueblo* crisis entailed intense planning, a rapid military buildup, and then withdrawal of most U.S. naval assets. The buildup had provided a degree of assurance to U.S. policy makers who had to deal with a highly unpredictable nation. With the effort, the United States was at least prepared to retaliate if diplomacy broke down and *Pueblo*'s crew was harmed or if the ROK attacked North Korea. U.S. Forces Korea and the ROK Army were better prepared for war, and South Korea was reassured of the U.S. commitment to deal with the North. Yet, the situation was frustrating. Diplomacy, not military force, would predominate until the crisis finally ended in December. It would be a long road for all.

USS *Pueblo* (AGER-2) was one of several intelligence collection ships operating worldwide in 1968. The ship, with a complement of only eighty-three crewmen, was virtually unarmed when it was surrounded by North Korean patrol boats on 23 January 1968. *U.S. Naval Institute Photo Archive*

A Shershen patrol craft such as this was one of at least six P-4 patrol boats and Shershens that confronted *Pueblo* off Wonsan while NKAF MiGs flew overhead.
*U.S. National Archives and Records Administration*

Desperate to locate *Pueblo* and to see whether the DPRK was preparing to invade South Korea, the National Command Authorities approved a Black Shield aerial reconnaissance mission to overfly the North. A CIA Oxcart aircraft (a relative of the SR-71 Blackbird shown here) flew the first mission.
*U.S. Naval Institute Photo Archive*

Both satellites and Oxcart aircraft photographed Wonsan, North Korea, the port to which the North Korean Navy escorted *Pueblo*. An Oxcart reconnaissance aircraft took this image of Wonsan Harbor and helped to locate *Pueblo* just days after the DPRK seized it.
*U.S. National Archives and Records Administration*

Gen. Earle Wheeler, the chairman of the Joint Chiefs of Staff, was at the center of both the *Pueblo* and EC-121 shootdown crises. He helped to outline contingency plans to the National Command Authorities and to shape the forces that might have to retaliate for both incidents.
*LBJ Library*

Within days of the *Pueblo* seizure, President Lyndon Johnson briefed Congress on the steps his administration was taking to deal with the crisis.
*LBJ Library*

Director of Central Intelligence Richard Helms (*left*) and Secretary of Defense Robert McNamara (*right*) briefed Congress about the *Pueblo* crisis on 31 January 1968.
*LBJ Library*

Outgoing secretary of defense Robert McNamara and his replacement, Clark Clifford, shouldered much of the burden for dealing with the *Pueblo* crisis throughout 1968.
*LBJ Library*

Presidential adviser McGeorge Bundy, U.S. ambassador to South Korea William Porter, and LBJ deliberate about the Korea problem.
*LBJ Library*

The EC-121 was carrying thirty-one crewmen when North Korean MiGs shot it down in international waters. The wreckage was found approximately ninety miles from the North Korean coast.
*U.S. Naval Institute Photo Archive*

# 6

# DENOUEMENT

As the U.S. carriers withdrew from the Sea of Japan in March 1968, the longest part of the *Pueblo* crisis remained ahead. However, the remaining nine months of the story would focus on diplomacy rather than military posturing. The crisis would still have its military side, but U.S. hints at military coercion would be few and widely spaced. The military focused instead on contingency planning and structural improvements to enhance U.S. and ROK readiness for anti-infiltration operations and general war.

## Diplomacy for the Long Haul

The basic North Korean demand—the "Three As"—had already become familiar by the February meetings. The North wanted the United States to admit that *Pueblo* had entered North Korean territorial waters on an espionage mission. After apologizing, the United States was to assure Pyongyang that such acts would not recur. The United States, however, was unwilling to apologize for acts that might not have been committed.[1] By mid-March the talks were essentially in a logjam. Talking with Benjamin Fleck, State's country director for Korea, on 16 March, British ambassador Michael Wilford sensed stalemate. He reported to his superiors at the Foreign Office:

> Fleck said that they were in fact very near the end of the line at Panmunjom. The initiative for calling the next meeting there lay with the North Koreans, but the Americans would not force the pace unduly as they could not see any useful move which they could make if the North Koreans put an end to the present exchanges. . . . The Administration are at a loss to know what further positive steps they can take to effect the release of the *Pueblo*'s crew. But I detect no sign that they see violence as in any way useful to achieve their end. I think that they accept that it may be many months before the crew is released and that in the meantime they must play it cool and hope for the best.[2]

The talks continued despite the lack of progress. On 8 May, the North proposed a document designed to resolve the crisis. The draft "apology" would have the United States admit that *Pueblo* had repeatedly violated North Korean territorial waters to spy on North Korea. The United States "solemnly apologizes for the grave acts of espionage committed by the U.S. ship," the draft continued, " . . . and gives firm assurance that no U.S. ships will intrude again in future in the territorial waters . . . of the DPRK." The document concluded with a request for the DPRK to "deal leniently" with *Pueblo*'s crew.[3]

The U.S. negotiators responded with an alternative proposal. The United States would not affirm charges it held to be false. Maj. Gen. Gilbert Woodward, USA, the U.S. negotiator, would not sign the document itself. Rather, he would write a short note onto the apology document. The note would only acknowledge receipt of the crew. Woodward would sign that note—not the document itself. This proposal, called the "overwrite solution," would give the North Koreans propaganda mileage by allowing them to say that the United States had "signed" the document. The DPRK appeared to consider the proposal in September before finally rejecting it in October.[4]

## Readier for War?

The need for intelligence did not diminish as the United States entered the second phase of the *Pueblo* crisis—the prolonged negotiations. First, the CIA had to head off a plan to use reconnaissance aircraft merely to pressure the North. In response to a State Department contingency plan to pressure Pyongyang to release the crew by increasing airborne reconnaissance against North Korea, the CIA shot back that the assumption was "at least dubious." The deputy director of intelligence wrote that the North was unlikely to take the threat seriously. Moreover, he warned that even if North Korea were to feel pressured by such activity, they were at least as likely to harden their position as to concede anything on behalf of the crew. "What we know of the North Korean mentality suggests a pronounced tendency toward increased obstinacy and belligerency in the face of pressures, even in their dealings with their communist neighbors, the Soviet Union and China," he noted. Options such as tactical reconnaissance, jamming, and peripheral reconnaissance were even less desirable. The United States avoided such posturing during both the *Pueblo* and EC-121 crises.

Observing North Korea and obtaining useful intelligence was complicated because U.S. analysts had to weed out numerous rumors that the North was preparing for war. U.S. decision makers had already had a taste of this in February when they received reports of an impending attack on the ROK. On 9–10 February, the U.S. intelligence community received reports that the Soviets and North Koreans were planning nuclear strikes on Seoul and Osan Air Base. The reports actually related only to a command post exercise, but the lower-level officials who received the reports were not advised of their tenuous provenance. Director of Central Intelligence Richard Helms ultimately advised LBJ on 13 February that "the report on a possible air attack by North Korea on Seoul was unnecessarily alarming. There was nothing to it."[5]

In a similar vein, National Security Adviser Walt Rostow in May forwarded three misleading CIA field reports to President Johnson that ostensibly revealed evidence of preparations for war. For example, a 3 May CIA field report noted a "militant mood" among students in the DPRK; the impending outbreak of war was an accepted fact, the report said, and the country was organized in a "semi–war state." Another report transmitted the same day claimed that the North intended to divert America from the Vietnam War by invading the South in the near future. Referring to the latter in a memo to President Johnson, Rostow wrote that the intelligence community was working on a fresh assessment of the North's intentions. (He also warned LBJ that he might be asked to approve another reconnaissance flight over the DPRK.) The CIA also reported "rumors" of increased draft calls, mobilization of reserves, unusual troop movements and deployments, and the buildup of stockpiles near the DMZ, but such indicators of impending hostility were not supported by reliable evidence.[6]

The U.S. intelligence community was able to weed out false alarms and develop a model for anticipated behavior because it was watching North Korea very closely. In an August memo, State assured LBJ that the intelligence community was "keeping the closest watch on the situation."[7] The Korea Task Force told Undersecretary of State Nicholas Katzenbach that the intelligence establishment was trying to fill information gaps.[8] Black Shield reconnaissance missions against the DPRK continued intermittently throughout the crisis, so the United States maintained a detailed imagery baseline similar to the one produced immediately after the seizure.[9] The United States had a range of sources that could be used to corroborate one another. For example, U.S. analysts had learned to be skeptical of letters going from North Koreans to Korean expatriates in Japan. One intelligence estimate noted: "The 'war is coming' tone of letters . . . appears to reflect official propaganda; such letters almost certainly suit the regime's purposes since all outgoing mail is carefully censored."[10]

The intelligence community had also refined its understanding of what *should* occur if Pyongyang were preparing a large attack. But instead of detecting evidence of impending attack, the United States continued to receive "negative indicators"—evidence that specific preparations essential for an attack were not being made. For example, the DCI observed that there was "no evidence—in this nation of chronic shortages—of unusually large imports of food or medicines, or other unusual international transactions."[11]

Consequently, in May the intelligence community again ruled out an invasion. Moreover, it assessed that the North was unlikely to take action that it considered likely to provoke a second Korean War. However, a new Special National Intelligence Estimate projected that Pyongyang would continue to provoke incidents along the DMZ and conduct terrorist acts within the ROK interior. The SNIE also left itself an out by concluding that "Pyongyang might be tempted to go well beyond incidents along the DMZ." However, the national intelligence community foresaw another form of miscalculation as the principal danger: the North might press so hard that *South* Korea would order extensive retaliation, thereby setting off an escalatory cycle toward general war.[12]

The national-level analysts reasoned that the North probably was not committed to "any particular sequences of moves or to any timetable." North Korean theoreticians understood the amount of time and effort it would take to develop a revolutionary movement in the South. Consequently, the SNIE anticipated that the pattern of DMZ incidents and internal terrorism could continue for a long time. In fact, for the current North Korean strategy to succeed, it need not even escalate to major violence.

In other words, the United States could reasonably expect more of the same. With this background, Department of Defense planners addressed two related issues during the remainder of the *Pueblo* crisis: how to better prepare for general war should the situation escalate to that point and how to give the South the military assistance it sought without emboldening it to launch a war on its own. First, CINCPAC updated OPLAN 27, its basic plan for the defending the ROK.[13] In May, the JCS also asked CINCPAC to analyze potential North Korean provocations and suggest appropriate U.S. responses. CINCPAC was also to identify particular scenarios that warranted further planning. On receiving CINCPAC's response, the JCS in August directed CINCPAC to develop draft plans to counter some of the scenarios. These would be available when the North downed the EC-121.[14]

This planning doubtless took a lot of effort. However, a far more difficult (and costly) problem was upgrading infrastructure, especially on the South's handful of relatively undefended jet-capable air bases. As described by the U.S. embassy in Seoul, the U.S.–approved ROK military shopping list was long. It included

> extensive hardening of forward positions . . . improvements in infrastructure . . . particularly construction for airfield dispersal and hardening . . . ; facilities to permit rapid receipt and forward movement of external combat and logistic support; selected improvements in mobility and communications; . . . [and] the availability in the area . . . of ammunition war reserves for all services.[15]

U.S. planners worried that U.S. Air Force aircraft deployed to the ROK were especially vulnerable. More than 150 aircraft were jammed together on six unhardened bases, most of which were a few minutes' flying time from the North. Moreover, with only a few crowded bases, it would take longer to "flush" sufficient aircraft into the air to counter a surprise attack.

In the fall of 1968, CINCPAC (and the JCS) concluded that a surprise attack on the NKAF bases would be costly. CINCPAC's Command History notes that the study estimated "US/ROK aircraft losses . . . at 70 aircraft after the first wave and 110 aircraft after the second wave in an attack centered around aircraft on the ground." The study concluded that "US/ROK aircraft, POL stocks and terminals, radar sites, communications centers, and surface to air missile sites were vulnerable to low altitude surprise attack" and "recommended extensive hardening, dispersal and shelter construction."[16]

The overcrowding problem was so acute and the aircraft so vulnerable that in September, Secretary of Defense Clifford introduced a proposal that the United States reduce its deployed contingent of 151 aircraft on the peninsula by half. The JCS and CINCPAC fought the proposal by arguing it would send the wrong signals to both North and South. The fighters remained deployed even after the end of the *Pueblo* crisis.[17]

The JCS and CINCPAC supported their case for keeping the aircraft by noting that a program to build 171 shelters for all fighters in Korea was under way in 1968 and would be completed by 1969. In fact, $78 million was spent on base and aircraft shelter protection, improved petroleum and ammunition storage, and other facility upgrades in 1968. The buildup in air munitions had also paid off; by early in the crisis the U.S. Air Force units on the peninsula had sufficient stockpiles for forty-five days of combat.[18]

Although the United States was spending money on infrastructure enhancements, the two U.S. divisions in South Korea remained "understrength and not rated as having attained combat ready status."[19] General Bonesteel's crucial manpower requirement, the addition of 8,500 personnel, remained unmet. The JCS endorsed it in October, but the DOD staff was skeptical.[20] The U.S. divisions still had significant logistics shortfalls as well. Even near the end of the *Pueblo* crisis, DOD reported that U.S. forces in Korea were "inadequately supported" from a logistics viewpoint. They simply could not compete with Vietnam.[21]

Readying the ROK was the second component of the long-haul military strategy during the *Pueblo* crisis. To counter the large number of North Korean intrusions, General Bonesteel had already initiated a program to better defend the DMZ and South Korea's seaward approaches and to support ROK counteragent teams in the interior.[22] Following the Blue House raid and *Pueblo* seizure, he managed to airlift equipment to Korea to support this program.[23]

The United States sought to provide arms to the South on a larger scale as well, probably to compensate the ROK for its support in Vietnam and for its deep disappointment at the U.S. failure to retaliate for the Blue House and *Pueblo* incidents. Providing arms aid was a delicate process, however, because the United States did not want to encourage a war by giving the ROK too many offensive weapons. The State Department's country team strongly believed that Seoul was prepared to initiate hostilities:

> There are therefore grounds for serious concern that the ROK national leadership may be contemplating military moves which may range from substantially larger retaliatory actions to a preemptive strike against the North to effect unification. . . . ROK national leadership believes that if unification can be effected rapidly by military means, the great powers will not intervene and will accept the fait accompli. . . . [Full U.S. support for the ROK military acquisitions plan] . . . is not justified in terms of present U.S. objectives in Korea because it could lead to a military force capable of independently taking courses of action inimical to the U.S. national interests.[24]

In other words, the United States had to be selective in choosing what arms it would supply. The ROK had been offered a supplement of $100 million in military aid in addition to the $400 million already promised for 1968. The shopping list, tailored to ROK requests, included a squadron of F-4D fighters, M-16s, and support for the ROK national police.[25]

From North Korea's perspective, then, the *Pueblo* crisis had unpleasant and unintended effects. It accelerated the U.S. program to enhance its readiness to conduct both counterinsurgency and general war on the Korean peninsula. More seriously from a prestige perspective, *Pueblo* indirectly provided the South with highly publicized (and prestigious) new equipment for its arms race against the North.

## End Game

The stalemate continued into the fall. Faced with the lack of progress (and a complete hiatus in the talks between 31 October and 17 December), the United States sent low-key military signals to the North. In mid-September, the State

Department made an unusual proposal to the U.S. embassy in The Hague. As a subtle warning to the North that its economic interests might be imperiled, State suggested that U.S. embassy personnel inquire about the status of four fish factory ships the Dutch were constructing for the DPRK for delivery between October 1968 and July 1969. The U.S. government was desperate for a lever to use against Pyongyang, and seizing North Korea's fishing assets had a certain appeal. In State's pressure ploy, U.S. embassy officials would ask either the Dutch government or the shipyard questions regarding ships' delivery date, who would crew the ships en route North Korea, when title would pass to the DPRK, and so on. Such questions would imply U.S. interest in seizing the ships, but the "ultimate object, of course, would be that such an inquiry on our part get back to the North Korean government."[26]

By mid-October, the DPRK appeared to be on the verge of rejecting the latest U.S. proposal for resolving the crisis. Writing that the United States would have to wait and see what the North's response really would be, State advised Ambassador Porter on 12 October that in the interim "we will activate whatever additional pressures might move them to a favorable decision, e.g., threatening noises toward ships being built in Netherlands."[27]

Unnamed U.S. government officials evidently leaked the idea to the *New York Times*. A version of the "plan" appeared on the front page of the *Times* on 26 November 1968. The article said that some U.S. officials believed the key to obtaining release of the *Pueblo* crew might be two fish-processing ships under construction in Rotterdam. The *Times* continued that Washington was weighing issues such as where to seize the ships, what to do if they were flying a non-Korean ensign, what to do if they were escorted by a Soviet warship, and so on. The article also said that the U.S. Navy might shadow the fish factory ships for the entire thirty-day transit from Rotterdam to North Korea. In a helpfully unclassified message, State summarized the article for the U.S. embassy in The Hague.[28]

In his book about the *Pueblo* incident, Mitch Lerner suggested that the threat to seize the fishing vessels hit home. Kim Il Sung's legitimacy rested on North Korea's ability to pursue self-sufficiency (*chuche*). The North had demonstrated an independent, self-sufficient foreign policy in seizing *Pueblo*. However, the political benefits of retaining *Pueblo* were beginning to wane. Meanwhile, the hard cash that fish factory ships could earn were critical to

North Korea's economic independence—another key component of Kim Il Sung's self-sufficiency program. With its utility to DPRK foreign policy objectives already diminished, *Pueblo* could become an outright liability if retaining it endangered vital North Korean economic interests.[29]

As the talks faltered in late October, LBJ sent another signal: he canceled a planned U.S.–ROK exercise called Focus Retina. The exercise included movement of an airborne brigade to the ROK and was to have started on 20 November. Undersecretary of State Katzenbach, who reasoned that Pyongyang might perceive Focus Retina as a pressure tactic, argued that an announcement that the exercise was to start in November would "considerably reduce the chances of any North Korean concessions in the *Pueblo* negotiations, since they would appear to be making concessions under threat." But Focus Retina was merely postponed. In a message designed to reassure South Korea that the U.S.–ROK relationship remained strong, the United States announced that the exercise would occur the following spring.[30]

The State Department next sought to influence the North through unpublicized naval activity. A carrier battle group (presumably led by USS *Hancock*) was scheduled to operate in the Sea of Japan between 2 and 4 December before steaming on to Sasebo on 5 December. State felt that having some vessels operate north of the thirty-eighth parallel ("but well off the North Korean coast") would have "some utility, in terms of the *Pueblo* negotiations and general posture *vis à vis* Korea." A second internal memo opined that naval operations north of the thirty-eighth parallel would convey "a signal of firmness to North Korea, thus erasing any impression that might have been made by our cancellation of Focus Retina."[31]

USS *Hancock* accordingly operated in the Sea of Japan during the first week of December. *Hancock*'s presence seemed to hearten the State Department. The department's next message to American embassy Seoul had an upbeat tone:

We hope also that recent visit of CVA *Hancock* will have reminded them [North Korea] that winding-down of Vietnam war could liberate resources to improve US-ROK military posture and that they would be well advised to reduce sources of tension, both by releasing *Pueblo* crew and by desisting from infiltration attempts such as Ulchin.[32]

State hoped to send Moscow a message as well. It hoped the Soviets might conclude that *Hancock's* visit was a response to the major North Korean raid on Ulchin—it was not—and might also realize that increasing U.S. naval power was becoming available to deal with North Korea as the war in Vietnam began to wind down.[33]

With the *Pueblo* talks essentially recessed for more than a month, State in early December began to craft the Johnson administration's last attempt to resolve the crisis. Writing to LBJ in a subparagraph entitled "Time for a Squeeze Play," Katzenbach described the approach of Christmas and the end of the administration as affording an opportunity to issue the North an ultimatum without a high risk of breaking off the talks. The United States would offer to do one of two things: (1) "overwrite" a North Korean apology document with phraseology merely acknowledging receipt of the crew, or (2) actually sign the North Korean document but orally repudiate it before and/or after signing it.[34] General Woodward, the U.S. negotiator, would read a version of the following statement disavowing the written admission of U.S. guilt:

> The position of the U.S. government with regard to *Pueblo,* as consistently expressed in the negotiations at Panmunjom and in public, has been that the ship was not engaged in illegal activity, that there is no convincing evidence that the ship at any time intruded into the territorial waters claimed by North Korea, and that we could not apologize for actions which we did not believe took place. The document which I am going to sign was prepared by the North Koreans and is at variance with the above position, but my signature will not and cannot alter the facts. I will sign the document to free the crew and only to free the crew.[35]

The United States would emphasize that the North would have to accept one of the offers in time to get the crew home for Christmas. If the North rejected both proposals, the administration would withdraw them and would make no further offers during its remaining few weeks in office.[36] State elaborated on this stratagem in a message to U.S. embassies in Seoul and Moscow on 11 December 1968: "Our hope is that North Koreans will calculate that they are not likely to get more from President-elect Nixon than President Johnson and will accept one of choices offered."[37]

On 17 December, the North accepted the U.S. proposal to sign a document prepared by North Korea along with an oral disclaimer (a "pre-repudiated apology"). General Woodward and General Pak signed the documents on the morning of 23 December, and General Woodward made the prearranged disclaimer. The North released the crew in Panmunjom that same morning. The crew returned to San Diego on 24 December.[38] *Pueblo* remained in North Korea.

USS *Pueblo* itself was not forgotten once the crew was home, however. In thanking his *Pueblo* diplomatic team, Secretary of State Dean Rusk said, "Now the next thing is, let's get that ship back."[39] Thoughts immediately turned once again to seizing the fish factory ships under construction in the Verolme Shipyards in Rotterdam, but State rejected this course of action because it would potentially jeopardize the principle of freedom of the seas.[40]

The Joint Chiefs continued planning to regain *Pueblo* as well. In a memo to the new secretary of defense, Melvin Laird, on 28 February 1969, the JCS argued that North Korea's retention of the *Pueblo* hurt U.S. credibility as a defender of freedom of the seas. The JCS proposed a plan with escalating steps starting with a diplomatic track: the United States would demand *Pueblo*'s return (1) privately in meetings with the DPRK representatives at Panmunjom, (2) publicly in the same venue, (3) before the UN, and finally (4) before an international adjudicatory body. Should these diplomatic courses fail, the United States would inform the North that "if shared use of the high seas depends upon effective power rather than law, N.K. can expect her share to be far more limited than that prior to *Pueblo* seizure." The JCS recommend that the United States then undertake military action once these steps were exhausted.[41] There is no evidence that this proposal found any resonance in the new administration. If anything, any residual focus on reclaiming the ship was interrupted by the new surge of planning demanded by the EC-121 shootdown.

However, the U.S. Navy chafed at the eighty-mile buffer the JCS had imposed along the DPRK's east coast. The restricted area potentially constrained bilateral naval exercises with both the ROK Navy and the Japanese Maritime Self-Defense Force. The navy resisted any implied acceptance of limits to its freedom of navigation. To make the point, it still sought the option (at least in principle) of occasionally operating destroyers along North Korea's coasts.

## Lessons Learned

A number of organizations collectively devoted many man-years to developing the lessons learned from the *Pueblo* incident. The published results show that they first addressed the immediate issue: how to safely operate a fleet of virtually unarmed intelligence collection ships. The *ultimate* lesson learned, however, does not appear in those interim reports: Operating an unarmed U.S. Navy collector near potentially hostile areas demands far more support than is warranted by the intelligence "take." The demands for on-call aircraft and warships to quickly respond to a rapidly emerging threat to a slow-moving AGER made the price tag too high to justify retaining the old (and maintenance intensive) AGERs. A warship could better perform the collection mission on an "as required" basis.

Even before the lessons-learned process was under way, the fleet took steps to protect its shipboard intelligence collectors worldwide. For example, in its "Nice Time" Caribbean patrols, USNS *Sergeant Joseph P. Muller* was initially directed on 30 January to extend its standoff distance from Cuba from six to ten miles. (On-call fighter support would be available.) After the JCS and Commander in Chief, Atlantic, rethought the problem in February, they assigned a destroyer to escort *Muller*. The ship would operate four to six miles seaward of *Muller*, and USMC F-4s in Key West would support both ships. As for the Mediterranean, the JCS initially directed *Georgetown* on 30 January to remain in port in Naples until further notice. If *Georgetown* was to operate in the eastern Mediterranean, a destroyer would have to operate between it and the coast. Its authorized closest point of approach to land was extended from twenty-five miles to thirty-five miles. Naval Forces Europe also directed the ship's crew to attempt an emergency destruction drill. To his likely horror, the theater commander discovered that the crew would have taken eight hours to destroy *Georgetown*'s sensitive equipment and documents! The commander directed that steps be taken to reduce the entire process to half an hour. Despite these concerns, *Georgetown* was back operating off the Egyptian coast by mid-February (with several ships, including the carrier *Roosevelt*, on standby to protect it).[42]

The first review of shipboard intelligence-collecting procedures was done secretly and quickly in the early stages of the *Pueblo* crisis. Evidently, in early

February 1968, President Johnson asked George Ball to conduct a "'no holds barred" review of the *Pueblo* incident. The review board, which comprised Adm. David McDonald, Gen. Mark Clark, and Gen. Laurence Kuter, was to establish the facts of the case; assess the mission's planning, instructions, and conduct; and make recommendations regarding future surface ship intelligence collection operations. In addition to looking at the mission approval process, operating instructions, and communications support, the Ball Committee was to review the "adequacy of interagency arrangements for monitoring approved aerial and ship operations, particularly with respect to continuing political assessments of sensitive operations." The committee would also review the adequacy of emergency assistance arrangements for surface intelligence collectors.[43]

After briefing Robert McNamara and Dean Rusk, Ball phoned LBJ on 7 February 1968 and advised that the report was nearly done. He told the president that the committee had agreed that "we ought to perform these missions in a somewhat different fashion . . . that we probably shouldn't send them into waters of this kind without protection."[44]

In his autobiography, Ball commented that he was greatly surprised when his committee agreed on a report so critical of those in command, and he ordered all final copies destroyed to avoid a press leak. The report "raised serious doubts as to the exact position of the *Pueblo*, was severely critical of the planning, organization, and direction of the whole enterprise, and recommended a number of measures to avoid a similar disaster." As summarized in a memo for the record, the Ball report made four points:

1. It would be wise to abandon efforts to conduct covert electronic intelligence (ELINT) collection activities at sea. ELINT ships could then operate without radio silence and could be protected by armed naval vessels. (*Pueblo* had operated under radio silence until the crew determined that North Korea had detected it.)

2. The government should review the sensitivity of coastal areas of ELINT interest before dispatching *Pueblo*-type ships on new missions.

3. ELINT ships should carry adequate destruction devices to ensure quick destruction in times of emergency.

4. Instructions to the skippers of intelligence collectors should be reviewed.

Apparently the instructions regarding the use of weapons in self-defense were ambiguous.[45]

The Joint Chiefs also conducted an "elaborate examination" of the incident in a search for lessons learned. Approximately three months after *Pueblo* was seized, the chairman, General Wheeler, wrote that he was unconvinced that U.S. contingency plans for the DPRK were as "current and specific as they realistically should be" in view of the North's military posture. Moreover, Wheeler was unaware of any U.S. plans to respond to North Korean provocations short of all-out attack. He directed that the Joint Staff review all plans for the North and analyze contingencies short of all-out war with the DPRK. He also wanted to review sensitive intelligence collection. Although he did not mention the date of the review, General Wheeler later testified before Congress that the JCS "did make changes, a number of them, having to do with the validation process, various rules or procedures for ships' captains, [and] the provision of destruction devices."[46] Interestingly, it was the chairman's opinion that the risk evaluation system in effect at the time of the seizure was adequate.[47] This perspective may explain why the DIA director's prepared testimony to Congress in the spring of 1969 revealed no change in DIA risk assessment methodology between the *Pueblo* seizure and the EC-121 incident.[48] The key change seems to have been the JCS ensuring that the entire chain of command began to use the same risk assessment methodology. That is, the lower levels of the chain began to use the same methodology used in Washington.

The next publicized set of reviews, which began after the crew returned to the United States, followed the naval board of inquiry held in San Diego between 20 January and 13 March 1969. The DOD reviews coincided with ongoing congressional hearings that began on 4 March 1969. (The Special Subcommittee on the USS *Pueblo* of the House Armed Services Committee held hearings on *Pueblo* during March and April. That summer, it issued a blistering report on the *Pueblo* incident and the EC-121 shootdown.)[49] On 14 March 1969, Deputy Secretary of Defense David Packard requested a reassessment of measures being taken to prevent "compromise" of intelligence collection ships. The navy was to examine tasking procedures, onboard classified material allowance, and improved destruction techniques.[50] The navy's response addressed the ten broad areas of concern shown in table 5.

Table 5. U.S. Navy *Pueblo* Lessons-Learned Topics

*Command and Control*

Criteria and procedures for tasking intelligence collection ships

Planning policy for employment of forces to protect intelligence collection ships

Preparation of intelligence collection ships where quick withdrawal may be required

Adequacy of written guidance for captain and crew concerning contingency
   planning and interpretation of rules of engagement

*Emergency Destruction*

Objectives of the destruction device retrofit program

Strategy for use of emergency destruction equipment

Effect of destruction mechanisms on communications capability during crisis
   situations

Capability of ships to endure hostile fire

Determination of minimum essential classified material required aboard intelligence
   collection ships

Need for improved destruction techniques

*Source:* Draft response to deputy secretary of defense attached to memo from EA and naval aide to assistant secretary of the navy, "Reponse to Mr. Packard's Questions of 14 March on *Pueblo*," 18 April 1969, Double Zero files, *Pueblo*, NHC.

The navy assured the DOD that it planned to work with the National Security Agency to streamline the tasking of AGERs. The navy proposed semi-annual meetings with the NSA to coordinate signals intelligence objectives that the AGERs might satisfy. In a proposed agreement with the NSA, cognizant naval commanders would have sole SIGINT operational control of the AGERs—there would be a single line of command tasking the AGERs. (Under the earlier AGER missions, the NSA and the navy had alternated tasking.) Additionally, review, coordination, and approval of sensitive maritime collection operations would now be in accordance with the JCS directive "Peacetime Reconnaissance and Sensitive Operations" (SM-701-68).[51] (The "68" designation suggests that the directive was either revised or created in 1968. It likely postdated *Pueblo*'s seizure and incorporated lessons learned as developed in the JCS lessons-learned process that General Wheeler mentioned.)

In fact, SM-701 and associated documents released by CINCPAC and CINCPACFLT contained revised criteria for evaluating the risks of intelligence collection missions and assigning a risk category. SM-701 identified which aspects of a mission were to be evaluated and specified criteria to be used in making a risk assessment. It mandated the assignment of one of four categories of risks. CINCPACFLT confirmed that it was now using the same risk assessment methodology. This decision introduced consistent risk assessment methodology that had been lacking in the approval process for *Pueblo*. The new instructions also reminded the operators that "risk level will vary from mission to mission" and—particularly relevant to *Pueblo*—that risk level "is susceptible to change during a particular mission."[52]

SM-701 also mandated more rigorous planning in support of sensitive collection operations. Foremost, intelligence collection ships would "normally be restricted to areas outside of sensitive areas" (specified by the JCS in other publications) to avoid needing rescue. If a mission were conducted in *or adjacent to* a sensitive area, its operations would be planned and approved in accordance with SM-701-68. The directive required each unified and specified command to develop contingency plans and to dedicate forces in support of each intelligence collection ship patrol. It mandated that the theater commander must specify alert forces, estimated reaction times, command and control capability (C3), and procedures. The plan (or plans) must be a workable document containing alternative contingency responses. In particular, contingency plans must recognize the operational constraints imposed by the very limited speed and maneuverability of AGER/AGTRs. Additionally, the commander had to actually *test* the plan to ensure a demonstrated capability to respond. Navy policy now carried this a step further and explicitly prohibited the use of an intelligence collection ship without adequate alert forces if the risk assessment rose above category 4 (minimum risk). Evidently complying with this guidance, CINCPACFLT now directed that intelligence collection mission proposals include "requirements for and availability of supporting forces (direct and standby)."[53]

In mid-May 1969, as the navy introduced the new procedures, the secretary of the navy reminded the CNO that he remained concerned about "proper and timely *Pueblo* follow-up action." Vice Chief of Naval Operations Adm. B. Clarey warned the key navy operations staff components that "this subject will be raised frequently in the future." He accordingly directed that the deputy chief of naval operations (fleet operations and readiness) form a task force to ensure follow-up of *Pueblo* corrective actions. Administrative procedures for tracking outstanding *Pueblo* action items had been established and in use for a year, but Admiral Clarey directed that these become more extensive and better documented.[54]

The navy was hardly slacking off in its responsibilities. More than thirty AGER follow-up actions had already been initiated by May 1969, including several tasked by the deputy secretary of defense. Although not all of the results of this staff work have been declassified, the subject headings of those that have been are wide ranging. They include compiling lessons learned, producing a damage assessment, reviewing command and control coordination for special project ships and cruisers operating independently in sensitive areas, developing standardized protection for future AGER operations, eliminating operations former conducted in radio silence, and evaluating operational intelligence support.[55]

The navy had begun to provide far better protection for its surface collection ships even while the *Pueblo* crisis was ongoing. A combatant ship was assigned to escort a collector on two patrols in the Mediterranean. A warship escorted the collector during its entire eastern Mediterranean patrol on 9–17 February 1968, and another warship joined it as it steamed off the North African coast. The navy placed a second collection ship, which had been operating in an unspecified area for years, under continuous naval escort after *Pueblo*.[56]

The DOD showed that it could do a better job of supporting its surface collection ships immediately after the *Pueblo* incident as well. In *Assault on the* Liberty, for example, James Ennes wrote that USNS *Sergeant Joseph P. Muller* was on an intelligence patrol off Cuba in February 1968 when its engines failed. A destroyer was escorting *Muller* (there had been no escort before the *Pueblo* incident) and remained within five miles of its position. *Muller* evidently quickly patched into the National Military Command Center, and fighter aircraft scrambled from Florida to come to the disabled ship's assistance. *Muller* was drifting toward Cuban territory, and the destroyer's repeated attempts to tow it failed as one towline after another parted. Just as *Muller* was about to enter Cuban territorial waters, the final towline held.[57]

The *Muller* incident thus contained both good and bad news for the JCS. The planning and command and control arrangements to support sensitive surface collection operations worked smoothly. However, the *Muller*'s engineering failure so close to a sensitive area was an unpleasant reminder of how risky these operations could be. Although the *Liberty* and *Pueblo* incidents probably had a greater influence on the navy's decision to cancel the AGER program, experiences like *Muller's* likely also played a role in it. Even when things went well, collection by old, unarmed SIGINT collection ships was awfully risky.

After *Pueblo* was seized, the United States also modified the way reconnaissance missions were flown off North Korea. The JCS revised its guidance for reconnaissance missions flying off the DPRK four times during the *Pueblo* crisis. At the time of the seizure, the JCS imposed an eighty-mile restriction on such missions off the coast. On 25 January, PARPRO aircraft were restricted to daylight flights, and then only under fighter escort. The requirement for close fighter escort ended on 28 January 1968. After that, the reconnaissance aircraft received support from fighters on combat air patrol. The JCS suspended the fighter escort requirement for reconnaissance flights being flown overland along the DMZ but mandated strip alerts on 5 February. Finally, on 2 July 1968, the JCS reduced the over-water restriction from eighty miles off the North Korean coast to forty miles. Strip alerts were still required.[58]

In conjunction with preparing its Fresh Storm contingency plans, CINC-PAC also revised the rules of engagement for U.S. forces operating near North Korea. After *Pueblo* was seized, CINCPAC polled the Strategic Air Command and his subordinate subunified commands about proposed rules changes. In July 1968, CINCPAC forwarded a consolidated rules of engagement message to the JCS. The draft rules were significant because they would now authorize "hot pursuit" of offending North Korean ships/aircraft into/over North Korean territory. The State Department objected to giving blanket "hot pursuit" authorization to U.S. forces in Korea.[59] They lost. The JCS issued the new rules of engagement in July 1969. Although he admitted that General Bonesteel had imposed tighter rules on his forces, the chargé d'affaires at the American embassy in Seoul commented:

> We note that we lost our principal point—that authorization for immediate pursuit by aircraft or ships, if attacked into the territorial waters and airspace of North Korea should be separately approved for specific operations, missions or projects and not be made general in applicability. The Rules of Engagement as published do just the opposite—they are generally applicable unless modified for specific operations, missions, or projects.[60]

The rules of engagement suggested by the JCS directed that

> immediate pursuit may be conducted as necessary and feasible. In event US/ friendly forces in Korea are attacked by a hostile aircraft or vessel, immediate pursuit may be conducted into territorial seas or airspace of North Korea and international waters until the immediate threat to the security of US/friendly forces has been successfully countered.[61]

Despite such discussions, as of early 1969 the DOD was making only relatively minor (but important) adjustments to existing programs. A broader question had yet to be answered: was the AGER program worth its increasing costs? A related query about whether all of the SIGINT flights off North Korea were completely justified had yet to be asked. Both questions would be topical by decade's end.

In the interim, intelligence consumers continued to push for more intelligence. Even on the day the *Pueblo* crew was released, Undersecretary of State Kazenbach wrote to LBJ: "Our limited intelligence makes it difficult to estimate the precise nature of the threat to South Korea" and "our intelligence both as to intent and capability needs improvement."[62] Katzenbach's statements are significant considering that the DPRK had been a high-priority target for intelligence collection even *before* it seized *Pueblo*. With intelligence consumers so avid for information, it would be hard to cut back on promising but risky collection programs. Missions such as that flown by the ill-fated EC-121 that North Korea downed in April 1969 were hardly likely to be disapproved.

# 7

# ROUND TWO

North Korea's downing of a Fleet Air Reconnaissance Squadron One (VQ-1) EC-121M raised harsh questions. Had the United States learned nothing from the *Pueblo* incident? North Korea had twice surprised Washington during a sixteen-month period. Many of the men who had been in leadership positions during the *Pueblo* crisis held the same positions during the EC-121 crisis. In the aftermath, Congress had hard questions for them. The evidence suggested that the attack was deliberate and premeditated, but did anyone know why the North did it? Why did the intelligence community allow U.S. reconnaissance planes to begin approaching within nearly forty miles of the North Korean coast (without fighter escort) while the *Pueblo*'s crew was still in North Korean hands? Why were no forces close by to assist the EC-121? The lessons learned from *Pueblo* had not saved the EC-121. What more did the United States need to learn?

## Watching the North

When it came to intelligence collection, *Pueblo* was an anomaly. Aircraft had been the preeminent collection platforms against the DPRK for decades. North Korea claimed that even after *Pueblo* was seized the United States flew

RB-47s, RB-57s, RC-130s, and EC-121s over its territory. In addition to the very active VQ-1 based in Japan, Guam, and elsewhere, the U.S. Air Force monitored the North with Okinawa-based collectors. An RC-135 strategic reconnaissance squadron was based there along with a three-aircraft SR-71 Blackbird detachment. Both were assigned to and were under the operational control of the Strategic Air Command.[1]

Although much of the "take" from the missions remains classified, VQ-1's annual report for 1969 shows how useful reconnaissance missions could be in mapping the DPRK's air defense environment. Over a three-year period the North had rapidly enhanced its air defense capabilities. VQ-1 obtained evidence to show this. Knowing the location of the DPRK's ever-growing collection of radar sites would be highly useful information for contingency planners who would have to ascertain radar detection ranges and determine which sites needed to be destroyed or jammed to effectively blind the NKAF's air defense system. During 1969, VQ-1 had detected growing numbers of key radar types focused on the DPRK: GCI (Bar Locks), early warning (Flat Faces), missile control (Fan Songs), and height finders (Side Net and Rock/Stone Cakes).[2]

Collecting signals intelligence from airborne platforms could be dangerous. North Korea had severely damaged one U.S. collector only four years earlier. On 28 April 1965, two MiG-17s attacked a U.S. Air Force RB-47 flying eighty miles off the east coast of North Korea. The bomber used its tail cannon and barely escaped. The plane made an emergency landing at Tachikawa Air Base, Japan, but was so damaged that the air force described it as a constructive loss.[3]

Although NKAF fighters routinely scrambled in response to reconnaissance missions, the next four years were uneventful.[4] In fact, the number of NKAF reactions to U.S. PARPRO missions dropped during 1967. Some 35 missions flown from January to March 1967 elicited only six NKAF fighter reactions. The reaction rate dropped dramatically for the rest of the year: 172 reconnaissance missions flown from April through December 1967 generated only five fighter reactions, and no more than one in any month.[5]

The NKAF reacted in other ways to reconnaissance aircraft after 1965. It had begun working on intercept techniques—including air-to-air missiles—against U.S. reconnaissance aircraft off its coasts.[6] Brig. Gen. Ralph Steakley, director of the JCS Joint Reconnaissance Center, commented on one incident in which a North Korean fighter approached "really close" to a U.S. aircraft but evidently was flying at 25,000 feet, too low to intercept it.[7] The North had also been practice-firing surface-to-air missiles against targets flying at the altitude used by the Black Shield reconnaissance aircraft.[8] Beyond that, the NKAF MiG-19s and MiG-21s occasionally reacted to photoreconnaissance missions.[9]

The air force became cautious after the April 1965 RB-47 shootdown attempt. For two years after the incident, the Strategic Air Command flew reconnaissance missions over the Sea of Japan only during darkness. During these two years, the NKAF demonstrated no hostile intent.[10] Consequently, the United States resumed normal day and night missions over the Sea of Japan in late 1967. These missions had fighter escorts for an unspecified time after the 1965 shootdown attempt, but the escorts were discontinued when the flights were not challenged. In any case, the escorts were expensive and "relatively ineffective," in the words of General Wheeler.[11]

## Risk Assessment

Although the lessons learned during the *Pueblo* crisis had resulted in the implementation of some changes, the basic national-level criteria for assessing the risks to reconnaissance missions remained unchanged in April 1969.[12] Some of the challenges that had faced those who approved *Pueblo* in December 1967 survived to plague those who would have to approve the EC-121 mission. The validation system still required a relatively small number of people at different levels of the chain of command to review and approve hundreds of proposed surveillance missions in a very short period. Moreover, North Korea's behavior seemed no more predictable in March 1969 than it had been in December 1967 when *Pueblo*'s patrol was approved. The key difference, of course, was that the DPRK had demonstrated that it would attack U.S. intelligence collectors at sea as well as airborne collectors.

General Bonesteel had lobbied for yet another SNIE on North Korea when he visited Washington in November 1968. He got his wish on 30 January 1969. Approximately ten weeks before the EC-121 was shot down, the director of central intelligence released an updated SNIE. Unfortunately, it said little more than his May 1968 assessment had said. SNIE 14.2-69, "Confrontation with Korea," concluded that the DPRK was unlikely to provoke major hostilities with the United States, let alone invade South Korea. Pyongyang would, however, continue its campaign against the ROK and thereby risk provoking ROK escalation that could potentially lead to the outbreak of general hostilities.

The drafters seemed unwilling to treat the *Pueblo* experience as anything more than an anomaly.[13]

As late as February 1969 the North seemed quiescent. The U.S. embassy in Seoul reported that activity along the DMZ was at a "notably low level." The embassy could offer no clear-cut reason for the lull but suggested that the season and associated heavy snows had slowed the usual infiltration program. The South Korean prime minister speculated that the North might not have wanted to misbehave and thereby strengthen President Park's campaign to push through a constitutional amendment that would allow him a third term in office. He also believed that Kim Il Sung might have considered it wise to lie low while the new Nixon administration was formulating its policies toward Asia.[14]

Thus, as the risk assessment process for the April 1969 batch of PARPRO missions began in March, the DPRK may have looked less threatening than usual. Of course, the North had made no discernible defensive preparations before seizing *Pueblo* either. During the year before *Pueblo* was seized, North Korean fighter reaction to PARPRO missions had been infrequent and low key. During 1967, the DIA had prepared three special risk assessments on North Korean fighter reactions to airborne intelligence gatherers. In March 1967, it had written that the "risk appears somewhat greater now than at any time since the hostile engagement of 28 April 1965" (the attack on the RB-47). This assessment was written after NKAF fighters had challenged six PARPRO missions. The response rate dropped 80 percent during the rest of the year. In December 1967, the DIA had endorsed the resumption of daylight signals intelligence missions against the ROK: "North Korean reactions to daytime flights are likely to be minimal providing the aircraft stay at a reasonable distance from North Korean sovereign airspace." However, the DIA also advised that the NKAF would be more capable of reacting to daylight flights because its large force of MiG-17 (daylight-only, clear air mass) fighters could now participate in intercepts along with MiG-19s and MiG-21s.[15]

The proposed mid-April EC-121 mission probably underwent a more complex validation process than did the *Pueblo* patrol. Because the aircraft was going to engage in an ELINT mission, CINCPAC would have cited the mission in the list of Pacific-area ELINT missions it forwarded to Washington in early March. In theory, the DIA would then have reviewed the ELINT mission proposal to ensure that it did not duplicate other ELINT missions and that it was not "marginally productive." By mid-March, the DIA would have met with representatives of other Washington agencies to ensure that they agreed that the proposed mission had merit. By the third week of March, the Washington staffers would have completed their interagency scrub of proposed reconnaissance missions. They would then marry it up with the overall proposed monthly reconnaissance schedule for the Pacific that CINCPAC would have just submitted.[16]

The risk assessment process was influenced by a related basic risk assessment of the particular track the reconnaissance aircraft would fly. There were 130 different approved reconnaissance tracks in the Korean area at that time.[17] The tracks reflected airborne sensor capability, the type of aircraft flying the mission, and the nature of the target being monitored. A standard track flown by an EC-121 SIGINT aircraft, for example, would be much different from the track a photoreconnaissance aircraft would have to take. The risk assessment for a track was based on changes in the political situation, observed reaction to reconnaissance activities, and so on.[18]

In April 1969, the EC-121 was to fly a track over the Sea of Japan that EC-121s had flown eight times since November 1968.[19] The JCS's decision to reduce the standoff distance from eighty to forty miles in July 1968 seems to imply that the risk assessment for these missions was lower than it had been earlier in 1968. The delay of more than two months between when CINCPAC requested the modification and its approval suggests that the decision was carefully considered. In fact, the JCS approved the proposal quickly in early May 1968 but was unable to secure State Department concurrence until 2 July 1968. In February 1969, even the forty-mile restriction was rescinded provided that the JCS was notified of any air or naval operation that would bring U.S. forces into the formerly restricted area.[20]

The approval of the proposed April mission implies that there had been no significant NKAF fighter reactions any of the other eight times EC-121s had flown that track, including as recently as 13 March 1969.[21] Indeed, between January 1968 and April 1969, the United States had flown 976 flights within sixty miles of a line drawn parallel to the east coast of Korea and north of the DMZ.[22] Put another way, the United States had flown 190 uneventful reconnaissance flights (49 of them by VQ-1 planes) over the Sea of Japan from January through March 1969.[23] The NKAF simply did not appear to challenge this level of flight activity.[24] With that background, the chain of command and the DIA would likely have designated the EC-121 mission proposed for 15

April as category 4: "hostile intent remote, intercept actions unlikely, defensive patrols possible."[25]

Once the risk assessment was complete, the Joint Reconnaissance Center would have briefed the Joint Chiefs on the proposed worldwide reconnaissance schedule. Given the volume of collection activity then going on over the Sea of Japan, it is unlikely that this routine EC-121 mission received special attention. General Wheeler observed that the JCS really had time to focus only on unusual missions (or unusual incidents) from previous months: "Unless there was some event which would cause us to really focus on it, we would say, 'Well, last month this particular program went off without incident.' There would be no reason to expect, or require, a detailed examination. We would look at them . . . in chunks."[26]

## North Korea's Motivations

The mission validation process in Washington was evidently completed on schedule. The review process was based on pattern analysis and documented behavior. As in the *Pueblo* approval process, it was very hard for the EC-121 mission's risk assessors to "think outside the box," particularly when North Korea appeared to be quiescent. Their failure to understand the North's decision-making process hindered U.S. planners' ability to foresee the shootdown. Even today, that process is speculative. The available evidence suggests that the shootdown was deliberate, but the "why" remains uncertain.

One school of thought argues that the EC-121 downing was the result of internal power rivalries in the DPRK. The State Department desk officer advised the British ambassador that internal political turmoil—perhaps a new hard-line defense minister—might have contributed to the shootdown.[27] An effort by the partisan generals discussed earlier to demonstrate that their proposed policy of confrontation and high-tech military buildup was appropriate may, that is, have been a contributing factor.

After attaining power under contentious circumstances, the partisan generals likely needed to show quick and spectacular results to support their takeover of anti-ROK operations. In relatively quick order, they staged the Blue House raid and seized the *Pueblo*. Such blatant, unconventional provocations against the United States might have yielded several benefits for Kim Il Sung.

They afforded personal triumphs—a critical incentive for a regime that was becoming, and remains, highly personalized; they provided a propaganda tool demonstrating an external threat that warranted sacrifices made in the North in fulfillment of the ambitious Seven-Year plan; and they also strained U.S.–ROK relations. U.S. support remained the center of gravity for Seoul, and any action that might endanger this support was worth considering.[28] Indeed, the U.S. failure to retaliate for either incident and Washington's active discouragement of ROK retaliation likely helped make the case for the planners of the EC-121 episode.

When, by early 1969, the new policies seemed to have made no progress toward unification, Kim reportedly began to criticize the generals. At a meeting of the Fourth Party Committee of the Korean People's Army (KPA) in January 1969, Kim criticized the defense minister for advocating high-tech weapons inappropriate for Korea's terrain. Kim accused him specifically of being interested only in highly sophisticated fighters while Korea's terrain called for slow, low-flying aircraft.[29] In addition to stressing inappropriate technology, the group as a whole was criticized for failing to fortify the country properly with tunnels, wasting military supplies, spare parts shortages, and attempting to form their own clique in the military. Continuing this theme at the next KWP congress held in November 1970, Kim warned that the "random import of sophisticated military arsenals irrespective of conditions should be avoided." By November 1970, the director of the Liaison Bureau (i.e., with South Korea) had been replaced by a nonmilitary man. Ten other high-ranking party generals, including Defense Minister Kim Ch'ang-bong and the chief of staff, reportedly had been removed as well. The British Foreign Office also noted the exceptional turmoil in the DPRK hierarchy. Between 1966 and 1970, two of the five members of the Presidium and two other full and seven candidate members of the Political Committee of the KWP had lost their jobs. The number of candidate members had also dropped from eleven to seven.[30]

Thus, facing an uncertain fate as early as January 1969, the proponents of sophisticated armaments may have sought one last opportunity to prove their case. What better way to justify the cost of a complement of expensive fighters than by using a pair of them to destroy a U.S. reconnaissance aircraft? Better still if the shooter could be a supersonic MiG-21, the newest, most glamorous, and most expensive aircraft in North Korea's arsenal. (The records thus far declassified do not identify the type of MiG that shot down the EC-121.) Downing a U.S. aircraft would achieve many of the benefits gained during the *Pueblo* crisis. It would provide a dramatic demonstration of North Korean capability against the overwhelmingly more powerful United States. Concurrently, it could also undermine U.S. credibility by demonstrating America's unwillingness to retaliate on its own behalf, let alone that of the ROK. Most important, downing the EC-121 might afford a way for the builders of a costly high-tech military to redeem their policies and remain in power.

North Korea's one victory during the "second Korean war" was in its handling of the *Pueblo* affair. By staging a shootdown, the partisan generals could replicate elements of the *Pueblo* seizure. Several things commended a shootdown. There was a high probability of tactical success because the operation would be easy to plan and execute against apparently unprotected U.S. operations; success could be further ensured by picking on an isolated U.S. asset. A shootdown would demonstrate that expensive conventional military assets were paying for themselves and would support central DPRK foreign policy objectives by demonstrating U.S. irresolution.

For the plot to work, however, the NKAF would have to make the right selection from the menu of U.S. reconnaissance aircraft flying along the North Korean periphery. Aircraft flying south of the DMZ were defended by ROK and U.S. fighters flying on strip alert in the ROK. As much as the DPRK might like to shoot one down, an A-12/SR-71 was too hard too destroy, even with surface-to-air missiles. The RC-135s likely stayed well out to sea and were flying fast and high enough to complicate a shootdown attempt. The EC-121, however, would be relatively easy to catch and bring down. Its two-hundred-knot cruising speed, long dwell time, and low altitude must have combined to make an inviting target.

Two factors could have influenced the shootdown's timing. First, the partisan generals needed to do something sooner rather than later in view of their resounding lack of success throughout most of 1968. A more immediate factor may have been Kim Il Sung's impending birthday on 15 April. The North Korean people and media always placed tremendous emphasis on this anniversary. Given this level of cultural emphasis and press treatment, the military might have conducted the shootdown as a birthday present. Certainly, the intelligence community quickly offered this as an explanation in the early days of the postshootdown crisis.[31]

With approval to conduct the shootdown, the NKAF may have made some low-key preparations. U.S. personnel in South Korea noticed that something was amiss. On 11 April 1969, U.S. Forces Korea advised CINCPAC that "during recent armistice commission meetings, the North Koreans have been particularly vehement and vicious in warning UN forces about provocative actions." Saying it was trying to keep the situation "cool," USFK suggested that surveillance flights remain at least fifteen nautical miles from the DMZ and preferably even farther away while over land. USFK warned that "aircrews [should] be especially alert and prepared to abort at the first indication of any North Korean reaction."[32] In an oral history shared three years after the shootdown, General Bonesteel referred to the anomalous behavior:

> I warned CINCPAC to be very careful about four days before the plane was shot down. I was specifically talking of Air Force flights, but we knew that the ROKs [*sic*] were doing something that was damned suspicious. I recommended they have a very close watch or tie-in with radars watching the . . . airfields and if they got any scramble to get the hell out of there.[33]

On receiving Bonesteel's warning, CINCPAC sent a message of his own to CINCPACAF, CINCPACFLT, and USFK advising the exercise of all caution during PARPRO operations near North Korea. CINCPACFLT in turn recommended that all PARPRO missions flying over the Sea of Japan increase vigilance. Such a warning might account for the fact that the EC-121 was directed to fly no closer than fifty miles to North Korea (instead of maintaining the usual forty-mile standoff distance).[34]

## The Shootdown

The tale of the shootdown is relatively short. VQ-1's EC-121 flew its ill-fated 15 April mission out of Atsugi Naval Air Station on the outskirts of Tokyo. It carried a crew of six officers, one marine, and twenty-four navy enlisted men, mostly communications and avionics technicians. The mission plan called for the aircraft to fly a daylight track from Atsugi into the Sea of Japan, to orbit there for several hours, and then to land at Osan Air Base, approximately forty miles south of Seoul.[35] Once on station, the EC-121 would have flown at an airspeed of two hundred miles an hour and an altitude of nine to sixteen thousand feet.[36] Table 6 provides a chronology of the shootdown events.

**Table 6. CE-121M Shootdown Chronology, 15 April 1969**

| | |
|---|---|
| 0700 | EC-121 departs Atsugi, Japan |
| 0717 | EC-121 transmits routine voice message |
| 1234 | NKAF MiGs scramble in response to EC-121 |
| 1300 | EC-121 transmits routine teletype report |
| 1322 | Contact lost on MiGs |
| 1336 | Contact regained on MiGs |
| 1338 | EC-121 is advised that MiGs have approached between 51 and 55 miles |
| 1340 | EC-121 is advised that MiGs have approached to within 50 miles |
| 1345 | Unidentified U.S. tracking site issues immediate precedence spot report (date-time group 150445Z) regarding NKAF fighter response to mission aircraft |
| 1347–1349 | MiGs shoot down EC-121 |
| 1350 | U.S. radar sites in ROK confirm that EC-121 has disappeared from radar screens |
| 1403 | Unidentified U.S. monitoring site issues immediate precedence follow-up (date-time group 150503Z) to original spot report of NKAF fighter response advising that two NKAF aircraft are heading east toward EC-121 |
| 1404 | Two F-102s scramble from Osan, ROK, to Sea of Japan |
| 1453 | Additional fighters take off to relieve first pair; HC-130 SAR aircraft departs Tachikawa, Japan |
| 1444 | U.S. monitoring facility in ROK issues CRITIC message advising that Korean air surveillance facilities reflect possible shootdown of EC-121 by NKAF aircraft |
| 1453 | Second set of U.S. fighters departs en route to search-and-rescue scene |
| 1542 | HC-130 SAR aircraft departs Tachikawa |
| 1740 | HC-130 arrives on scene |

*Sources:* This chronology combines times provided in four different reports: COMSEVENTHFLT 240151Z April 1969, "EC-121M Shootdown/SAR," 24 April 1969, folder "091 Korea (BP) EC-121 Shootdown," box 31, Wheeler Records, RG 218, NARA; House Armed Services Committee, "Review of Department of Defense Worldwide Communications, Phase I," 10 May 1971, 14–15; HASC Report, 1675–76; and HASC Report (draft), 109–10. The times vary slightly depending on the source. A flash precedence situation report transmitted by CINCPAC after the shootdown stated that the EC-121 acknowledged three warning messages just before the shootdown. See ADMIN CINCPAC 151113Z APR 69, contained in Double Zero 1969 files, NHC. This study relies more on timelines used in subsequent investigations because the authors of these studies presumably had reconciled the inconsistencies in the earlier reports.

*Notes:* All times are local Korea/Japan time. CRITIC messages report information of such urgency that they take precedence over all other messages; they must be delivered to the National Command Authorities within minutes.

108 Flash Point North Korea

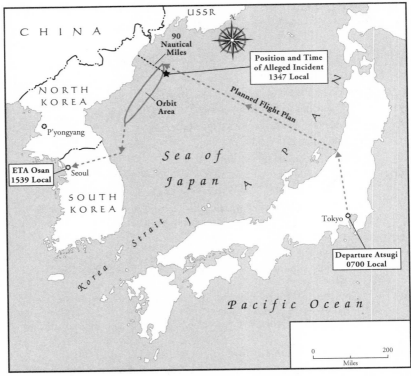

**EC-121 Flight Track–15 April 1969**

The EC-121, radio call sign Deep Sea 129, took off at 0700 local time on a standard Beggar Shadow reconnaissance mission over the Sea of Japan.[37] It flew nearly due north across Japan's main island of Honshu before turning northwest toward the North Korean coast. Army, navy, and air force units monitored its progress and would later provide warnings when the danger became apparent. After flying more than 600 miles and assuming station over the Sea of Japan, the EC-121 began a racetrack reconnaissance pattern whose major axis, oriented northeast to southwest, was approximately 120 miles long.[38] North Korean fighters evidently scrambled shortly after the EC-121 arrived on station, at 1234, but did not act in a way that would cause the mission to be aborted. The MiGs probably began flying a barrier combat patrol that they maintained for perhaps an hour. While the MiGs were on station, the EC-121 transmitted its last broadcast, a routine teletype message, at 1300 (approximately forty-seven minutes before the shootdown).[39]

At 1322, U.S. monitoring sites temporarily lost contact with the MiGs. When they were reacquired fourteen minutes later, the situation was about to get serious. (Under any circumstances, the EC-121 would have received little warning if MiGs were airborne near the coastline and the EC-121 was only ninety miles away. Even if the MiGs flew at subsonic speed all the way from the coast, they would require only ten minutes to reach a target ninety miles out. If any portion of the run was supersonic, they would require far less time.) At 1338, one of the monitoring stations supporting Deep Sea 129 transmitted a condition 3 warning—notification that hostile aircraft were within fifty-one to fifty-five miles of the EC-121M. CINCPAC reported that the EC-121 acknowledged the warning. The MiGs had flown over water nearly forty miles toward the EC-121. The EC-121 was probably ninety miles off the North Korean coast at this time, and the MiGs were heading straight for it. At 1340, the monitoring station issued a condition 5 warning—an admonition that the MiGs had now closed to within fifty miles of the mission aircraft. The EC-121 acknowledged this warning as well and started to abort the mission. CINCPAC also reported that the EC-121 received and acknowledged a second condition 5 warning approximately seven minutes later. This second receipt was the EC-121's last transmission before the shootdown. At about the same time, the MiGs evidently reached 30-mm cannon range of the EC-121, now probably fleeing on an outbound run away from the North Korean coast. Time-distance factors suggest that they had made a subsonic approach to get into firing position. At approximately 1347, they shot down the EC-121. It crashed at 41 degrees, 12 minutes north latitude, 131 degrees, 48 minutes east longitude some ninety miles southeast of Chongjin, North Korea. A shocked President Nixon noted that the downing "was a complete surprise in every sense of the word and, therefore, did not give us the opportunity for protective action that I would have taken had it been threatened."[40]

Even today, few details of the shootdown are public knowledge. President Nixon commented that U.S., Soviet, and North Korean radars had tracked the EC-121 and the MiGs. Although North Korea consistently claimed that the EC-121 had penetrated "deep" into North Korean airspace, the United States maintained that the aircraft never even approached it. National Security Adviser Henry Kissinger also stated that the aircraft had been directed to approach no closer than forty miles from the Korean coastline and that in fact it had approached no closer than forty-eight miles. The DOD press release issued the day after the shootdown confirmed that normal standing instructions called for reconnaissance aircraft to remain forty miles offshore, but this particular mission had been directed to remain fifty miles away from the DPRK.[41]

In his biography of Henry Kissinger, Seymour Hersh stated that his sources in the National Security Agency claimed that the shootdown was accidental, an outgrowth of a North Korean command and control mistake involving a single aircraft.[42] This assertion is doubtful. The air picture was unlikely to be so complex or the skies so crowded as to cause confusion in the area of the crash. The shooters were on station well before the shootdown. The EC-121 had been flying a simple racetrack pattern for more than three hours, so its movements were predictable. If the official record can be believed, the mission aircraft remained at least thirty-six miles away from the outer limit of the DPRK's twelve-mile territorial limit (or a total of fifty miles from the coastline). If it resembled other air defense systems in the communist world, and it probably did, the North Korean air defense system was characterized by centralized command and control. The military hierarchy would have severely discouraged local initiative, particularly for such an unusual long-range over-water intercept. In other words, an uncomplicated air defense picture, the distance the shootdown occurred from North Korean territory, the radar tracking methodology, and the rapidity of the North Korean press and diplomatic response suggest that the shootdown was deliberate. To be precise, it was premeditated murder.

How did the NKAF bring down the EC-121? Most likely, the shooters were MiG-21 Fishbeds, the most capable fighter then in the NKAF's inventory. A case can be made that the MiGs had been previously deployed to a staging base much closer to where they actually intercepted the EC-121; that is, at the northern end of its track. At the time, NKAF east coast MiG-21s were based only at Wonsan and Songdong Ni. These two airfields were more than twice as far from the intercept site as the Hoemun Ni and Chongjin air bases, which were located in far northeastern North Korea.[43] The combat radius of a MiG-21 carrying two air-to-air missiles and using fuel tanks on a subsonic intercept is well over four hundred miles.[44] However, the two MiGs had probably been loitering on combat air patrol for perhaps an hour before they started flying east toward the EC-121. Fuel limitations could become problematic even if the MiGs saved fuel by not going supersonic. Given the pilots' relative inexperience in long-range over-water intercepts, the NKAF planners would have wanted the aircraft to carry as much reserve fuel as possible. Significant fuel savings could have been gained by deploying the aircraft more than 150 miles closer to the desired intercept point. CINCPACFLT's initial assignment of Hoemun Ni as its number one priority in retaliatory contingency planning on 16 April offers a clue to U.S. planners' thoughts.[45] Home to only fifty older MiG-15s and MiG-17s, this base was far less important militarily than either Songdong Ni or Wonsan. However, if it was the base from which the MiGs launched en route to the EC-121, Hoemun Ni would have been the preferred target for a retaliatory strike.[46]

Had the MiGs deployed to Hoemun Ni, they (and the target) would still have been well within the range of North Korea's ground-controlled intercept (GCI) radars—essential to such a long-range over-water intercept. GCI coverage extended out two hundred miles from the radars, and NKAF MiGs did not operate outside the GCI envelope.[47] The GCI controllers might even have been familiar with this particular EC-121 track, which EC-121s had already used five times in 1969—three times in January and once each during February and March.[48] Even if they did not recall the track, the GCI controllers could ascertain its boundaries by simply tracking the EC-121 as it flew its predictable racetrack orbit. With MiGs already airborne, the GCI controller would only have to vector them to arrive at the northern extent of the EC-121's orbit at about the same time that the EC-121 was to arrive there. Once they reached close range, one of the MiGs shot the aircraft down with cannon fire. It is unclear if the MiG fired an AA-2 Atoll heat-seaking air-to-air missile. North Korean press reports for the week after the crisis mentioned that a "single shot" downed the aircraft; however, the recovered fuselage fragments showed only shell holes.[49]

In summary, the limited evidence available to the public can be used to make the case that North Korea flew two frontline MiG-21s to Hoemun Ni a few days before the shootdown to allow the pilots to become familiar with local flight conditions. The Fishbeds flew a barrier combat air patrol near Hoemun Ni (or slightly over water) between 1234 and 1336 hours while the EC-121 worked its way southwest and then northeast again on its racetrack pattern. As the EC-121 approached the northeastern extent of its orbit, GCI controllers directed the MiGs to initiate a subsonic attack run. The likely descent of the EC-121 to avoid its attackers might have complicated the attack, but the MiGs evidently managed to complete their strafing runs. The aircraft wreckage showed that the plane had been attacked with cannons and machine guns.[50]

After the shootdown, the United States suspended other PARPRO flights in the theater; ordered *Pueblo*'s sister ship, USS *Banner,* back to port in Sasebo; and immediately initiated an intensive search-and-rescue (SAR) effort. A U.S. Air Force H-130 flew to the EC-121's last known position. That evening, USS *Dale* (DLG-19) and USS *Henry W. Tucker* (DD-875) departed for the search area, to be joined by USS *Sterett* (DLG-31) and USS *Mahan* (DLG-11). Early the next morning, a navy P-3 located the crash site at 41 degrees, 14 minutes north latitude and 131 degrees, 50 minutes east longitude. The P-3 observed some debris in the area and dropped smoke markers. On the evening of 16 April, two Soviet warships (Kotlin- and Kashin-class destroyers) entered the SAR area, launched small boats, and began recovering debris. As the rescue effort continued on the seventeenth, USS *Dale,* USS *Sterrett,* and the Kotlin destroyer transferred debris they had found to the USS *Tucker.* All told, some twenty-six aircraft and four ships participated in the search. The SAR terminated at 1900 on the nineteenth, with two bodies but no survivors being found.[51]

## North Korea Responds

After the incident, North Korean forces, especially those with air defense missions, assumed a high state of alert. NKAF aircraft that had been near the west coast moved inland. The North's overall posture was defensive, just as it had been after the *Pueblo* incident; it did not appear to be preparing for more provocations.[52] The British also discerned no evidence that the North intended further provocative action.[53]

North Korea broadcast its version of events quite quickly—about two hours after the incident.[54] North Korean media coverage (for both domestic and international audiences) remained unwaveringly hostile and unrepentant throughout the crisis. (To this day, the North Korean media lauds both the seizure of *Pueblo* and the EC-121 shootdown as major accomplishments!) Had there been confusion in the hierarchy, as might be expected after an accidental downing, the North might not have issued a press release so quickly or been so consistent in its story. Instead, the Korean Central News Agency (KCNA) and Pyongyang Home Service repeatedly made the following points:

- With a "single shot," the KPA downed a U.S. reconnaissance aircraft flying at "a high altitude" and "deep" into DPRK airspace. As if to leave no doubt about the certainty of Pyongyang's cause, virtually every press comment claimed that the aircraft had been "deep" in North Korean airspace.[55]

- The United States had engaged in an extensive aerial reconnaissance program against North Korea for years. The press claimed that in 1965, RB-47 and L-19 aircraft had penetrated DPRK airspace. North Korea also claimed that after the *Pueblo* seizure, RB-47s, RB-57s, EC-121s, and RC-130s had conducted "aerial espionage" several hundred times against the North.[56]

- Defense Minister "Order Number 24" commended the KPA's "896 Unit" for conducting the shootdown. The citation warned that the "situation remains tense" and exhorted the unit to "step up military and political training."[57]

- Even before the shootdown, the United States had been intensifying provocations along the DMZ and had been conducting exercises such as Focus Retina. The very first English-language KCNA report on the shootdown devoted its first paragraph to saying that Washington was "intensifying the war provocation maneuvers" against North Korea and flying the reconnaissance mission "while perpetrating grave provocations along the Military Demarcation Line."[58]

- Most commentary warned that North Korea would retaliate if there were further provocations. For example, the Pyongyang Home Service stated, "our people and the KPA will return retaliation for the retaliation of the U.S. imperialists and all-out war for all-out war."[59]

At the height of the crisis, during the last week of April 1969, the North Korean government issued a lengthy statement encapsulating its position. Broadcast to both domestic and international audiences, the statement incorporated the above themes and added other familiar North Korean foreign policy constructs. The following quotes from its text summarize the DPRK's public posture throughout the EC-121 crisis:

The U.S. imperialists' reconnaissance planes have in recent months flown about the territorial air of our Republic to commit acts of espionage on several occasions and the [EC-121] had intruded deep into the territorial air of the Republic to conduct hostile acts of espionage. . . . Our counterattack and self-defense measures . . . are a justified act which fully conforms to international law. . . . The latest intrusion into the territorial air . . . was perpetrated precisely as a link in the chain of premeditated maneuverings to ignite a new war. . . . To maintain and consolidate peace in Korea, all foreign troops should be withdrawn from South Korea . . . the question of Korean unification can be solved at any time by the Korean people themselves. . . . The entire Korean people and the People's Army . . . must sharpen their revolutionary vigilance and must be fully prepared to return retaliation for "retaliation."[60]

Finally, the North Korean press highlighted a familiar propaganda theme (and policy objective): all its citizens were armed and the whole country had been turned into an impregnable fortress. This readiness for combat was due as much to widespread revolutionary commitment as to admitted growing technical capabilities:

> Our Red worker peasant militiamen, armed with the great revolutionary ideas of the respected and beloved leader, have striven to increase their combat capacity to match a hundred foes. . . . Our worker-peasant militiamen have grown up as crack shots who know how to handle various weapons and combat-technical equipment. . . . An all-people defense system with the People's Army as its backbone has been firmly established.[61]

In other words, the official commentary portrayed a North Korea imperiled by a multidimensional U.S. threat, the U.S. presence as the key factor for instability on the Korean peninsula, the benefits of speedy U.S. withdrawal for the cause of unification, and the need for heightened North Korean readiness and vigilance until that occurred. The shootdown fit neatly into the overall texture of the North's strategy and tactics. It also provided a self-fulfilling prophesy; as it marshaled forces, the United States *did* become more threatening to the North, thereby justifying increased readiness and more committed revolutionary activity.

About two hours after the shootdown, the DPRK also requested a meeting of the Military Armistice Commission (MAC) at Panmunjom for three days hence, on 18 April. The coincidence of the request also suggested premeditation. Although some observers thought the United States would defer the meeting until the following week to allow more time to develop a strategy, Washington agreed. Interestingly, the North's strategy for this meeting was to avoid even mentioning the shootdown despite the ferocity of its press coverage.[62]

North Korea's follow-up to the shootdown was thus fairly simple: a domestic and international propaganda campaign entailing hostile accusations against the United States. In contrast, the U.S. response was multilayered. With no hostage crew to consider, the United States would seriously consider military retaliation against the North. It quickly marshaled the forces to hurt North Korea in several ways.

# 8

# A TENTATIVE

# RESPONSE

North Korea's reason for downing the EC-121 is still a mystery. President Nixon's decision not to retaliate is nearly as intriguing. After all, the new president had criticized President Johnson during the election campaign for mishandling the *Pueblo* incident. He was naturally inclined to retaliate, and his autobiography treats his forbearance toward the North as a mistake. Some—but certainly not all—of his advisers urged retaliation. Yet, the accounts of the national-level participants portray a slow-motion response to the shootdown. No senior-level crisis committee immediately convened to formulate a response to the provocation, as had been the case during the *Pueblo* incident. President Nixon was informed of the shootdown about 0720 (Washington time) on the fifteenth, yet the cabinet did not meet to discuss the incident for more than a day. Henry Kissinger later said that much of that first day was spent in unfocused and "inconclusive planning exercises." When Nixon was finally presented with the two preferred options on the morning of the sixteenth, he avoided making a final decision.[1]

As the National Command Authorities pursued an unusually slow decision-making process, the Joint Chiefs of Staff and CINCPAC began moving forces and formulating contingency plans. Adm. John S. McCain Jr.

(CINCPAC) urged retaliation and offered a wide menu of options. However, unlike after the *Pueblo* seizure, the Seventh Fleet had no major combatants near Korea when the EC-121 was shot down. The necessary forces did not reach the preferred launch point until midnight local time on 21 April. While they were en route, the flurry of planning message traffic suggested that retaliation was imminent, but President Nixon had already ruled out retaliation by the time they got there. The White House did not abandon thoughts of retaliation for some future provocation, however, and several ships remained tethered to Northeast Asia until late May. Additionally, the president was determined to ensure that PARPRO flights had extensive airborne protection—at least for the time being.

## Force Generation

When North Korea seized USS *Pueblo*, CINCPAC quickly moved USS *Enterprise* and its escorts to Korea. The battle group had been en route from the United States to Vietnam and was conveniently near Japan when the seizure occurred. The United States had no standing requirement to keep a carrier near Korea, however; in those days, virtually everything that floated was committed to Vietnam or on essential port calls for maintenance. Consequently, it took days to position naval forces to retaliate following the EC-121 shootdown—much to the surprise of some national decision makers.

On the evening of the shootdown, the JCS evidently issued a warning order advising CINCPAC of the impending requirement to redeploy forces to Korea.[2] Commander, Seventh Fleet, also directed his units to prepare to deploy an attack carrier task force to Korea. He directed three attack carriers to "remain topped off on fuel, ammunition and other assets insofar as possible without degrading the Southeast Asia effort." The fleet commander envisioned that USS *Enterprise* and USS *Ranger* would respond first.[3]

In fact, the U.S. attack carriers—USS *Ranger*, USS *Ticonderoga*, and USS *Enterprise*—were committed to Yankee Station and supporting strikes against Vietnam. To relieve them without disrupting the war effort would require planning, turnover of responsibilities, and so on. Nevertheless, twenty-one hours after the shootdown, the JCS sent a flash precedence execute message directing CINCPAC to move three carrier task groups (with suitable anti-submarine warfare, antiair warfare, and cruiser bombardment capability) to the Sea of Japan at best sustained speed of advance.[4] During the afternoon and evening of the sixteenth, the three attack carrier groups and the USS *Hornet* antisubmarine warfare group detached from Yankee Station and began steaming north. The carriers USS *Kitty Hawk* and USS *Bonne Homme Richard* were yanked from port calls in Hong Kong and Subic Bay, respectively, to relieve them. The redeployment happened so quickly that the United States lacked carrier support for the war in Vietnam for only a day.[5]

The navy redirected other units as well. The battleship USS *New Jersey* had completed its deployment and was steaming home. It was only seventeen hundred miles from Long Beach, California, when CINCPACFLT ordered it back to the Seventh Fleet. Reversing course, *New Jersey* recrossed the Pacific at twenty-five knots and arrived in Japan on 22 April. After eight hours in Yokosuka, it raced on to take up station in the Sea of Japan.[6] Similarly, the Seventh Fleet began moving nuclear and diesel submarines into the operating area to provide early warning and to support poststrike search-and-rescue operations. USS *Diodon* (SS-349), USS *Haddock* (SSN-621), and USS *Pomfret* (SS-391) would operate in two patrol boxes from 19 April until at least 25 April.[7]

Steaming separately, the task groups arrived at a preassigned holding point west of Kyushu, Japan, on the morning of 20 April. By midday on the twenty-first, all Task Force 71 units had transited the Tsushima Strait and entered the Sea of Japan. They would arrive at the rendezvous point, Defender Station (37 degrees north latitude, 113 degrees, 100 minutes east longitude), by that evening.[8]

Always a man for details, President Nixon was personally interested in the location and duration of these naval special operations. When briefed about Task Force 71's operations around midday of the twenty-first, he directed that it sail north of the projected contingency launch point and specified that the task force should remain in the Sea of Japan for no less than twenty-four hours.[9]

As the Seventh Fleet was positioning ships in the Sea of Japan, CINCPAC also wanted to beef up his counterair capability in Korea. Within four hours of the shootdown, the commander of the Fifth Air Force directed that all of his conventional forces be brought to maximum readiness for deployment to forward operating bases by midnight local time.[10] Following the resolution of the *Pueblo* crisis, the U.S. Air Force presence in Korea had dropped to 95 aircraft.[11] The JCS decided to raise its presence back to the 151-aircraft limit established during the crisis.[12] The Sixteenth Tactical Fighter Squadron, which was en route from the United States to Southeast Asia, was directed to fly instead from Guam to Kadena, Okinawa, and thence to Kunsan, ROK. The Fifth Air Force also moved F-4 fighters from Misawa and Yokota, Japan, to the peninsula. Finally, the JCS directed that the U.S. Marine Corps F-4B Phantom squadron in Iwakuni raise its readiness for contingency operations. The JCS also alerted the USMC KC-130 tanker squadron to provide refueling support and deploy to forward bases.[13]

On the ground in Korea, General Bonesteel directed that HAWK and Nike Hercules surface-to-air missile readiness in Korea be "increased significantly." Had the NKAF attacked just then, the effectiveness of the HAWK batteries against the MiG onslaught would have been questionable. A recent combat evaluation had revealed that many of the HAWKs in Korea were unreliable for combat. Bonesteel submitted an urgent request for five hundred more HAWK missiles for U.S. and ROK units.[14]

Still concerned about the vulnerability of U.S. installations in Korea, CINCPAC requested that eight infantry security companies be airlifted to Korea.[15] Bonesteel also asked for guidance regarding what information he might share with the South Koreans. Once again, he was told that he would have to be circumspect. As with *Pueblo,* the contingency planning would be a U.S.–only affair.[16]

Overall, U.S. Forces Korea was better prepared for war than it had been at the beginning of the *Pueblo* crisis, but many U.S. and ROK Air Force units remained vulnerable to air attack because the shelter-building program was far from complete. Only 55 of the planned 170 shelters had been erected, and only 1 of these had had its concrete cover installed. The program was not scheduled to be completed until September 1969.[17] CINCPAC expressed continuing concern with the readiness situation:

> The general logistics posture has improved over the last year and will support the initiation of combat, although important deficiencies still exist which would affect the sustaining power of U.S. and ROK forces to prosecute military

operations. Some of the most important of these deficiencies are lack of repair parts, shortage of common items of ground ammunition, inadequate in-country distribution system, vulnerable loc's [lines of communication], deficiencies in the POL distribution system, and a shortage of support personnel.[18]

As during the *Pueblo* incident, U.S. Forces Korea would be largely a bystander in the EC-121 crisis. General Bonesteel had not controlled the EC-121, and most of the subsequent posturing would be done by forces not under his direction. Nevertheless, he directed the U.S. and ROK commands to "tighten command and control" and to maintain a "high state of vigilance" against the DPRK. The ROK enhanced its state of air defense readiness. Despite these preparations, British observers on 17 April noted that the U.S. embassy and the UN Command were "playing down" the incident, which was no direct concern of theirs. There were few visible preparations in South Korea other than brief alerts at certain airports and police admonitions for special vigilance.[19]

Although General Bonesteel's force would not be involved in any U.S. retaliation for the shootdown, it would likely be on the receiving end of any North Korean response. Concerned with this scenario, the JCS on 19 April directed that USFK prepare to make some high-visibility, low-cost defensive arrangements. They were not to disrupt USFK operations, alarm the ROK, or provoke the North. On the twenty-first, the JCS approved most of Bonesteel's proposed defensive actions, although the Joint Chiefs recommended moving several units and deferring the establishment of additional combat air patrols because they might provoke Pyongyang. The JCS further advised that the measures be implemented only when General Bonesteel concluded that they were essential for defense. The JCS subsequently also directed CINCPAC to review other vulnerable flights and shipboard activity near the Korean peninsula that might require protection.[20]

## National-Level Meetings

As was mentioned above, the National Command Authorities responded to the crisis in a remarkably desultory manner. National Security Adviser Henry Kissinger subsequently wrote: "We set the crisis machinery into motion with great deliberation, watching ourselves with rapt attention at each step to make sure we were not shooting from the hip."[21] The fact that the EC-121 shoot-down represented the administration's first crisis contributed to this halting approach to crisis management; however, Kissinger also doubted Nixon's underlying desire to retaliate: "I never had had the impression that Nixon had his heart in a retaliatory attack. He had procrastinated too much; he had not really pressed for it in personal conversation; he had not engaged in the relentless maneuvering by which he bypassed opposition when his mind was made up."[22]

For the national leadership, the crisis really lasted the five days between Tuesday morning, 15 April, when the president learned of the shootdown, and Saturday morning, 19 April, when he ruled out retaliation. In fact, President Nixon did not even meet with the National Security Council on this issue until Wednesday, 16 April. In Kissinger's view, Nixon had criticized Lyndon Johnson for his "Situation Room syndrome." LBJ had felt that world crises were best managed from the cramped and Spartan confines of the Situation Room in the White House basement. Nixon, on the other hand, was reluctant to assemble a staff in the Situation Room (or anywhere else) and begin micro-managing events at the first hint of trouble. Instead, "everything had to be played cool."[23]

On the morning of the fifteenth, the White House advised the State Department, Department of Defense, and CIA that the president's advisers wanted point papers addressing the range of available political, diplomatic, and military options. The papers were to go the National Security Council review group that afternoon, and then to a full NSC meeting scheduled for 1000 the next morning. The White House initially asked questions pertaining to four subjects: (a) retaliatory options, (b) measures that could/should be taken to prevent the North Koreans from retrieving any surviving crew members, (c) how quickly the United States could conduct an escorted reconnaissance mission similar to that being flown by the downed EC-121, and (d) worldwide North Korean assets against which the United States might retaliate. Laird warned right away that the United States might have to let the North retrieve any surviving crew members to save their lives in the forty-degree waters.[24]

A complex retaliatory plan addressing the reaction time, movement plan, force generation, tactics, defensive measures, and reinforcements needed to counter North Korean retaliation was to be delivered to the White House by the end of the day. Although the precise plan has not been declassified, it evidently demanded substantial air power. General Wheeler was to assess whether the United States could implement it and "still retain a sound air picture in Southeast Asia."[25]

State resorted to the crisis mechanisms it had used during *Pueblo:* a multi-agency Korea Working Group to generate the paperwork for the NSC and a State-only Korea Task Force to support the working group by tracking operational developments, responding to inquiries, and doing anything else that might be required.[26]

According to Kissinger, each agency prepared options reflecting its own parochial concerns. The options included seizure of a North Korean merchant ship, mining Wonsan Harbor, attacking an airfield, and shore bombardment. State weighed in with a memorandum opposing military retaliation —especially seizing a North Korean ship at sea; nevertheless, Kissinger noted growing interest in this particular option.[27] Kissinger was dissatisfied with the entire process. The options did not fit into a coherent strategy, offer a single operational plan, or produce any particular demand for North Korean reparations.[28]

U.S. options became better defined during the 16 April NSC meeting, as did the cabinet-level opposition to retaliation. The NSC concluded that North Korea had acted without encouragement from other communist nations. With that in mind, the NSC planners identified five U.S. objectives: (1) maintain U.S. use of international airspace; (2) deter similar hostile actions; (3) exact redress by retaliation or compensation; (4) increase international criticism of North Korea and decrease criticism of U.S. actions; and (5) maintain domestic support for U.S. overseas security commitments, including Vietnam.[29]

The NSC then reviewed ten alternative military courses of action, which included the following:

1. Show of force
2. Repeat the EC-121 reconnaissance mission with combat support
3. Single out "select military combat" actions such as:
   a. destruction of North Korean aircraft flying off the coast of North Korea
   b. selected air strike against a military target
   c. shore bombardment of North Korean military targets

    d. ground raid across the DMZ
    e. attack on military targets near the DMZ by artillery or missiles
    f. submarine attacks on North Korean naval vessels
    g. blockade
    h. mining
    i. seizure of North Korean assets abroad[30]

Kissinger likewise characterized this meeting as "unfocused and inconclusive." He felt that the participants haphazardly discussed military options without rigorously evaluating them.[31] The meeting did reveal major splits within the cabinet. Secretary of State Rogers, Director of Central Intelligence Richard Helms, and Secretary of Defense Melvin Laird all opposed military retaliation. Laird went so far as to put his objections in writing, the key objection being the fear of starting another war on the peninsula. The United States was no better prepared to fight two simultaneous wars in Asia than it had been during the *Pueblo* incident. Some also doubted that the administration could readily secure congressional or public support for the move.

There were counterarguments pertaining to U.S. credibility toward international communism in general and the North Vietnamese as well as the North Koreans. As Johnson had done in the earlier crisis, the decision makers linked Korea to Vietnam. Perceived weakness toward Pyongyang would encourage Hanoi to persevere. Kissinger evidently led the faction espousing this view, but Nixon realized that retaliation would be controversial. He was also influenced by a warning from Ambassador William Porter, the U.S. envoy who had served so well in Seoul throughout the *Pueblo* crisis. Porter had sent an urgent message in which he warned that U.S. retaliation would "play into the hands of the North Korean extremist leadership." Porter also warned that U.S. retaliation (still a U.S.–only affair) might embolden Seoul to attack the North.[32] "I stressed that a strong American reaction, which could not be revealed in advance to President Park, would be taken as a signal by the South Koreans to go North," Porter later explained. ". . . I said that they would believe that we had acted that way—in not consulting with them—in order to say that we did not urge them to go in."[33]

With these countervailing influences, Nixon focused on two options. Option 1 (the "hard option") would require an air strike against one NKAF air base; option 2 (the "soft option") merely called for resumption of escorted

PARPRO flights. At Nixon's behest, Kissinger directed that two papers be prepared. He assigned National Security Council Asia staffer Richard Sneider the task of writing the soft-option paper. Col. Alexander Haig (Kissinger's military aide), Larry Eagleburger, and Mort Halperin were to draft the hard-option paper. The Haig group's product also included a warning to Moscow not to interfere and a presidential statement delineating the limits of American tolerance in Vietnam.[34]

As this staff work was going on, President Nixon spent much of the day inquiring about the status of a North Korean fish factory ship then believed to be en route from Europe to the DPRK. The previous night, the NSC review group had submitted a memo to the White House on North Korean ships being built in the Netherlands—the same ships whose seizure had been a topic during the *Pueblo* crisis. Declassified NSC documents show that Kissinger continued to track one of the fish factory ships believed to be en route to Korea. On 16 April, Nixon was informed that the ship was near Cape Town and should reach Singapore on 3 May. Immediately after the formal NSC meeting he had a long session with Rogers, Laird, and Kissinger. He had a follow-up meeting with them (and General Wheeler) later that day. The tone of H. R. Haldeman's diary entry for that day suggests that Nixon had not ruled out retaliation: "P almost has to retaliate in some fairly strong fashion."[35]

The decision on whether to retaliate remained unmade on the seventeenth. Nixon was preparing for his 18 April press conference and devoting most of his attention to that. He had decided to announce the resumption of escorted PARPRO flights. However, option 1 (an air strike against one NKAF base) remained an open issue. After meeting with the president on the morning of the seventeenth, Kissinger told Haldeman that the United States would bomb the airfield at noon on Monday, 21 April. Later in the day, Kissinger called Haldeman to obtain his views on retaliation. Kissinger felt that retaliation would be internationally influential and would mobilize domestic support, but that it would "lose the doves" and might jeopardize Congress's appropriation of funds for an antiballistic missile system.[36] Kissinger did assemble and chair a special crisis management group peopled by middle-level representatives from State, Defense, CIA, and the JCS. Unfortunately, the group had no clear-cut directives to implement because the National Command Authorities had not really committed to using force. Consequently, the group's discussions remained theoretical.[37]

Nevertheless, the NSC did oversee a number of policy papers with an eye toward both diplomatic and military responses. On 17 April, papers reviewing the history of the *Pueblo* incident in the UN, the best diplomatic tack to take in the UN, and the best way to protest to the DPRK were in preparation. At the same time, the CIA was preparing a rationale/justification for the EC-121 flight and the DOD was preparing strike tactics that kept the carriers "in the south" until launch time.[38]

Another study produced on 17 April concluded that there would be little legal justification for Washington to retaliate for the shootdown so long after the fact. Had the United States responded immediately, it might have argued that the engagement was not really over—the MiGs might have returned and renewed the attack. After so much time had passed, however, a claim of self-defense was no longer justifiable. Another legal justification—that for reprisal—had been superseded by the UN Charter. Article 2 required members to resolve international disputes without endangering international peace and security. Unilateral use of force by the United States could probably not be legally justified until all "remedies of peaceful settlement" had been exhausted. Nevertheless, the more narrow the U.S. retaliation or reprisal, the more "proportional" (and therefore legally acceptable) it might be. From this vantage point, the best (and only) target would be the home base of the fighters that destroyed the EC-121.[39]

## Planning to Retaliate

As the NSC was deliberating, the JCS, SAC, and CINCPAC continued preparing contingency plans. Admiral McCain was clearly thinking about the *Pueblo* response when he urged retaliation on 16 April:

> The CVA's are again steaming north to join forces with USAF tactical air in South Korea. No guidance has been provided as to the possible mission of the CVA groups. During the elapsed transit time a mission should be assigned that will provide for positive action upon the immediate arrival of the CVA strike groups into the Sea of Japan. This could inject an element of surprise, particularly in view of the fact that past performance might lull the North Koreans into a false sense of security.[40]

He concluded by warning that anything less than retaliation would justify a North Korean perception that the United States was a "paper tiger."[41]

During the first few days after the shootdown, the Joint Chiefs produced six or seven plans ranging from attacks on North Korean airfields to destruction of hydroelectric plants.[42] Other plans recommended by the Pacific Command included seizing a fish factory ship believed to be steaming from Rotterdam to the DPRK and using a Talos surface-to-air missile–equipped cruiser to down a North Korean military aircraft. Both proposals evidently received considerable attention from the National Command Authorities. Plans such as submarine mining of North Korean ports received less.

At the time the shootdown occurred, the United States had no contingency plans to attack a *single* North Korean airfield. On the fifteenth, the Joint Staff discussed two potential candidates for retaliatory strikes. On the west coast, Onchon Up airfield, twenty-five miles from Pyongyang, hosted sixty MiG-15/17s and ten MiG-21s. Although it had no antiaircraft artillery, the base was defended by three probable SA-2 sites. Moreover, all 320 MiG fighters on the west coast could readily concentrate to engage the U.S. attackers.[43]

Approximately twenty-five MiG-15/17s and ten MiG-21s were based at Songdong Ni on the east coast. Located approximately thirty-five miles north of Wonsan, the airfield had twenty-seven aircraft revetments; nineteen petroleum, oil, and lubricant tanks; and eight ammunition storehouses. It was protected by only one SAM site, although it did have moderate antiaircraft defenses. East coast targets were preferable because they had fewer SAM and MiG defenses than those on the west coast. Moreover, it would take less time to marshal the strike force required to hit Songdong Ni than Onchon Up, and the JCS anticipated fewer casualties at the former. West coast targets would likely exact 5–8 percent casualties for the U.S. strike force, while 5 percent or less of the attacking force would be lost in an attack on Songdong Ni. A less demanding target, Songdong Ni remained topical in subsequent contingency planning.[44]

The Joint Staff also quickly outlined the relative advantages of using land-based aircraft compared to carrier air. Table 7, which summarizes the comparison, suggests that land-based and carrier-based aircraft both offered strong advantages. This may explain why CINCPAC and the Joint Staff subsequently developed separate plans for B-52s and carrier air.

Table 7. Comparison of Land-Based and Carrier-Based Aircraft for Use in Retaliation against North Korea

| Land-Based Tactical Air | Carrier-Based Air |
|---|---|
| Implies ROK involvement; not purely USA-NK affair; UNC implications | Keeps attack purely NK-USA affair. If NK retaliates on ROK, it made first move across the DMZ. |
| Best against western NK targets due to USA-ROK force disposition | Limited sea space in Yellow Sea for attack against western NK targets; closer to CHICOM threat; longer to resupply lines for sustained action |
| Less tactical surprise; NK's radar are oriented southward | Probably greater tactical surprise, especially from Sea of Japan |
| Can risk lower air defense force level | High air defense force level required; cannot risk carrier loss |
| Easy to generate necessary strike force levels; aircraft munitions available in area (163 strike aircraft) (less 14 SIOP)* | Three CVAs yield 128 aircraft |
| Can mount strike more quickly; forces in area | Need 72 hours minimum to reach area |
| Tanker requirements cut into SIOP/B-52/other needs | Organic tanker support |
| Easier to support sustained operations from established bases | Support of sustained air operations more difficult |

Source: Joint Staff briefing book, "Fact Book: EC-121 Shootdown in Sea of Japan," 20 April 1969, folder "091 Korea (BP) EC-121 Shootdown," Records of the U.S. JCS, Records of Chairman (Gen.) Earle Wheeler, 1967–70, RG 218, NARA.
*Single Integrated Operations Plan (the nuclear war plan)

On 16 April, CINCPACFLT assigned four contingency targets. Listed in priority order, they were the airfields at Hoemun Ni, Songdong Ni, and Wonsan; and the missile facility and naval base at Song Jon Pando. Commander, Seventh Fleet, began developing a plan that called for all-night A-6 attacks on the airfields followed by three simultaneous early-morning strikes.[45]

On 17 April, as this preliminary planning continued, Admiral McCain sent a strongly worded message to General Wheeler again urging retaliation:

If there were ever a circumstance in recent U.S. history where prompt and decisive action is required in the interest not only of the U.S. but international

well-being, it is this recent destruction of the EC-121 reconnaissance aircraft . . .
a quick and telling blow should be made against the North Koreans so as to
make clear that their aggression will not go unscathed. There are numerous
options ranging from a show of force to large scale conventional attacks against
the entire AOB [air order of battle] which could be used to drive home to the
enemy that the U.S. will not permit this challenge to go unanswered.[46]

On that same day—two days after the shootdown—the JCS finally issued
formal orders to investigate retaliation options when it directed CINCPAC to
quickly prepare separate strike plans against two east coast airfields: Songdong Ni and Wonsan (the latter became the preferred target). In fact, the JCS
requested two versions of each plan. The first plan, ultimately designated
Fracture Maple, would use twelve to twenty-four carrier-launched A-6s against
one of the airfields. The Intruders would conduct "night full-systems" attacks
against aircraft and revetments, support facilities, POL storage facilities, run-
ways, and taxiways.[47] If twenty-four A-6s were required, they would launch
from two carriers (one A-6 squadron was on each carrier) and fly against a
single target. The twenty-four aircraft would strike the selected airfield in fifty
minutes using a common initial point. The plan was subsequently changed
to reduce time over target to twenty-five minutes for the same number of aircraft. The Strategic Air Command was at the same time preparing plans to
use SR-71s and drones to collect poststrike imagery for bomb damage assessment purposes.[48] However, on the seventeenth, the JCS also directed that neither this plan nor the B-52 strikes be conducted on Sunday, 20 April 1969.[49] The
next day the JCS postponed the strike until after 20 April.[50]

By 19 April, Task Force 71 also had prepared plans for long-range strikes
against Wonsan. The carrier-based A-6s would fly the missions from launch
points in the Yellow Sea and from a holding point south of the Tsushima Strait.
If the North retaliated, the fleet would be prepared to conduct a second set of
strikes. In these, the fleet would fly forty-four night sorties followed by three
daylight strikes against the three airfields.[51]

The fact that the all-weather, night-attack-capable A-6s were central to
U.S. retaliatory planning had a major impact on Seventh Fleet operations for
the next two months. As will be discussed below, the White House became
reluctant to part with this capability. Only the pressing needs of the shooting

war in Vietnam would persuade the administration to pursue an alternative naval approach to dealing with the DPRK.

The second plan requested by the JCS called for Guam-based B-52s to attack the airfields at Songdong Ni and Wonsan. This plan had two versions. Twelve B-52s would participate in the first, and twenty-four would participate in the second. In a draft response to Henry Kissinger on 17 April, General Wheeler also compared the advantages of using B-52s with using carrier air. He noted that the B-52s would deliver up to 108 bombs each compared with 12 to 18 per tactical aircraft. B-52s could mount the strike more quickly than tactical air; however, the B-52s were "somewhat more vulnerable" than carrier air. Loss of a strategic bomber might have a more damaging effect on the U.S. image than loss of a tactical aircraft. The use of B-52s so close to Soviet territory might also elicit an adverse Soviet reaction.[52]

Even after the United States ruled out immediate retaliation for the EC-121 shootdown, the secretary of defense wanted more plans. In particular, on 9 May the JCS directed the SAC to develop a plan for a maximum of three B-52s to attack a single North Korean target, probably an airfield. The attack would rely on surprise and would be conducted on a "no-notice" basis. The JCS continued its strike planning, and on 3 June directed CINCPAC and CINCSAC to develop two plans to strike the Chongjin power plant should the North commit another major provocation. As with the other plans, one version of this plan would use B-52s and the other would use aircraft assigned to CINCPAC.[53]

CINCPAC proposed several other plans on 17 April as well. Fracture Pine called for positioning a cruiser off Wonsan to shoot down identified North Korean aircraft. Fracture Apple would direct the fleet to impound or harass fishing boats and North Korean coastal craft found beyond the twelve-mile limit. A third plan called for CINCPAC to seize a fish factory ship ostensibly in transit from the Netherlands to North Korea. The fourth called on USS *New Jersey* to fire on selected targets in the Wonsan complex.[54]

CINCPAC's proposal to use a Talos surface-to-air missile to shoot down an NKAF aircraft elicited high interest at the upper level as late as 19 April. This plan could be executed several ways. In one version, two Talos-capable cruisers (USS *Chicago* and USS *Oklahoma City*) would be stationed sixty miles off the east coast ports of Wonsan and Hungnam an hour before sunrise. They would fire on MiGs flying from the two airfields during a two-, four-, or eight-hour period. (CINCPAC hoped that the operation would be nearly a total surprise. In fact, the command hoped that the presence of U.S. fighters flying combat air patrol near the shooters would "flush the birds for easy shooting.") A variant of the plan would have directed simultaneous Talos shoots on both Korean coasts, but the two-coast option was not recommended because of concerns about potential Chinese responses to the Yellow Sea shooter.[55]

On 19 April, the plan to take a North Korean fish factory ship surfaced again when CINCPAC pushed hard to seize *Keumgang San,* last reported to be near Cape Town, South Africa, on 15 April. The intelligence community expected *Keumgang San* to arrive in Singapore on 3 or 4 May. CINCPAC wanted to seize it after it departed Singapore en route to North Korea. A single U.S. warship (within rapid reaction range of reinforcements) would prepare to board the factory ship. The boarding party would use sufficient force to stop North Korean or Dutch crew members from resisting effectively or scuttling the ship. A Seventh Fleet ship would tow the ship to a port within U.S. territory.[56]

Unfortunately, it turned out that *Keumgang San* was owned and flagged by Holland and crewed primarily by a Dutch crew; only two North Koreans were aboard. Nevertheless, CINCPAC urged Washington to make immediate plans to seize the ship after making "suitable arrangements" with The Hague. The JCS rejected the proposal on the twenty-sixth. Pointing out that this course of action had already been rejected after the *Pueblo* seizure, the JCS noted that high-level conferees had concluded back then that it would be counterproductive because it "would introduce new and serious maritime consequences." Additionally, the Dutch were not expected to cooperate. The JCS concluded that "we must wait until the ship is delivered and the North Koreans attempt to employ it." Even then, the Joint Chiefs were pessimistic. Their message warned that not one North Korean fish factory ship or fishing boat had sailed into international waters since the *Pueblo* was seized. Nevertheless, the JCS directed CINCPAC to come up with a plan to seize a North Korean vessel in international waters.

CINCPAC responded within two weeks with Fringe Swoop, a plan to seize the fish factory ship in international waters following its delivery to the North. This plan called for taking the factory ship in the Sea of Japan (south of 42 degrees, 17 minutes north latitude) using a surface-action group com-

prising four destroyer-type ships. Once aboard, the boarding party would
steam or tow the vessel to Guam. The factory ship would be impounded there
until North Korea apologized, made suitable compensation for the EC-121
shootdown, and released *Pueblo*.[57]

## Diplomacy

Unlike the *Pueblo* incident, the military had primacy in the EC-121 crisis. With
no captive U.S. ship or crew, there was little need for diplomacy and negotiations. Nevertheless, the State Department was briefly active via Panmunjom
and in addressing audiences in Moscow, Seoul, and Tokyo. Additionally, State
helped craft diplomatic courses of action should the United States actually
retaliate.

Moscow was initially the most significant audience. At 0300 EST on the
fifteenth, State's action officers arrived at work to start preparing a response
to the shootdown. During the next three hours they took measures to notify
the USSR, the ROK, and Japan about the incident. Search and rescue was
apparently uppermost on their minds. By 0500 they had fired off a message
to Moscow formally asking the Soviet Union's support in the search-and-rescue effort. State quickly followed this up with a phone call to Moscow at 0600
to ensure that the American embassy in Moscow had in fact approached the
Soviets. Just after noon, Secretary of State Rogers submitted a similar request
to the Soviet ambassador, Anatoly Dobrynin, in a meeting held at the State
Department.[58]

As the crisis developed, State used the 18 April Military Armistice Commission meeting at Panmunjom as the venue in which to protest to North
Korea. The protest was a mild one. President Nixon wanted the meeting to
focus on the substance of the U.S. complaint. Major General Knapp, USAF, the
U.S. delegate, was told to make a calm, reasonable, and restrained presentation
and to avoid procedural hassles. Accordingly, General Knapp characterized
the downing of a plane that had never entered North Korean airspace as a
"calculated act of aggression" unjustified by international law. The shootdown,
he noted, was part of a pattern of armistice violations. He demanded that
Pyongyang "acknowledge the true facts of the case" and "take appropriate
measures to prevent similar measures." Interestingly, in this meeting the

United States demanded neither a formal apology nor reparations. Moreover, the North Korean representative did not mention the shootdown at all in his prepared statement, even though he had the opportunity to speak first in this particular meeting. His rejoinder to General Knapp was simply to ask (three times) about the flag of the aircraft. General Knapp walked out of the meeting the third time this question was asked. The Panmunjom meetings did not reconvene for several months.[59]

The Soviets protested both in Washington and in Moscow about Task Force 71's operations in the Sea of Japan. The first deputy foreign minister met with the U.S. ambassador in Moscow and accused the United States of "heating up" the situation in an area close to Soviet borders. The Soviet ambassador to the United States issued a similar low-key protest. The United States responded that it hoped the Soviets would use their ties with Pyongyang to moderate tensions in the area. The American ambassador warned that the United States could not continue to tolerate the "indignities" and losses being exacted by the North. In other words, the Soviet Union apparently had less influence on U.S. actions than it had during the *Pueblo* crisis, when Premier Kosygin may have helped persuade President Johnson to reduce the U.S. naval presence in the Sea of Japan. After the EC-121 shootdown, there was no give in the U.S. position. The State Department history comments that the United States finally withdrew Task Force 71 solely for military reasons (particularly for reasons imposed by the war in Vietnam).

The South Koreans continued to warn Ambassador Porter that U.S. failure to retaliate would encourage the North to initiate more provocations. President Park reminded Ambassador Porter that after Blue House and *Pueblo* incidents he had advised Washington to warn North Korea that any additional incidents would lead to immediate retaliation. The United States had refused, only to be confronted again. The North had struck the United States and ROK three times and was "riding high," he warned, and it would probably attempt another provocation by August 1969.[60]

Despite the private warning to the ambassador, South Korea's public response was less bellicose than it had been after Blue House/*Pueblo*. South Korean press commentary "did not generate undue public concern," and by 17 April had already shifted away from calling for retaliation. President Park himself called for restraint in a 25 April press conference.[61] South Korea also offered to provide the United States with whatever support it required. On

18 April, the United States advised the ROK that it was planning to resume reconnaissance flights. The prime minister approved of this decision and authorized fighter support from the ROK. Ambassador Porter recommended that U.S. Forces Korea serve as the conduit to provide reconnaissance flight schedules to the ROK.[62]

The Japanese were initially sympathetic toward the U.S. loss. The Foreign Office accepted the facts of the case and concluded that the attack was unprovoked and illegal. On 18 April, State directed the American ambassador to notify Tokyo that reconnaissance flights were about to resume. As far as the Sea of Japan missions were concerned, only the reconnaissance aircraft—not the fighters—would use Japanese territory. The Japanese responded cautiously, fearing that the decision would increase tensions and raise the possibility of conflict that might involve Japan. The Japanese Foreign Office and media were nervous about Task Force 71's Sea of Japan operations and urged that the force be quickly withdrawn.[63]

State also addressed diplomatic courses of action should the United States retaliate. A draft timeline had State providing little warning of impending retaliation to any U.S. ally. At most, State planned to notify Seoul five hours before the event. Japan would receive two hours' notice, and the Soviet Union, People's Republic of China, and key U.S. allies would receive one hour of advance notification.[64]

State planners also addressed postretaliation diplomacy in Panmunjom and the UN Security Council. They recommended that the United States say nothing in Panmunjom. There were better venues, and the real audience for such an announcement would be world opinion, not the DPRK. As for the UN Security Council, State recommended that the United States merely circulate a letter justifying the retaliatory attack. To do more would facilitate condemnation of the United States or even invite a North Korean appearance before the United Nations.[65]

In sum, this crisis demanded a relatively limited diplomatic effort. The military role, however, would also become quite limited. Once President Nixon decided against retaliation, U.S. military concerns would focus on contingency forces to retaliate against future provocations and to support PARPRO missions. Despite the extensive planning by government leadership, Nixon spoke only of option 2 in his 18 April press conference. He commented that PARPRO flights were legitimate and that the EC-121 had been flying well outside North Korean airspace. He announced that the flights were going to resume immediately and would have appropriate fighter escort. Very much concerned about the related issue of U.S. credibility in Southeast Asia, Nixon had also made an unannounced decision. The United States would undertake intensive bombing against North Vietnamese and Viet Cong bases in Cambodia. After the press conference, Kissinger met with Nixon and agreed to poll key cabinet officials about retaliation. At the end of the day, he advised Nixon that Laird, Rogers, and Helms remained opposed. The next morning, 19 April, President Nixon canceled an NSC meeting scheduled to deal with Korea because he had decided not to retaliate.[66]

## Watching and Waiting

CINCPAC had assembled an impressive armada in a short time. At its peak strength there were twenty-nine combatants: three attack carriers; three cruisers; seven DLG/DDGs; nine destroyers; and one antisubmarine warfare group comprising seven ships, including the carrier USS *Hornet*. During 23–25 April, the task force conducted limited air operations in the Sea of Japan. The air wing commanders completed their strike plans in a series of conferences held aboard USS *Enterprise*. VQ-1 also flew missions to establish an ELINT barrier north of the Tsushima Strait during the force's transit and then a barrier oriented east to west once the task force was on station. The effort was not entirely wasted. The task force received useful "real world" training in its interactions with the Soviet Pacific Fleet.[67]

While the task force refueled and resupplied under way off Okinawa on 19 April, two Soviet Bear bombers made a reconnaissance run on its units. Once the task force was in the Sea of Japan, Badger bombers made another fourteen overflight attempts between 20 and 25 April. Unlike during the *Pueblo* incident, the bombers remained at medium or high altitudes and flew during daylight. All were intercepted and escorted by fighters from the attack carriers. The closest intercept occurred eighty nautical miles from the nearest carrier.[68] The Soviet surface response was also measured. Three AGIs monitored the task force. Additionally, a Krupnyy-class guided missile destroyer and two Kotlin destroyers departed Vladivostok on 19/20 April and accompanied the task force until 26 April.[69]

The U.S. Navy's response to the downing of the EC-121 was characterized by repeated schedule changes. On 19 April, the JCS had originally ordered Task Force 71 to steam from its holding point and transit the Tsushima Strait to the preferred launch point. Once there, the task force was to depart the Sea of Japan and operate in the Yellow Sea until 25 April (Korea time), when its units could detach for normal operations. While steaming south to the Yellow Sea on 23 April, the task force was ordered to reverse course and return to Defender Station. Moreover, on the twenty-first, the JCS first slipped the final detachment date from the Yellow Sea operating area from 24 to 25 April and then extended the departure date to 26 April.[70]

The uncertain nature of these special operations complicated scheduling and demanded great flexibility on the part of fleet planners and logisticians. The commander of the Seventh Fleet commented:

> The extremely fluid and fast changing situation precluded scheduling of UNREPS [underway replenishments] . . . in the normal manner. The uncertainty of future operations and highly classified nature of directives by TF 71 hampered the adequate dissemination of information to CTF 73 to permit proper logistics planning.[71]

President Nixon made an interim decision before 25 April to reduce the size of Task Force 71, and this preliminary decision evidently was quickly relayed to the fleet. The interdepartmental coordinating committee established by Kissinger discussed the withdrawal on 28 April. It recommended that the drawdown continue, and the president then gave final approval to the redeployment originally ordered on 25 April.[72]

On the twenty-sixth, Task Force 71 departed the Sea of Japan. However, there was a proviso. In keeping with the 25 April decision, the JCS directed that one attack carrier task group remain near Korea for another ten days. USS *Enterprise* (and its invaluable A-6s), USS *Sterett,* and six escorts thus continued to linger in the Yellow Sea.[73]

Although President Nixon had ruled out retaliating for the EC-121, he sought to maintain an immediate retaliatory capability as well as an ability to protect the PARPRO missions that he had ordered to resume on 18 April. Because it was the only navy aircraft capable of the all-weather night attack envisioned in the U.S. contingency plan, the A-6 was the logical protector. But the Intruders were also vital for the shooting war in Vietnam. Only the large-deck attack carriers had them, and to complicate matters, only one A-6-capable carrier was scheduled to be in the western Pacific between July and October. Additionally, after 1 July 1969 the number of carriers deployed to the western Pacific was scheduled to drop from five to four, and it would be difficult to devote *any* carrier to dedicated operations in Northeast Asia.[74] CINCPAC was anxious to return his forces to Yankee Station.

The JCS initially extended the *Enterprise* battle group's stay in the Sea of Japan for only ten days, but then, acting at White House direction, tethered it to Korea until 25 May. The JCS also warned that there was "considerable high level interest in maintaining a CVA with all weather capability in the Korean area on a permanent basis." Perhaps with this requirement in mind, the JCS in late May extended *Enterprise* operations in the Sea of Japan until 31 May. On that day, the JCS advised the Seventh Fleet commander that the National Command Authorities still had not made a final decision. A carrier (with A-6 capability) would remain within twenty-four hours' steaming time of Korea for the indefinite future.[75]

In the meantime, a flurry of messages and staff papers from CINCPAC and the JCS sought to free *Enterprise* and rescind the president's decision for A-6 aircraft to be committed to potential Korean contingency operations. Between them, the two staffs formulated a plan in which carriers (with or without A-6s) would deploy into the Sea of Japan for two days, undergo upkeep in Yokosuka or Sasebo, Japan, for eight to ten days, and then operate in the Sea of Japan for another few days before continuing with Southeast Asian operations. After 1 July the JCS would fulfill the commitment by having the remaining four carriers visit the Sea of Japan on the inbound and outbound legs of their western Pacific deployments.[76]

In mid-June, the JCS finally received firmer guidance. The resulting compromise resembled the one that had followed the *Pueblo* seizure. An attack carrier (with or without A-6s) would remain within twenty-four hours' steaming time of the Sea of Japan for twenty to thirty days a month. Carriers going to/from Southeast Asia would rotate through the Sea of Japan. All CVAs operating in the western Pacific could be rotated through to meet this requirement.[77]

In addition to committing more forces to supporting contingency plans against North Korea, CINCPAC also had to craft a more effective plan for supporting PARPRO missions over the Sea of Japan. Right after President

Nixon had announced at his 18 April press conference that the reconnaissance flights would resume, the JCS had directed CINCPAC to resume the missions and to ensure that each had four fighter escorts.[78] On greater reflection, however, the Joint Chiefs rescinded the directive. Within hours of issuing the first order it told CINCPAC to formulate his own plan to resume and protect these sensitive missions.[79]

Meanwhile, President Nixon had discovered that the Defense Department had suspended PARPRO activity worldwide (a decision clearly not blessed by Nixon beforehand) and was incensed. In his autobiography, he wrote:

> Even worse, we discovered that without informing the White House, the Pentagon had also canceled aerial reconnaissance in the Mediterranean and the North Pacific—two of the most sensitive areas of the globe. I was surprised and angered by the situation. The North Koreans would undoubtedly think that they had succeeded in making us back off the reconnaissance flights.[80]

Perhaps to dissipate some of the president's anger, the JCS twice directed CINCPAC to fly C-130 Commando Royal SIGINT missions along the DMZ and over water in the Sea of Japan. On 23 April, the JCS sent CINCPAC a flash precedence message ordering a "regular" Commando Royal mission as soon as possible. The ten-hour mission would approach no closer than thirty-six miles from North Korean territory and was given a category 3 risk assessment—higher than normal. Ground-controlled intercept coverage was mandatory, and carrier-based aircraft would protect the C-130 while it was over water. Determined not to have a repeat of the EC-121 shootdown, the commander of Task Force 71 committed six F-4 Phantoms from *Enterprise* ("with ample CAP [combat air patrol] backup") to escort the C-130. The commander wanted a show of force to deter North Korea: "Believe this stationing, number and presence of CAP will be apparent on North Korean radars."[81] On 29 April, the JCS demanded another similar "one-time" mission. Neither message explained the reason for or urgency of the missions (or why the missions were ordered when the DOD had grounded its force of PARPRO aircraft).

On 30 April, the White House provided further instructions: the fighter escort was to remain fifty miles away from the Korean, Soviet, and Chinese coastlines. On that same day, the JCS directed CINCPAC and SAC to resume reconnaissance flights as soon as possible. The National Command Authorities were clearly determined to protect the PARPRO missions this time. Although the reconnaissance aircraft had to remain outside the fifty-mile prohibited area, associated barrier combat air patrol aircraft could fly within the zone—up to twelve miles from the North Korean coast. If an NKAF fighter provided "reasonable certainty of intent to attack," the protecting fighter could even enter the twelve-mile limit to counter the attack or defend itself.[82]

Several problems had to be resolved before the PARPRO missions could be restarted: ground-controlled intercept capability had to be enhanced, the escort size and type had to be determined, the available land-based fighter inventory had to be matched with the scheduled PARPRO missions, and PARPRO missions needed to be reduced or consolidated.

CINCPAC and Washington took a two-pronged approach to the GCI problem. They proposed immediately increasing the number of EC-121 College Eye airborne warning and control aircraft in the theater from eleven to fifteen. This number of aircraft would allow twenty-four-hour GCI support for PARPRO missions if necessary. Additionally, on 29 April the JCS directed that CINCPAC dispatch a GCI-capable ship to the Sea of Japan "at best speed."[83]

The problem of providing fighter escort to each PARPRO mission was more daunting. Approximately 105 PARPRO missions were then being flown off Korea each month. If four fighters escorted each mission, the equivalent of five fighter squadrons and the twenty-six KC-135 tanker aircraft required to support them would have to be devoted solely to PARPRO support! CINCPAC simply did not have the resources to provide such robust protection to each reconnaissance mission flown off Korea.[84]

CINCPAC quickly began to pursue alternatives. Fighters could be assigned to provide barrier combat air patrols. Instead of accompanying the mission aircraft, they would go on station astride likely NKAF avenues of approach to the mission aircraft. Additionally, CINCPAC wanted to reduce the number of aircraft protecting over-water missions from four to two. U.S. fighters on strip alert would protect the reconnaissance missions flown over the ROK. CINCPAC recommended that PARPRO missions be flown simultaneously so that one barrier combat air patrol could protect more than one mission. Finally, CINCPAC recommended that marginal aerial reconnaissance tracks be eliminated.[85]

Neither the JCS nor CINCPAC was convinced that even these precautions would prevent a determined NKAF attack against a PARPRO aircraft. A point paper prepared for a meeting between General Wheeler and Melvin Laird contained a stark warning: "The plan provides a substantial measure of protection, but it will not insure the safety of each recce sortie if the enemy is determined to destroy a recce aircraft and accepts the risk of losing some of his force in the effort."[86]

## EC-121 Aftermath

With the new plans completed and the elements in place, the Pacific Command prepared to resume its aerial reconnaissance program. The shootdown had led to a three-week cessation of VQ-1 flights against North Korea. These flights resumed on 5 May but occurred farther away from North Korea and less frequently. Before the shootdown, VQ-1 flew forty-nine surveillance missions against North Korea during 1969. For the remaining eight months of that year the squadron flew only twenty-two such missions. Moreover, smaller, jet-engined EA-3s replaced the slower EC-121s. Even as late as September 1969, the overall number of reconnaissance flights remained below that before the EC-121 shootdown, although the intelligence community was exerting strong pressure to increase aerial reconnaissance activity against the DPRK. Drones, however, might have begun to compensate for the collection shortfall. By October 1970 a high-altitude SIGINT version of the venerable Firebee drone had begun to operate along the North Korean periphery.[87]

There was still residual dissatisfaction in Washington with the way the U.S. response to the downing had played out. President Nixon was still fuming. Privately, he told Kissinger, "They got away with it this time, but they'll never get away with it again."[88] Kissinger himself was unhappy. In his memoirs he wrote, "I judge our conduct in the EC-121 crisis as weak, indecisive, and disorganized. . . . I believed we paid in many intangible ways, in demoralized friends and emboldened enemies."[89]

Nixon, Kissinger, and Haig all faulted the National Command Authorities' decision-making process. Their memoirs paint a picture of a secretary of defense who was not forthcoming and was sometimes even obstructionist. The national security adviser had difficulty getting updates on the status of carrier task force movements, and Laird did not inform the cabinet that his suspension of PARPRO missions was worldwide, not just off Korea. Moreover, the memoirs fault the DOD for taking three weeks to resume PARPRO missions that should never have been stopped in the first place. In the aftermath of the crisis, Colonel Haig prepared a memo for Kissinger's signature that demanded that ongoing studies of worldwide reconnaissance activity be forwarded to the 303 Committee. The memo would "focus the attention of the Secretary of Defense on the 303 Committee's charter" and "serve to preclude the type of *unilateral activity* which caused the standdown of reconnaissance activity at the time of the Korean shootdown."[90]

Comments such as these suggest that underlying rivalries and tensions contributed to flawed communications within the command authority. Given the strong personalities involved (and the fact that this was the Nixon administration's first crisis), it could hardly have been otherwise. The failures were also likely born of the administration's underlying lack of knowledge of the true impact of Vietnam on worldwide U.S. military readiness. The administration seemed to approach the crisis with the assumption that the United States *should* have had major forces lurking off Korea ready to respond immediately. In fact, the U.S. Navy was stretched very thin and lacked the resources to invest in prolonged contingency operations outside Southeast Asia. Haig, at least, also failed to understand how quick the navy's response to the EC-121 crisis really was. His memoirs imply that days—not just about twenty-seven hours—elapsed between the shootdown and the first carrier movements north from the South China Sea to Defender Station.[91]

Kissinger also blamed the administration's decision-making methodology.

> We made no strategic assessment; instead, we bandied technical expedients about. There was no strong White House leadership. We made no significant political move; our military deployments took place in a vacuum. To manage crises effectively, the agencies and departments involved have to know what the President intends. They must be closely monitored to make certain diplomatic and military moves dovetail. In this case, we lacked both machinery and conception. We made no demands North Korea could either accept or reject. We assembled no force that could pose a credible threat until so long after the event that it became almost irrelevant.[92]

Summarizing the episode, the State Department's country director for Korea, James Leonard, told the British ambassador that the new administration leaders had faced their first crisis "unbriefed" about the availability and location of forces. By the time they knew what their options were, it was too late to react. They instead found themselves looking at ways to reduce the risks and increase the efficiency of future aerial surveillance efforts. Leonard added that the top leadership was now fully briefed and could make decisions quickly regarding Korea. He concluded that the North Koreans "would be most unwise to count on continued immunity if they do the same thing again."[93]

The administration sought to deter similar actions against U.S. forces and personnel by preparing for immediate retaliation. In his 18 April press conference, President Nixon simply said that he had ordered a resumption of aerial reconnaissance flights and repeatedly promised that they would be protected. In private, he attempted to ready U.S. allies for the shock of retaliation. On 28 April, Kissinger told the British ambassador that Nixon was taking "with great seriousness" the possibility of another attack on a U.S. ship or aircraft. Although the president hoped "he had got the message across," Kissinger warned that "immediate and rather drastic measures" would follow another attack and said that London should know of this because "expressions of shock would doubtless come from some European countries, should the United States retaliate." In that event, the president would be doubly appreciative of "steady British nerves" and "whatever indications of sympathy we could offer him."[94]

Kissinger elaborated on this warning in June. He advised the British ambassador that retaliation would "probably be taken against a military target or targets, would be commensurate with the provocation, and would not include attacks on the civilian population or an urban center." Kissinger continued that the United States had no evidence to suggest that another such incident was imminent. The British Foreign Office commented: "Neither have we. But in view of the intransigence and bellicose mood of the North Korean regime, the possibility of future incidents cannot be entirely discounted."[95]

# 9

# LESSONS
# LEARNED

Within hours of the EC-121 shootdown, U.S. decision makers were once again assembling sets of lessons learned from encounters with North Korea. This occurred at several levels. Some sought to answer pointed questions from President Nixon or Congress, which was then holding hearings on the *Pueblo* incident. As the military provided rapid answers to short-fused questions, the national-level decision makers began to summarize what they had learned during the shootdown. A third set of inquiries occurred over the next several months as the Department of Defense, the Joint Chiefs of Staff, and two congressional subcommittees initiated a thorough review of the PARPRO program, its associated command and control, and contingency planning.

These inquiries would significantly influence U.S. intelligence collection against North Korea. They likely set the stage for the death of the surface-ship collection program and sharply reduced the number of PARPRO missions flown against the North. Conveniently, the pressure to collect intelligence may have concurrently subsided temporarily. Starting in mid-1969, the number of DMZ incidents dropped sharply. Even under the hawkish Nixon administration, the North's threat seemed to drop sufficiently to warrant withdrawal of one of the two U.S. infantry divisions stationed in the ROK in 1971.

The threat from the North was merely dormant; it was only a matter of time before the next provocation occurred. The number of ground forces was steadily growing in Pyongyang's favor. The next time the North engaged in a provocation, however, the United States would be far better prepared. The U.S. response to North Korean violence in the Joint Security Area after the so-called tree-trimming incident in August 1976 suggests that U.S. decision makers learned several lessons from the EC-121 shootdown.

## Initial Lessons

Almost immediately after the shootdown, the JCS asked for a review of the PARPRO program. In part, this likely resulted from a memo General Wheeler, the chairman of the JCS, addressed to the director of the Joint Staff on 17 April. Stating that he expected "searching questions" about the shootdown and the overall requirements for PARPRO missions, Wheeler asked the staff to address nine topics that concerned the PARPRO program. Six of the topics pertained to the shootdown itself, but three addressed the overall intelligence collection program:[1]

> A worldwide assessment evaluating portions of reconnaissance tracks on which protection might be called for against hostile intercept capabilities. This assessment should include an estimate of the resources required to provide a postulated degree of protection to the reconnaissance platforms.
>
> An assessment, in collaboration with NSA, of the value and use made of the intelligence products of previous similar missions over the Sea of Japan. [Wheeler commented that the National Security Agency had already started this study and would provide results to the Defense Intelligence Agency.]
>
> A description of the current mission of USNS *Valdez* and an evaluation of the mission requirement and a risk assessment.

Given the urgency of this project, Wheeler expected an interim status report by 21 April, only four days later. The immediate requirement to evaluate the utility of worldwide PARPRO missions likely prompted the JCS to "farm out" the project to theater commanders worldwide. On 19 April, the JCS directed a comprehensive review of the PARPRO program to identify which PARPRO missions were essential and which might be eliminated. Meanwhile, the commander of the Seventh Fleet ordered that a board of investigation be convened at Atsugi Naval Air Station, Japan, on 21 April. The board was to review the shootdown itself as well as the subsequent search-and-rescue effort.[2]

National Security Adviser Henry Kissinger asked the director of the Joint Staff to provide his own impressions of the interagency response group Kissinger had created on 17 April. Vice Adm. Nelson Johnson responded that the small group worked well. He liked it because it kept control above the departmental level; it was small and authoritative (each attendee was the direct and *permanent* deputy of his principal); it maintained security; and it used a "master scenario" timeline that permitted integration of political, diplomatic, and military actions. Kissinger himself also must have endorsed the structure and procedures of this initial crisis group. He would use them as the model of and guidelines for the Washington Special Action Group that was convened to address so many Nixon-era crises.[3]

Both CINCPAC and the JCS ordered further formal investigations of the shootdown. Even before the military posturing ended, CINCPAC on 26 April appointed a board of evaluation to review the incident. At the JCS level, the acting chairman, Gen. John McConnell, established a flag-level fact-finding body on 5 May. The general officers were to assess the command and control aspects of U.S. military involvement in the incident, especially reaction times for the military commands responding to the incident. They were to establish timelines for both the transmission of operational information and for operational responses, including those during the period well after the EC-121 search-and-rescue effort concluded.[4]

On top of these investigations, Deputy Secretary of Defense David Packard announced that he had ordered a comprehensive review of vulnerable intelligence collection efforts. On 29 May, he notified Kissinger, Helms, Attorney General John Mitchell, and Alexis Johnson (State's undersecretary for political affairs) that he had ordered a review of overseas reconnaissance and intelligence missions "that are particularly vulnerable to harassment, damage or capture."[5] The review would consider all platforms—surface and ground as well as air. Assisted by representatives from State, the CIA, the National Security Council, and the attorney general's office, Gardiner Tucker, the "acting principal deputy director defense research and engineering," was to evaluate the following by fall 1969:

- the intelligence value and cost of such activities including the effects of reduced collection,

- the nature and extent of various vulnerabilities, including the likelihood of interference,
- the means available for protection, including their cost and likely effectiveness,
- alternative means of collection that are available or can be developed, including their adequacy, vulnerability and cost, and
- command and control arrangements for warning, communications, and responding to incidents.[6]

This effort may also have been supported by the work of Gerald Dinneen, an intelligence specialist and National Security Agency consultant. Seymour Hersh wrote that the Dinneen study questioned the need for at least the most provocative PARPRO operations.[7]

These reviews had significant ramifications for the national intelligence collection program. First, the navy's unarmed fleet of surface collectors was probably eliminated as a result of them. No new AGERs were commissioned, and the remaining two AGERs, USS *Banner* and USS *Palm Beach,* were soon decommissioned. The last AGTRs would remain in service only a little longer.[8] Armed combatants would be the preferred platforms to conduct future surface collection patrols.

The number of airborne PARPRO missions evidently also dropped sharply. The 303 Committee had approved more than eight hundred sensitive collection programs for January 1968. Eleven years later, the NSC would endorse only half that number. In February 1979, the JRC proposed only 430 airborne missions during March 1979. State, DOD, JCS, and CIA had approved some 402 airborne missions for February 1979. Korea continued to be a target for some of these missions. In fact, the March 1979 schedule included a new SR-71 track against the DPRK: the Blackbird would take off from Kadena and fly along the southern half of the DMZ, approaching to within six miles of North Korean territory.[9]

Evidently, some adjustments were also made to the conduct of the PARPRO missions. The JCS noted that the advisory system used to warn ongoing PARPRO missions of threatening fighter reactions was satisfactory.[10] However, the Dinneen study resulted in new guidelines that specified closer monitoring of ongoing PARPRO missions.[11] Admiral Hyland, the former commander in chief of the Pacific Fleet, thought the new guidelines were an improvement: "I think we're now much better able to handle some of those aerial collection flights. We have ways now of knowing much sooner and much more accurately whether countermeasures are being taken. We can get the word to get them out, beat it before anything can be done to them."[12]

CINCPAC sought to enhance the command, control, communications, and intelligence associated with Pacific Command PARPRO missions. In its board of evaluation report released on 27 May, CINCPAC talked of creating upgraded command posts ("single integrated all source centers") to respond to emergencies. CINCPAC's ability to process crisis-related information was hampered by physically fragmented information processing that was supported by "inadequate and non-integrated communications networks." CINCPAC proposed the creation of interconnected "information centers" (later called Joint Area Information Centers) in Korea, Japan, Okinawa, and the Philippines to consolidate information processing. These facilities would support local commanders and component commanders as well as CINC-PAC. They would process all source information regarding military operations and exercises, provide updates on forces operating in the area, and display the status of all scheduled or ongoing reconnaissance missions. They would have liaison officers from other U.S. government agencies. Their existence would facilitate "immediate and complete peacetime interchange of information" by all commands in the area.[13]

A month later (in late June), however, CINCPAC began referring to the expense of this initiative. Given the "austerity expected in the FY 70 budget," the commander in chief urged his component commanders to try to achieve some of the functionality of the Joint Area Information Centers without a large outlay of funds. He urged the components to "align the facilities of their existing command centers to include the JAIC functionalities." He also directed them to provide long-range plans to improve the exchange of information up and down the chain of command to provide adequate command and control during crises. Their proposals would be due during October 1969.[14]

Congress subsequently investigated the communications shortfalls associated with the shootdown (along with those during the *Pueblo* incident). While the House Armed Services Committee found nothing to show that the messages in question would have provided warning adequate to save the EC-121, the committee's report did highlight apparent delays in reporting the threat up the chain of command. Collection units in the theater had transmitted three messages revealing that the North Korean aircraft were tracking the EC-121. The first spot report took one hour and sixteen minutes to reach Washington. The Joint Reconnaissance Center did not receive the first follow-up to this spot report until three hours after its probable transmission. Sent at flash precedence, the second follow-up to the spot report took thirty-eight minutes to reach Washington. Congress faulted personnel problems rather than equipment problems and sought to reorganize the defense communications system. It also highlighted the urgent need to upgrade secure telephones.[15]

Some of the review participants seemed upset that there had been no "off the shelf" contingency plans to retaliate for the shootdown. H. R. Haldeman wrote in his diary that Kissinger was unhappy at the lack of a plan and intended "to force a whole range of contingency plans."[16] Kissinger must have remained concerned about the North's residual threat. Although he altered his April demand to have a full set of Korean contingency plans available within two weeks, Kissinger still wanted a thorough review of U.S. planning on the peninsula. On 1 May, he suspended the two-week project until an earlier project on North Korean planning was complete. In a March 1969 memo, Kissinger had directed a study of U.S. contingency planning for Korea that reviewed potential responses to limited as well as full-scale North Korean attacks. Kissinger had also directed CINCPAC to address potential U.S. responses to a unilateral South Korean attack on the North. The plans were to contain integrated political and military courses of action. This project had primacy over others and would require at least a month to complete. Additionally, in June, the National Command Authorities directed CINCPAC and the Strategic Air Command to quickly prepare close-hold plans for a retaliatory strike on the Chongjin power plant. General Wheeler explained that highest authority would consider using the plan in the event of another provocation similar to the EC-121 shootdown. With only three days' notice, SAC was to deliver a plan for B-52s to strike the plant; CINCPAC would produce a plan that had the same objective but used only the aircraft under its control. Both commands were to estimate the number of aircraft required to inflict moderate to heavy damage, estimated U.S. losses, and the amount of notification required to execute the strikes.[17]

Kissinger followed up on this assignment in person. In a meeting with Admiral McCain in San Francisco during August 1969, he asked CINCPAC for a list of available contingency options being developed to retaliate for North Korean provocations. Admiral McCain forwarded a draft of the proposed list to the JCS in late August. He warned that the options were still in draft form and that most had not been approved by the JCS. In July, the JCS had increased the number of actions that required concept plans from seven to twenty-three. CINCPAC forwarded the massive plan, "OPLAN 5020 A-Z," and its twenty-six annexes to the JCS in October 1969. Each annex addressed one of the twenty-three actions proposed by the JCS. CINCPAC considered some of the plans infeasible but prepared the package to illustrate the existing limitations of each of the plans. The JCS approved this OPLAN in December 1969.[18]

## The Peninsula Calms Down

Despite the EC-121 shootdown, 1969 turned out to be a much quieter year on the Korean peninsula than either 1967 or 1968. The number of incidents along the DMZ dropped more than 80 percent, and associated casualties also dropped sharply (see table 8). Commentators characterized this period of "good behavior" as an outgrowth of the continued purge of Korean Worker's Party officials and the 1966–1968 infiltration campaign's stark failure. As discussed earlier, the instability along the DMZ may have been associated with the decline of the partisan generals who had fought with Kim Il Sung during World War II and who deeply believed that South Korea was ripe for popular insurrection encouraged by the North. A British Foreign Office paper written in 1970 provides a retrospective of the turbulence between 1966 and 1970:

> In October, 1966, the Central Committee of the Korean Worker's Party (KWP) approved a reorganization of its Political Committee and the creation of a Secretariat. It seemed probable at the time that the membership of these bodies and the ranking order within the Party leadership would remain stable for some time to come. Appearance lists, however, soon began to give signs of change from 1967 to 1969 and it was evident that considerable reshuffling was taking place. The Central Committee met in plenary session at the beginning of December, 1969, and then from then until August this year the ranking order observable from appearance list remained constant.[19]

**Table 8. Casualty Rates in the DMZ, 1967–1969**

|                       | 1967 | 1968 | 1969 |
|-----------------------|------|------|------|
| Number of incidents   | 462  | 542  | 99   |
| Americans killed      | 16   | 14   | 5    |
| South Koreans killed  | 75   | 81   | 5    |

*Source:* CINCPAC Command History, 1969, 4:132, NHC.

Not only had the partisan generals been unsuccessful in fomenting rebellion in the South, they had risked starting a war that the North was ill prepared to fight. In his study of the North Korean leadership, Dae-Sook Suh concluded:

Kim's generals became more and more adamant, eventually transforming their military prominence into political influence and took Kim and the North to the brink of a precipice with the seizure of the *Pueblo* and the shooting down of the American EC-121 spy plane. Kim had to purge most of his loyal comrades in arms from the partisan days. By the time of the Fifth Party Congress, Kim had experienced the trials and tribulations of independence [from the PRC and Soviet Union] and returned to the normalcy of building a socialist state in the North.[20]

The U.S. embassy in Seoul also ascribed the reduced number of DMZ incidents to the North's desire to replace a failed policy with a more effective one. Armed confrontation had neither reduced popular support for the ROK government nor forced the United States to abandon Seoul. Rather, the North's provocations had encouraged the South's populace to rally behind the government, Washington to increase its presence and military spending on the ROK, and Seoul to enhance its counterinfiltration capability. When belligerence appeared counterproductive, the power elite in Pyongyang evidently decided on a policy that would deny the United States and ROK the ability to "hype" the KPA's military threat. By reducing the number of DMZ incidents, Pyongyang removed this propaganda point. Its replacement strategy entailed infiltrating agents for the long-term subversion of the government who would be useful without creating a strong U.S.–ROK military response.[21]

Despite the North's less confrontational stance, the United States continued to provide better protection for all PARPRO missions throughout the western Pacific. In part, the orders mandated greater standoff distances. For example, surveillance missions that had been allowed to approach to within twenty miles of the People's Republic of China now had to remain fifty miles away.[22] On 5 June 1969, CINCPAC directed U.S. fighters in Japan or Taiwan to go on strip alert any time a reconnaissance aircraft approached an area within two hundred nautical miles offshore of the Soviet Union or China. Nearby carriers would maintain fighters on deck alert. If a reconnaissance aircraft received a warning that hostile attack was imminent or probable, the fighters would launch. The strip alerts reduced the reaction time to support these missions, but CINCPAC commented that they still provided "very little protection against hostile attack by CHICOM and USSR fighters because of the time and distance to effect an intercept." Finally, the Seventh Fleet began routinely stationing two combatants in the Sea of Japan. These "PARPRO picket ships" were to provide warning and protection to ongoing PARPRO missions.[23]

As for Korea itself, CINCPAC continued the policy of placing fighters in the air whenever PARPRO missions entered certain areas offshore of Korea. Normally four fighters would be airborne at such times. These fighters did not have to escort the intelligence collection aircraft, but they did fly a combat air patrol that would afford quick response to NKAF fighter reaction. These combat air patrols went smoothly throughout 1969. The fact that the patrols flew nearly every day suggests that the United States still pursued a robust, albeit reduced, reconnaissance program against the DPRK. CINCPAC continued to warn that the fighter escorts for flights off Korea "did not guarantee protection of the reconnaissance planes from a concerted and dedicated air attack."[24]

As tensions in the peninsula relaxed, the Nixon administration reviewed a drawdown of air and ground assets deployed there. Initially, it merely replaced two Air National Guard F-100 Super Sabre squadrons with two U.S. Air Force F-4 fighter squadrons in June 1969. However, these squadrons (along with an F-106 interceptor squadron) were scheduled to redeploy in March 1970.[25] Additionally, that same year the administration proposed removing one of the U.S. infantry divisions stationed in the ROK. In 1971, President Nixon actually withdrew the Seventh Infantry Division.[26]

# Aftershocks

Seven years after the EC-121 shootdown, North Korea challenged the United States in ways that resembled its behavior during the *Pueblo* and EC-121 incidents. This time, the United States responded more effectively to the provocations. The U.S. response to the August 1976 "tree-trimming" incident was smaller, more rapidly executed, and more successful than the responses to the two earlier incidents had been.

On 18 August 1976, North Korean guards confronted a small U.S.–ROK working party that was attempting to trim a poplar tree in the Joint Security Area in Panmunjom. In the ensuing scuffle, they killed two U.S. officers and injured nine UN Command guards. The UN Command concluded that the attack had been premeditated. The incident coincided with Kim Jong Il's appearance before the first Non-Aligned Movement meeting held in more than a year. The meeting provided the DPRK with an opportunity to attack the United States before the world, and indeed, Kim Jong Il convinced the Non-Aligned Movement to condemn the United States for the incident.[27]

The day the incident occurred, Henry Kissinger convened a meeting of the Washington Special Action Group. The participants concluded that the murders were indeed premeditated. Reviewing the options, Kissinger recommended that the defense readiness condition on the peninsula be raised. Thus, for the first time since the Korean War, U.S. forces in Korea raised the DEFCON in response to conditions on the peninsula itself. The ROK simultaneously took similar measures. Occurring only a day after the tree-chopping incident, the change from DEFCON 4 to DEFCON 3 was a major step in enhancing readiness for war on the peninsula. Because extensive activity was required to effect this shift, many of the preparations were readily discernible to North Korea.[28] Kissinger's group further recommended that the United States "resurrect" a training exercise that called for flying B-52s over the DMZ.[29] On 19 August, at Kissinger's request, the Korea Working Group prepared a spreadsheet depicting a range of other actions that the United States might take against North Korea. By then, the United States had raised the DEFCON and deployed an F-4 squadron from Kadena, Okinawa (Japan), to Korea. The B-52s, a carrier battle group, and a stateside FB-111 squadron were alerted to support potential contingency operations. The United States was also reviewing options that included sending reinforcements to the peninsula, taking further military actions, and initiating unspecified "punitive measures."[30]

Certainly some of the measures would have been familiar to Pyongyang. For example, the United States quickly moved aircraft to Korean air bases, as it had during the *Pueblo* and EC-121 incidents. RF-4 reconnaissance aircraft and F-105 Wild Weasel fighter-bombers were deployed to Osan, Kunsan, and Taegu from elsewhere in the western Pacific. FB-111 bombers also were deployed from Mountain Home Air Force Base in Idaho to the peninsula. Some of the other steps would have been both atypical and more alarming to the North:[31]

- The United States increased the number of SR-71 flights along the DMZ.[32]
- The U.S. Second Infantry Division and ROK troops began relocating to prehostility outpost positions along the DMZ.
- The United States began moving missiles and nuclear weapons to forward storage areas.
- The UN Command began conducting extensive (and highly visible) prehostilities logistics activity.

The DPRK responded by quickly assuming a high state of alert. U.S. Forces Korea's intelligence officer saw the response as "reactive, urgent, and defensive." The alert betrayed a "general apprehension over the possibility of UNC retaliation." This was exactly the state of mind the UN Command wanted to engender.[33]

Also unlike the *Pueblo* and EC-121 crises, the UN commander was in the driver's seat. After all, the forces involved this time were under his command, and it was his staff who rapidly drafted the plan for Operation Paul Bunyan, the U.S. response to the tree-chopping incident. On 21 August, only three days after the incident, the commander deployed a well-armed 813-man U.S.–ROK force into the Joint Security Area with orders to chop down the poplar tree. Twenty-seven helicopters provided air support for the operation. As the ground unit moved into the area, B-52s from Guam were ordered to fly along the DMZ. USS *Midway* simultaneously launched forty combat aircraft.[34]

The sudden appearance, size, and armament of the UN Command's tree-chopping unit must have caught North Korea by surprise. Its behavior was indecisive. KPA troops certainly did not confront the UN troops as they felled the tree. In fact, at a hurriedly convened MAC meeting on 21 August, Kim Il Sung expressed "regret" over the 18 August incident. This response was unusual in that it was the first time North Korea had expressed doubt or regret over an incident it had provoked. A few days later, the North proposed dividing the Joint Security Area into two zones to avoid further conflict. The UN Command rapidly agreed.[35]

Thus, in response to a premeditated attempt by North Korea to humiliate the United States at the cost of U.S. lives, the United States responded quickly and decisively with measures that were far more confrontational than those used during the *Pueblo* and EC-121 crises. There was no delay while four carrier battle groups were assembled or hundreds of aircraft were deployed forward to the peninsula. The contingency planning appeared more focused. The commander who would have fought the war was adequately consulted. In his memoir of his years in the White House, Kissinger compared the U.S. responses to the tree-trimming and EC-121 incidents and found the latter wanting:

> No military forces could be moved for at least twenty-four hours, which turned out to be another error. An immediate mobilization of military strength would at least have put North Korea on notice that a grave offense had been committed. It might have elicited a gesture to indicate that it had backed down or admitted the need for some reparation. That is indeed what happened when the North Koreans beat two American officers to death along the DMZ in 1976.[36]

Although it may be argued that the participants had learned some lessons from the *Pueblo* and EC-121 incidents, the U.S. response to this crisis was perhaps more focused and more immediate because several variables had changed. The United States could likely take tougher steps because it was no longer burdened with the war in Vietnam. This was important because the theater decision makers in the tree-trimming incident felt that there was a high risk of war.[37] Moreover, there was likely a profound desire to restore national credibility after the ignominious evacuation of Saigon in April 1975. The penalty for not responding at all might thus have been more severe than that for making only a limited and focused response.

Moreover, the immediate U.S. objective—cutting down a tree while pro-ducing a show of force on a smaller scale than would have been required to make a significant statement in either the *Pueblo* or EC-121 incident—was more achievable. U.S.–ROK air assets were less vulnerable to NKAF attack because the shelter construction program had likely been completed years earlier. The ROK Air Force had also begun to strip away the North's air supe-riority, which was of concern during the *Pueblo* and EC-121 crises.

Even after the show of UN Command resolve, however, North Korea's provocations continued intermittently. In fact, the PARPRO aircraft them-selves remained in danger. North Korean media—always mindful in reporting U.S. reconnaissance activity on and near the peninsula—heatedly condemned such missions during the summer of 1981. The North then attempted, unsuc-cessfully, to down an SR-71. On 26 August, an SA-2 site on the southern tip of the Ongjin Peninsula in southwestern North Korea fired one SA-2 surface-to-air missile at an SR-71 flying in international airspace. The missile exploded several miles away from its quarry. The North was unapologetic, and even the following spring the North Korean media's treatment of alleged U.S. "spy flights" was "harsh" and contained "wild" language similar to that used before the EC-121 shootdown.[38]

Aerial reconnaissance missions flown near the peninsula still serve as potential targets for the North should it wish to foment a crisis. In fact, the North Korean press provides monthly and annual tabulations of the number of surveillance missions the United States allegedly flies against it. For example, the North claimed that the United States flew 1,760 "espionage" missions against it during 1999, and nearly 200 in June 2003.[39] The tone of recent press coverage is nowhere near as hostile as that preceding the attempt on the SR-71. Nevertheless, Pyongyang still characterizes these missions as "an extremely provocative and rash war maneuver."[40]

## Lessons Learned

Following the EC-121 shootdown, the NSC, Defense Department, Joint Chiefs of Staff, and CINCPAC devoted much effort to conducting lessons-learned review boards. Although not all of the "lessons learned" from the EC-121 have been declassified, it is apparent that several changes were made to the ways that sensitive operations were supported and possible responses to provocations deliberated.

*Command and control:* The NSC created the Washington Special Action Group, a sub-cabinet-level working group used throughout the Nixon administration to respond to crises. The Pacific theater commander made the case for a theaterwide set of command centers with far better communications than those available during the EC-121 incident.

*Collection platforms:* The lessons-learned boards reviewed the use of surface platforms as well as reconnaissance aircraft and evidently concluded that the dedicated auxiliary collection ships had to go. None remain.

*Collection effort:* The review almost certainly led to a reduction in the number of PARPRO missions. This decision reduced the costs of the program and simplified the fighter escort problem.

*Fighter support:* For 1969, at least, the United States learned the lesson that PARPRO missions off Korea required fighter escort. However, the JCS found more efficient ways to provide airborne fighter support to reconnaissance aircraft.

*Statecraft:* At a strategic level, U.S. elites must have concluded that the threat of force against North Korea might persuade (or dissuade) if it was credible. The U.S. response to the tree-trimming incident was more successful than that to either EC-121 or *Pueblo* in that it secured a North Korean apology. Moreover, the United States and ROK took extraordinary measures to prepare for *land* warfare on the peninsula. This response—not taken to the same extent in either the *Pueblo* or EC-121 crises—sharply increased the military threat to the North and may have been more persuasive than simply moving aircraft in and around the peninsula.

*DPRK unpredictability:* The DPRK's willingness to challenge another reconnaissance flight—even under the very conservative and combative new Reagan administration—in August 1981 suggests that deterrence of the North was ephemeral. Kim Il Sung seemed quite capable of ignoring earlier U.S. warnings and even previous U.S. military responses in his desire to demonstrate independence (and his intermittent need to heighten tensions on the peninsula).

The *Pueblo* and EC-121 incidents also instruct at a deeper level. It is to these longer-term issues that we now turn.

# 10

# CONCLUSIONS

The intelligence community and the military performed unevenly in the *Pueblo* and EC-121 incidents. Although it would be tempting to fault individuals for failing to anticipate either provocation, the problems that contributed to both incidents were more systemic than individual. In particular, they reflected the inherent risk of intelligence collection against a competent adversary and the fundamental challenges in analyzing—let alone predicting—North Korea's behavior. Command, control, communications, intelligence, and manpower shortfalls likely complicated the assessment process. The U.S. military, however, also demonstrated exceptional planning, mobilization, logistics, and deployment capabilities once the crises began. With this background, a concluding list of observations on the U.S. military's performance during the incidents, both positive and critical, follows.

## No Free Lunches

Collecting military intelligence against hostile countries can never be completely safe. The United States had willingly incurred risks (acceptable to all levels of the chain of command) by conducting a worldwide reconnaissance program since World War II. More than three dozen U.S. aircraft were attacked flying such missions between 1946 and 1969, and seventeen were actually shot down.[1] Other reconnaissance aircraft crashed in peacetime accidents. The fact that the United States continued to fly the missions suggests that all of the presidential administrations from Truman's through Nixon's felt that the mission "take" justified the risks. In other words, intelligence collection was and is inherently risky, but the United States has consistently accepted both the risks and the costs of military reconnaissance missions, particularly when the target is a threatening and unpredictable power such as the DPRK and even when the risks are higher than "minimal."

Two factors increased the risk to the collector in the case of North Korea in the late 1960s. *Pueblo* was attempting a new form of intelligence collection. It was unarmed, sufficiently close, and on station long enough for the North to develop a simple plan to seize it. In the case of the EC-121 shootdown, the United States incurred extra risk simply by flying an extraordinarily large number of PARPRO missions (on highly predictable tracks) against North Korea. These unique aspects of the Korean collection effort exacerbated the risks inherent in collecting against a government whose intentions were murky but almost certainly malevolent.

## Was It Worth It?

A track-by-track review of mission results to justify ongoing intelligence collection activity in 1968 would have demanded a great deal of time and skilled analysts. Yet such a review would have ensured proper management of collection programs and eliminated marginally productive collection. Had the process worked, it would have saved money by reducing flight activity and would have reduced risk by providing fewer opportunities for "something" to go wrong.

This thorough review process evidently did not occur after *Pueblo*. The Ball Report focused on the surface collection program, but the aerial reconnaissance program should have been carefully reviewed as well. If nothing else, a careful review would have shown congressional investigators that *all* U.S. reconnaissance programs were being carefully managed. Unfortunately, it took the EC-121 shootdown to force such a zero-based review. After the shootdown, Deputy Secretary of Defense David Packard directed the Department of Defense to review the worldwide reconnaissance program with the explicit objective of eliminating marginal reconnaissance tracks. This review likely contributed to significant reductions in reconnaissance activity given the much lower monthly total of U.S. reconnaissance flights being reported a decade later.

Reviews of the utility of ongoing collection activity are at the core of a well-managed reconnaissance program. There is a natural tendency for these not to happen because collectors and analysts naturally fall into two different communities of interest. It takes leadership to force members of these two communities to reach across the divide.

## Inscrutable Pyongyang

In 1968 (as now), it was difficult for intelligence analysts to understand North Korea's decision-making dynamics as they tried to anticipate Pyongyang's next moves. The U.S. intelligence community could discern only the broadest aspects of the process. Moreover, the significance of the political developments that *were* publicized, such as when Pyongyang published promotion and public appearance lists, was sometimes not apparent for years.

This remains a potential problem. Western analysts may be no closer today than they were in 1969 to understanding how and why decisions are made in the North. One can postulate broad regime objectives and strategies; however, any attempt to determine why one objective might be selected over another is both challenging and speculative. Further, in a one-man dictatorship such as North Korea, the leader can make decisions quickly and secretly.

Such limited knowledge invites misinterpretation by Western analysts—a potential stumbling block in any attempt to develop a systematic warning system. In his seminal work on strategic warning, Richard Betts commented:

> Miscalculation of an attacker's intent can be due to a combination of psychological factors and political premises—the vagaries of human intellect and cognition interact with assumptions about the stakes and alternatives in a crisis. Ironically, recklessness or miscalculation by the attacking state . . . can also enhance surprise if the victim seeks a rational explanation of warning indicators and *does not understand the attacker's mistaken judgments*. In a situation

where it seems clear to the victim that the enemy has more to gain from diplomacy than from war, it is easy to infer that indicators reflect defensive precautions or political coercion rather than preparations for an immediate strike.[2]

U.S. intelligence analysts should have tried to model the threat by looking at it from the North Korean perspective. Instead, U.S. risk assessment entailed projection. "Projection ('mirror-imaging')," Betts noted, "may flow from wishful thinking or unrecognized differences in culture or perceptions. The defender may assume his adversary will see the same alternatives and constraints in the situation, or the same linkages between facts, that he does."[3]

The U.S. analysts who approved the *Pueblo* mission used a Western, legalistic model and mistakenly assumed that Pyongyang would mirror Moscow. They assumed that Pyongyang held the principle of freedom of the seas to be sacrosanct, even though North Korea did not rely heavily on maritime trade and, in any event, routinely violated international law. They also assumed that since Moscow had AGIs that relied on freedom of the sea, Pyongyang would not want to upset the balance by attacking U.S. "AGIs."

Additionally, Western analysts underrated the salience of collection incidents to a North Korean regime stridently bent on demonstrating independence and power. While the USS *Pueblo* seizure and the EC-121 shootdown have been virtually forgotten by most Americans, both incidents remain a source of pride for the North. The North Korean media make glowing references to both incidents to this very day. In 1999, Pyongyang went so far as to sneak *Pueblo* from Wonsan on the east coast around the peninsula to the west coast and finally up the Taedong River to Pyongyang, where it is now a museum. The North Korean media also covers its life in this new incarnation.[4]

In addition to engaging in "mirror imaging," U.S. analysts may also have failed to appreciate the domestic costs Kim Il Sung faced by *not* attacking the EC-121, seizing *Pueblo,* or conducting a similarly egregious act, as well as the propaganda value such acts would have. In a subsection appropriately titled "The Logic of Craziness," Betts commented:

> Aggression can be rational. Rational does not mean "good" but simply that means are logically consistent with ends. Status quo powers seeking to deter aggression may err by assuming symmetry between their own and their adversary's valuation of what is at issue between them and also by worrying only about the positive gains the adversary seeks. . . . Too seldom do decision makers

in the victim state consider or appreciate the costs to the adversary, as he sees them, of not attacking. They often presume that continuation of the status quo leaves the enemy no worse off. If the deterrer focuses on only half the possible costs, he undervalues the stakes at issue, the enemy's incentives to take risks, and the full range of choices that the enemy sees. . . . The probability of armed conflict depends not only on the actual dangers of war to the attacker, but also on the perceived dangers of peace.[5]

A more sophisticated mission approval cycle would have relied on gaming North Korean attitudes toward U.S. surveillance from the North Korean perspective. Even a basic simulation might have produced an assessment that U.S. reconnaissance assets off the coast of North Korea were tempting targets. Unfortunately, the declassified records do not reveal that the United States ever attempted such modeling, even after *Pueblo*. The declassified Special National Intelligence Estimates do not warn of a threat to U.S. intelligence collectors even after *Pueblo* was seized. A rigorous SNIE that at least mentioned a heightened risk to U.S. collectors certainly would have served CINCPAC and the new Nixon administration well.

## The Challenge of Warning

Both incidents demonstrate that it is extraordinarily difficult to break the yoke of pattern analysis. Predictive analysis based on previous activity (or lack of the same) is persuasive. Convincing decision makers that an adversary is going to do something new and more belligerent is a hard sell, especially when there are counterarguments for why the adversary will not change its policy. Yet, intelligence failures occur when an adversary does try new approaches that may generate a new and unfamiliar set of indications. Betts put this problem succinctly:

> Historical context is of course a necessary and valuable grounding for strategic assessment, but not a reliable guide. The warnings at issue involve major changes from normal behavior. Extrapolations from past behavior and incremental changes are poor bases for anticipating dramatic shifts. Mathematical probability theory is no help in predicting one-time events when there is a small number of cases to use as a base.[6]

   The process of warning went off track when the United States attempted to apply flawed analytical assumptions to a nation imbued with a profound sense of operational security. There was essentially no tactical warning that North Korea might attack *Pueblo*. In the case of the EC-121, on the other hand, North Korean actions (such as the tone of pronouncements in Panmunjom) had become sufficiently ominous for COMUSFK, CINCPAC, and CINC-PACFLT to take precautionary measures. PARPRO missions were scaled back, and Commando Clinch overland reconnaissance flights were restricted from approaching the DMZ. The 15 April EC-121 mission was given a minimum standoff distance of fifty miles instead of the usual forty miles.

   Nevertheless, in both cases the North evidently was careful to avoid scaring off the quarry. In neither case did the North Korean military raise its alertness state before striking. As heated as its rhetoric was, the DPRK media did not warn of a possible attack on U.S. naval assets. In fact, the political context preceding the EC-121 shootdown provided little warning. The number of North Korean provocations across the DMZ had declined. The "second Korean War" appeared to be ending when the NKAF suddenly downed the EC-121.

   The small operations and terrorist acts preferred by North Korea are intrinsically hard to detect. By virtue of their small size and few participants, they produce few indications. The DPRK likely went to great lengths to mask even these when it was preparing to seize *Pueblo* and shoot down the EC-121. Additionally, the North denied the warnings that might be gained from pattern analysis by breaking the patterns. It tried new approaches that might generate a new and unfamiliar set of indications. Such "pattern breaking" is a long-term trend in North Korea's behavior.

   Consequently, not one U.S. agency asserted that *Pueblo* was at risk. Unfortunately, the argument could have been made. Since October 1966, North Korea's misbehavior had jumped several notches up the spectrum of violence. Well before Korean commandos boarded *Pueblo*, U.S. analysts acknowledged that Americans along the DMZ had been attacked and were at risk for further attack. The North had developed plans to assassinate President Park, and the most recent SNIE warned that even Vice President Humphrey might be a target for assassination teams during his mid-1967 visit. Yet, the planners approving the *Pueblo* mission assumed that international law would protect U.S. vessels operating outside North Korean waters. In retrospect, this is a remarkable assumption given Pyongyang's willingness to violate other international laws. Few analysts or decision makers would have made the same illogical conclusion about North Vietnam.

The National Security Agency came close to making the case for assigning a higher risk assessment to *Pueblo*'s proposed patrol. A slightly different format on its well-crafted threat assessment transmitted on 29 December 1967 could have stopped the *Pueblo* mission in its tracks. The drafter of the message merely needed to expand his message with two more paragraphs. One would remind his readers of the threat to U.S. personnel on the peninsula and make the case that the North could readily extend this threat to U.S. personnel *off-shore*. It might also remind its readers that the U.S. intelligence community could not confidently project the upper bound to North Korean violence in and around the Korean peninsula. The second additional paragraph would state what probably was really on the drafter's mind: *Pueblo*'s initial patrol should be assigned a risk assessment higher than "minimal" simply because it *was* the first extended patrol of an intelligence collector in a sensitive area. Additionally, the message itself should have been more widely disseminated or flagged as a "personal for" to a senior member of the operational side of CINCPAC and the JCS. This would have forced a discussion that evidently did not occur at the working level the day the *Pueblo* patrol was approved. The analysts who participated in that meeting seem to have become so accustomed to North Korean misbehavior that they lost sight of the possible danger. Instead, the worried NSA analyst took a half measure and prepared a message addressed solely to the Joint Reconnaissance Center that described what working-level analysts already knew. The NSA "analysis" did not get the attention it would have demanded as a formal warning message.

## The DPRK and U.S. Aerial Reconnaissance

North Korea is one of the few countries that broadcasts detailed press releases about alleged aerial reconnaissance activity being flown against it. Nearly every month the North Korean media summarize the alleged overall activity and then give a partial breakdown by type of aircraft. For example, the North accused the United States of instigating "190 cases of aerial espionage" against it during December 2002. The media cited dates and aircraft, such as U-2 missions on 28 December, an EP-3 mission on Christmas Day, and RC-12 and

RC-7B flights throughout the month. This particular account did not accuse the United States of violating North Korean airspace. Nevertheless, in a highly unusual event during March 2003, four NKAF aircraft—two MiG-29s and two MiG-23s—shadowed an RC-135 reconnaissance aircraft flying 150 miles off the North Korean coast. The MiGs reportedly flew to within fifty feet of the U.S. aircraft. Their pilots even made hand signals for the RC-135 to follow them back to North Korea before the RC-135 aborted its mission.[7]

Why do the media bother advertising U.S. surveillance activity? Since the treatments are in Korean, they are likely destined for a domestic audience. Publicizing the alleged U.S. surveillance activity does give the regime internal propaganda points. The flights can be characterized as representing a threat that justifies the tremendous sacrifices demanded of the North Korean people to maintain the country's distended military budget. For example, the broadcast cited above concluded: "their acts show that their aggressive ambition to militarily crush our country has not changed a bit."[8] Because it gains such propaganda mileage, the North is likely to continue frequent reporting of U.S. reconnaissance flights allegedly being flown against it.

Such coverage would also provide the background and justification for another North Korean attack on a U.S. reconnaissance mission. The media treatment has laid the groundwork to make a case for North Korea should it down another U.S. aircraft. However, Pyongyang has many other options if it wants to ratchet up tensions on the peninsula, and in recent decades North Korea has consistently leaned toward terrorism instead of military confrontation.

## Limited Communications

Although they were tied together by formal record message traffic, the analysts and operators who evaluated the risk to *Pueblo* and the EC-121 were physically and psychically worlds apart. The distances, time zone differences, and poor-quality secure voice communication systems complicated informal coordination. With informal communication so difficult, both groups probably did the bare minimum to ensure that the *formal* message was transmitted in time to meet the tight deadlines required by the national reconnaissance program's monthly approval cycle. With today's better informal secure communications (e-mail, secure VTCs, etc.), analysts have more opportunity to flesh out sub-tle reservations about impending operations. This does not eliminate sur-prise or miscalculation, but at least the Department of Defense has replaced the stilted communications modes used in 1968–69.

## Was Contingency Planning a Culprit?

Some national-level decision makers faulted the military for having inade-quate contingency plans to retaliate for the EC-121 shootdown. If this was the case, it is no wonder that Henry Kissinger was annoyed. After a year of deal-ing with the *Pueblo* crisis, the JCS should have had an elaborate menu of con-tingency plans for virtually every conceivable North Korean provocation. However, a perceived lack of contingency plans did not really delay the U.S. response to the EC-121 incident. The relatively slow speed of national-level deliberations and the time required to move three carrier groups from the South China Sea into the Sea of Japan likely took far longer than did drafting a simple plan to strike one North Korean airfield.

What really frustrated decision makers was the lack of assets to support immediate reprisals. Had naval assets—such as a Talos surface-to-air missile–equipped cruiser—been operating in the Sea of Japan when the shootdown occurred, the United States might well have retaliated. Talos could have allowed the United States to shoot down the very MiGs that attacked the PARPRO aircraft, or at least to readily engage the next group of MiGs that took off. Stationing ships off Korea afterward to be prepared to retaliate quickly after future provocations would have been difficult given the over-whelming competition from the war raging in Vietnam. Members of the new administration who might want this capability simply were unattuned to the tremendous strain the war in Vietnam had placed on the Pacific Fleet; hence their frustration. Once briefed about the demands of the Vietnam air war, the National Command Authorities settled instead for using land-based fighter patrols for deterrence and released all the aircraft carriers within a few weeks of the EC-121 shootdown.

It seems that reconnaissance operations in the late 1960s had a readily dis-cernible "break even" point. An intelligence collector—airborne or shipboard —operating alone was acceptable. However, when the plane or ship required protection, the collection effort suddenly became expensive and was hard to justify for long. Because the DOD likely became convinced that unarmed surface collectors could not operate without dedicated on-call support, further AGER conversions were canceled and auxiliary intelligence collectors decommissioned.

Even sustaining fighter escort for PARPRO missions was problematic. Maintaining a barrier combat air patrol was challenging, and flying fighter escort for each mission aircraft was expensive. Given the short-lived nature of fighter protection afforded to airborne collectors after *Pueblo*, it is unlikely that PARPRO aircraft enjoyed airborne fighter protection for even a full year after the EC-121 shootdown.

## More Bodies?

A typical Washington reaction to a perceived intelligence failure is to throw more bodies at the problem by creating a working group or task force. In fact, during both the *Pueblo* and EC-121 crises, working groups and task forces were created in Washington to orchestrate the U.S. diplomatic response to the crisis. If the national intelligence community took steps to better monitor the DPRK by assigning more analysts to the Korean problem, it is not apparent, although there must have been temporary surges in the numbers of analysts working the problem during peak points of the *Pueblo* crisis and during the probing House Armed Services Committee hearings of March–April 1969.

In fact, in his prepared testimony before Congress, the DIA's director, Lt. Gen. Joseph Carroll, revealed no significant enhancements in the way the DIA monitored Korea after *Pueblo*. He did not cite personnel shuffles, new products, new collection strategies, or even new analysis methodologies.[9] Perhaps the general felt that by advertising improvements he would highlight perceived shortfalls present before *Pueblo* was seized. On the other hand, such enhancements simply may not have occurred. Like other U.S. intelligence agencies both in the theater and in Washington, the DIA likely had to commit most of its Asian analytical resources to supporting the war in Vietnam. Moreover, the war was continuing as the U.S. military started to downsize in the early 1970s. A presumably shrinking DIA would still have had to devote a disproportionate share of its analysts to that war. In other words, the DIA may not have created a much larger Korea analytical cell because it could not pay the personnel bill.

## U.S. Military Responsiveness

The *Pueblo* and EC-121 incidents revealed an impressive U.S. capability to mass air and naval forces into the theater. Despite the complexity and size of the responses demanded during the two crises, the U.S. military responded quickly and professionally. Although General Bonesteel lost his manpower battles, the United States quickly (but temporarily) redressed the airpower imbalance on the peninsula. The deployment of so many assets would have allowed the United States to execute a host of retaliatory contingency plans, up to eliminating the entire NKAF using well-coordinated conventional strikes.

The justification for the surge in forces may be questionable. Admiral McCain (CINCPAC) warned after the EC-121 shootdown that the United States might be perceived as a "paper tiger" if it again assembled forces without using them. The South Korean leadership said the same thing. However, in both crises, senior U.S. leaders wanted the forces on station in the Sea of Japan and only reluctantly returned them to Vietnam. This is particularly true because neither administration ruled out the possibility of having to retaliate. Given the unpredictability of North Korea's behavior in 1968, no U.S. leader could say with absolute certainty that Pyongyang would not try, and perhaps even punish, the crew. Ambassador Porter in particular urged that naval forces be retained to reassure the South Koreans. State itself later sought to push for naval posturing in the Sea of Japan during critical junctures in the U.S.–North Korean negotiations over the *Pueblo* crew.

In the case of the EC-121 shootdown, the White House was profoundly unhappy that there were no U.S. forces on station to retaliate instantly. Afterward, the NSC evidently was determined to ensure that the United States had adequate airpower (notably A-6s) on station to retaliate immediately should the North conduct another such provocation. The Seventh Fleet extricated the carriers from these contingency stations in the Sea of Japan and the Yellow Sea only with the greatest difficulty. Evidently, only dire warnings that such a requirement would endanger the air war in Vietnam were sufficient to carry the day. In other words, the sea power committed to Korea during both crises had far more salience for the National Command Authorities than was then popularly known.

## Conclusion

The EC-121 and *Pueblo* incidents are instructive at several levels. They reveal the challenges and pitfalls of intelligence collection. They demonstrate the extent to which the United States relied on relatively fragile command, control, communications, and intelligence systems. They confirm the utility of military power, even when not used. But most of all, the two incidents confirm the continuing challenge posed in analyzing and deterring North Korea. That nation remains a complex and obscure entity. It will almost certainly continue to provide foreign policy surprises for the United States and the Republic of Korea.

# NOTES

## Abbreviations Used in the Notes

| | |
|---|---|
| BBC | British Broadcasting Corporation |
| CINCPAC | Commander in Chief, Pacific |
| CINCPACFLT | Commander in Chief, Pacific Fleet |
| CINCUNC | Commander in Chief, United Nations Command (in Korea) |
| CINCUSARPAC | Commander in Chief, U.S. Army Pacific |
| CJCS | Chairman, Joint Chiefs of Staff |
| CNO | Chief, Naval Operations |
| COMSEVENTHFLT | Commander, Seventh Fleet |
| COMUSFK | Commander, U.S. Forces Korea |
| DCI | Director, Central Intelligence |
| DCNO | Deputy Chief, Naval Operations |
| DDRS | Declassified Documents Reference System Database |
| DIA | Defense Intelligence Agency |
| DIRNSA | Director, National Security Agency |
| DOD | Department of Defense |
| FCO | Foreign and Commonwealth Office, London, England |
| FOIA | Freedom of Information Act |
| *FRUS* | *Foreign Relations of the United States* |
| HASC | House Armed Services Committee, U.S. Congress |
| INR | U.S. State Department, Bureau of Intelligence and Research |
| JCS | Joint Chiefs of Staff |
| JRC | JCS Joint Reconnaissance Center |
| KCNA | Korean Central News Agency |
| LBJ | Lyndon Baines Johnson Library, Austin, Texas |
| NARA | National Archives and Records Administration, College Park, Maryland |
| NHC | Naval Historical Center, Washington, D.C. |
| NMCC | National Military Command Center |
| NSC | National Security Council |
| NSF | National Security Files |
| PRO | Public Records Office, Kew Gardens, London, England |

| RG | Record Group |
|---|---|
| SECDEF | Secretary of Defense |
| SECSTATE | Secretary of State |
| SNIE | Special National Intelligence Estimate |
| USFK | U.S. Forces Korea |

## Chapter 1. Lightning Strikes Twice

1. U.S. House Armed Services Committee [HASC], Special Subcommittee on the USS *Pueblo, Inquiry into the USS* Pueblo *and EC-121 Plane Incidents,* HASC 91-12 (Washington, D.C.: U.S. Government Printing Office, 1969), 1620; hereinafter cited as HASC Report.

2. Ibid., 1622–23.

3. Ibid., 1620.

4. Ibid., 1621.

5. Ibid., 1624.

6. See Trevor Armbrister, *A Matter of Accountability: The True Story of the* Pueblo *Affair* (New York: Coward-McCann, 1969); hereinafter cited as Armbrister, *Accountability.*

7. The State Department's website contains the electronic version of *Foreign Relations of the United States 1964–1968* [hereinafter *FRUS*] vol. 29, pt. 1: *Korea,* which reveals some of the documents associated with national decision making during the *Pueblo* incident. Other National Security Council, State Department, Central Intelligence Agency, Joint Chiefs of Staff, theater-level military, and British Foreign Office documents scattered in more than a half dozen archives provide fragmentary pieces of the story.

## Chapter 2. An Intelligence Blank

1. Chart entitled "Korea Demilitarized Zone Area," in Director of Central Intelligence, "North Korean Intentions and Capabilities with Respect to South Korea," Special National Intelligence Estimate 14.2-67, 21 September 1967, folder "SNIE 14.2-67," NSF Country Files, NIEs, box 5, LBJ; hereinafter cited as SNIE 14.2-67, LBJ.

2. A third responsibility now assigned him, commander of the Combined Force Command, did not come into being until that U.S.–ROK command was created in 1978.

3. Germane academic sources include Dae-Sook Suh, *Kim Il Sung: The North Korean Leader* (New York: Columbia University Press, 1988); Hy-Sang Lee, *North Korea: A Strange Socialist Fortress* (Westport, Conn.: Praeger, 2001); Chuck Downs, *Over the Line: North Korea's Negotiating Strategy* (Washington, D.C.: American Enterprise Institute Press, 1999); B. C. Koh, "The *Pueblo* Incident in Perspective," *Asian Survey* 91 (January–June 1969): 264–80; Nicholas Sarantakes, "The Quiet War: Combat Operations along

the Korean Demilitarized Zone, 1966–1969," *Journal of Military History* 64 (April 2000): 439–58, hereinafter cited as Sarantakes, "The Quiet War."

4. Memo from INR/REA (Fred Greene) to U (Claus Ruser), "State of Intelligence on North Korea," 1 August 1968, folder "Korea 2 of 2," Senior Interdepartmental Group Files 1966–1972, Office of Executive Secretariat, box 8, RG 59, NARA; hereinafter cited as Greene, "State of Intelligence on North Korea."

5. Ibid.

6. SNIE 14.2-67, LBJ.

7. Director of Central Intelligence, update to "North Korean Intentions and Capabilities with Respect to South Korea," 29 February 1968, folder "NIE 14.2 North Korea," NSF Country Files, NIEs, box 5, LBJ; hereinafter cited as Update to SNIE 14.2-67, LBJ.

8. See "The South Korean Revolution" and "Disintegration of the Partisan Group," in Suh, *Kim Il Sung.*

9. Ibid., 247–48.

10. Ibid.

11. Memo, Thomas Hughes (INR) to Secretary of State, "North Korea's Program for the Reunification of Korea," 2 February 1968, folder "POL 32-4 KOR 1/1/67," Central Foreign Policy Files 1967–1969, box 2266, RG 59, NARA; hereinafter cited as Hughes, "North Korea's Program for the Reunification of Korea."

12. Memo, F. Brewer, China and Korea Section, Research Department, "Kim Il Sung on the 'Liberation' of the Republic of Korea," 10 July 1968, FCO 21/307, PRO. INR noted that Kim Il Sung had begun referring to "active reunification" as early as 1965, but that the North Korean media had been using the phrase with increasing frequency since late 1966. See Hughes, "North Korea's Program for the Reunification of Korea." Suh noted that the speech went a "step farther" than any other speech Kim Il Sung had made on the South Korean revolution (*Kim Il Sung,* 230–31). Kim also said, "The present situation requires us to conduct all our work in a more active, more revolutionary manner and subordinate everything to the struggle to accomplish the South Korean revolution by giving them support in their struggle and to reunify the country."

13. See Sarantakes, "The Quiet War," for an excellent discussion of this turbulent period.

14. DIA point paper, Lt. Comdr. J. Clay, untitled, 17 June 1968, folder "Korea 1 May 1968–30 April 1969 091," Records of the U.S. Joint Chiefs of Staff, Records of Chairman (Gen.) Earle Wheeler, 1967–70, box 29, RG 218, NARA; hereinafter cited as Wheeler Records, NARA.

15. SNIE 14.2.67, LBJ.

16. CIA, Office of National Estimates, "Security Conditions in South Korea," report, 23 June 1967, *FRUS,* 258–95.

17. Suh, *Kim Il Sung,* 231–32.

18. SNIE 14.2-67, LBJ; CIA Directorate of Intelligence, "Intelligence Memo: North Korea's Military Forces," February 1968, file "Korea Codeword Vol. 1, 1966, 1968," NSF

Country Files, Asia and Pacific, box 256, LBJ; hereinafter cited as CIA Directorate of Intelligence, "Intelligence Memo: North Korea's Military Forces."

19. CIA Directorate of Intelligence, "Intelligence Memo: North Korea's Military Forces"; CINCPAC Command History, 1969, 4:131–33, NHC; message, COMUSFK, "Korean Situation, Status of Actions," 19 February 1968, provided in response to FOIA request to U.S. Eighth Army.

20. SNIE 14.2-67, LBJ; CIA Directorate of Intelligence, "Intelligence Memo: North Korea's Military Forces."

21. SNIE 14.2-67, LBJ.

22. Letter from Kim Sung Eun (ROK minister of national defense) to Denis Healey (British defense minister), 22 February 1968, FCO 21/347, PRO.

23. Annex to memo, Director of Central Intelligence, "The Likelihood of Major Hostilities in Korea," SNIE 14.2-68, 16 May 1968, folder "NIE 14.2-68," NSF Country Files, NIEs, box 5, LBJ.

24. CIA Directorate of Intelligence, "Intelligence Memo: North Korea's Military Forces"; CINCPAC Command History, 1969, 4:132, NHC.

25. CINCPAC 230509Z January 1968, "Defense Analysis: North Korean Air Force," 23 January 1968, Seventh Fleet Files, NHC. The military normally cites message traffic using a combination of originator and date-time group. The first two digits in the date-time group refer to the day of the month; the next four digits refer to the time (Zulu time zone) using the twenty-four-hour clock. Thus, CINCPAC transmitted the above message on 23 January at 0509 Zulu time. I use the convention of citing originator and date-time group to designate most of the military message traffic cited herein.

26. CIA Directorate of Intelligence, "Intelligence Memo: North Korea's Military Forces"; SNIE 14.2-67, LBJ.

27. Although the growth of the North Korean SAM inventory was impressive, U.S. aircrews were familiar with the far more daunting air defense environment over Vietnam. The North Vietnamese had 191 SA-2 sites, versus the DPRK's 20 sites. The DPRK was also less well endowed with antiaircraft artillery (AAA). A list of key AAA categories follows (within the parentheses, the first number represents the total number possessed by the DPRK; the second number is North Vietnam's total for each category): 37 mm (350/3,200); 57 mm (350/2,000); 85/100 mm (200/1,200). The North Koreans had constructed sixty-four early warning/ground-controlled intercept radar sites, but the North Vietnamese had three times as many. These numbers would suggest that once its MiGs were eliminated, North Korea would be a far less intimidating target for U.S. planners than was Vietnam. See Joint Staff briefing book, "Fact Book: EC-121 Shootdown in Sea of Japan," 20 April 1969, folder "091 Korea (BP) EC-121 Shootdown," Records of the U.S. JCS, Records of Chairman (Gen.) Earle Wheeler 1967–70, RG 218, NARA; hereinafter cited as JCS, "Fact Book: EC-121."

28. CIA Directorate of Intelligence, "Intelligence Memo: North Korea's Military Forces."

29. Ibid.

30. Greene, "State of Intelligence on North Korea."

31. Ibid.
32. Ibid.
33. Ibid.
34. Director of Central Intelligence, update to SNIE 14.2-67, LBJ.


## *Chapter 3.* A Risky Patrol?

1. HASC Report, 1632–33; Memo, Korea Task Force (W. Brown) to Secretary, "Fulbright Letter on USS *Pueblo*," 20 March 1968, folder "POL 33-6 KORN-US 3/15/68," Central Foreign Policy Files, box 2269, RG 59, NARA; hereinafter cited as "Fulbright Letter on USS *Pueblo*."

2. The fleet comprised USS *Oxford* (AGTR-1), USS *Georgetown* (AGTR-2), USS *Jamestown* (AGTR-3), USS *Belmont* (AGTR-4), USS *Liberty* (AGTR-5), USNS *Valdez* (TAG-169), and USNS *Muller* (TAG-171).

3. Memo, Paul Warnke, "The *Pueblo* Incident," 5 February 1968, file "*Pueblo* Top Secret," Robert S. McNamara Papers, RG 200, NARA; hereinafter cited as Warnke, "The *Pueblo* Incident."

4. Draft Report of the Special Subcommittee on the USS *Pueblo* of the House Armed Services Committee, forwarded as enclosure in letter from Congressman L. Mendel Rivers to Secretary of Defense Melvin Laird, 1 July 1969, folder "Double Zero—1969—*Pueblo*," Double Zero Files 1969, box 119, NHC, 18–20; hereinafter cited as Draft Report.

5. Ibid.

6. Armbrister, *Accountability*, 121; "Fulbright Letter on USS *Pueblo*."

7. Armbrister, *Accountability*, 119.

8. Ibid., 119–20.

9. HASC Report, 1639; Warnke, "The *Pueblo* Incident."

10. HASC Report, 1640–45.

11. "Fulbright Letter on USS *Pueblo*."

12. Message from General Bonesteel to General Wheeler, "North Korean Posture," 24 January 1968, *FRUS*, 313.

13. Memo, Al Jenkins to Walt Rostow, "Bonesteel's 'Eyes Only' of July 21," 26 July 1967, *FRUS*, 261; message from General Bonesteel to Admiral Sharp, "Situation in Korea as of Mid-July 1967," 21 July 1967, *FRUS*, 262–66.

14. "Fulbright Letter on USS *Pueblo*."

15. Memo for the U.S. Intelligence Board, 25 October 1967, cited as footnote in *FRUS*, 283.

16. "Fulbright Letter on USS *Pueblo*."

17. Gen. Charles H. Bonesteel III, oral history, taped November 1972, in U.S. Senior Officer Oral History microfiche collection, University Publications of America, 346; hereinafter referred to as Bonesteel oral history. Also see Armbrister, *Accountability*, 120.

18. Memo, "Summary Minutes of Meeting," 24 January 1968, *FRUS* 475.

19. Ibid., 474.

20. Armbrister, *Accountability*, 186, 192.

21. Memo, Deputy Director of Intelligence to Director of Central Intelligence, "JRC Monthly Reconnaissance Schedule for January 1968," 2 January 1968, NSF, NSC Historical Archives, *Pueblo* Crisis, box 28, LBJ.

22. Letter from Vice Adm. Harold Bowen, regarding "Court of Inquiry to inquire into the circumstances relating to the seizure of USS *Pueblo* (AGER 2) by North Korean Naval Forces, which occurred in the Sea of Japan on 23 January 1968, and the subsequent detention of the vessel and the officers and crew," 9 April 1969, 79, CDROM 1981100100086, microfiche 1981-438A (www.ddrs.psmedia.com), DDRS; hereinafter cited as Court of Inquiry Report.

23. HASC Report, 1650.

24. Ibid., 1651; Armbrister, *Accountability*, 188.

25. Armbrister, *Accountability*, 188; HASC Report, 1638.

26. Bonesteel oral history, 340, 343, 346, 347.

27. "Fulbright Letter on USS *Pueblo*"; draft statement for use by Director, DIA, in testimony before the *Pueblo* subcommittee of the House Armed Services Committee, 20 March 1969, DIA Archives.

28. Armbrister, *Accountability*, 189.

29. Ibid., 191–93.

30. Undated DIA internal memo regarding DIAAP-4 coordination on *Pueblo;* draft statement prepared for use of Director, DIA, in testimony before the *Pueblo* subcommittee of the House Armed Services Committee, 20 March 1969, 1–11, DIA Archives.

31. Draft statement for use by Director, DIA, in testimony before the *Pueblo* subcommittee of the House Armed Services Committee, 20 March 1969, 1–11, DIA Archives.

32. Ibid.

33. Ibid.

34. DIA memo, "DIA Procedures for U.S. Reconnaissance Operations," 14 February 1969; Draft Report, 47b–47c.

35. DIA memo, "DIA Procedures for U.S. Reconnaissance Operations," 14 February 1969.

36. Armbrister, *Accountability*, 187.

37. Draft statement for use by Director, DIA, in testimony before the *Pueblo* subcommittee of the House Armed Services Committee, 20 March 1969, 11; memo, DIAXX to DIAAP-2, "Information for DIADR on the *Pueblo*" (undated), DIA Archives.

38. Memo for the record, Peter Jessup to Mssrs. Katzenbach, Nitze, and Helms, "Telephonic Approval by the 303 Committee," 16 January 1968, and memo, DDI to DCI, "JRC Monthly Reconnaissance Schedule for January 1968," 2 January 1968 (hereinafter cited as "JRC Monthly Reconnaissance Schedule for January 1968"), both in folder "*Pueblo* Crisis 1968, vol. 3, Day-by-Day Documents, part 1," NSF, NSC Historical Archives, *Pueblo* Crisis, box 28, LBJ; HASC Report, 1646.

39. "JRC Monthly Reconnaissance Schedule for January 1968"; HASC Report, 1654–55.

40. Armbrister, *Accountability,* 196–97; see HASC Report, 1654–55, for the DIRNSA message.

41. HASC Report, 1655.

42. Ibid.; Court of Inquiry Report, paragraph 14.

43. "JRC Monthly Reconnaissance Schedule for January 1968."

44. HASC Report, 1622–23; Court of Inquiry report, paragraph 12.

45. Court of Inquiry Report, paragraph 12.

46. Editorial, "The *Pueblo* Warnings," *New York Times,* 27 January 1968.

47. The Naval Court of Inquiry stated: "The particular FBIS reports were not seen at CINCPACFLT headquarters, nor at COMNAVFORJAPAN headquarters prior to the seizure. On being shown these reports, however, after the fact, the consensus was that they were similar to numerous other reports received from FBIS and were not a direct threat to *Pueblo.*" (Court of Inquiry Report, paragraph 60); "Fulbright Letter on USS *Pueblo.*"

48. Memo, H. Kissinger to R. Nixon, "*Pueblo,*" 21 April 1969, folder "*Pueblo,*" National Security Council Files, box 379, Richard M. Nixon Collection, NARA.

49. Ibid.

50. Memo, appendix (enclosure 1) responding to Fulbright question no. 9, "Representative North Korean Statements on Sea Incursions," folder "*Pueblo* Crisis 68, vol. 10 —Fulbright letter folder 6," NSF, NSC Historical Archives, *Pueblo,* box 31, LBJ; untitled response to Fulbright question no. 8, in ibid., box 31, LBJ; memo, "North Korean Warnings Related to Spy Ships Prior to USS *Pueblo* Seizure," undated, DIA document 125646, DIA Archives.

51. Memo, British Foreign Office Far Eastern Department study, "Changes in the North Korean Workers' Party Leadership since 1966," 30 September 1970, FCO 21/774, PRO.

52. CIA Office of National Estimates, "Security Conditions in South Korea," 23 June 1967, *FRUS,* 257–59.

53. Memo from Cyrus Vance to LBJ, "The Objectives of My Mission," 20 February 1968, *FRUS,* 391.

54. Armbrister, *Accountability,* 33.

## *Chapter 4.* Playing Catch-up

1. Minutes prepared by Tom Johnson, "Notes of the President's Meeting with the Joint Chiefs of Staff," 29 January 1968, box 2, Tom Johnson Meeting Notes, LBJ.

2. HASC Report, 1640–42.

3. Armbrister, *Accountability,* 28.

4. Memo from N. Davis to W. Rostow, "*Pueblo* Incident," 24 January 1968, NSF Country Files, Asia and Pacific, box 257, LBJ; Armbrister, *Accountability,* 34; Eighth Army Tactical Operations Center Log, entries for 240310I, 240332I, and 240730I, January 1968, copy provided in response to FOIA request to U.S. Eighth Army.

5. CIA briefing package for high-level *Pueblo* advisory group chaired by former undersecretary of state George Ball, 5 February 1968, folder "*Pueblo* Crisis 1968, vol. 6, Day-by-Day Documents, part 10," NSF, NSC Historical Archives, *Pueblo* Crisis, boxes 29, 30, LBJ; Armbrister, *Accountability,* 30, 34.

6. 5AF [Fifth Air Force] FUCHU AS JAPAN 251012Z JAN 68, no subject, 25 January 1968, NSF Country Files, Asia and Pacific, box 257, LBJ.

7. Warnke, "The *Pueblo* Incident"; HASC Report, 1658–59, 1662.

8. Warnke, "The *Pueblo* Incident"; Oral History Interview no. 10 with Adm. U. S. Grant Sharp, 6 June 1970, typescript held by U.S. Naval Institute library.

9. Memo from N. Davis to W. Rostow, "*Pueblo* Incident," 24 January 1968, NSF Country Files, Asia and Pacific, box 257, LBJ; and Armbrister, *Accountability,* 34.

10. Warnke, "The *Pueblo* Incident"; HASC Report, 1658–59; originator unknown, "Analysis of Communications/Command/Control Functions involved in USS *Pueblo* Capture," 30 January 1968, folder "*Pueblo* TS," McNamara Papers, RG 200, NARA.

11. 5AF FUCHU AS JAPAN 251012Z JAN 68, no subject, folder "Korea *Pueblo* Incident vol. 1, pt. A," NSF Country Files, Asia and Pacific, box 257, LBJ.

12. National Military Command Center, memo for the record, "USAF Actions Related to USS *Pueblo* Incident," 30 January 1968, Korea Crisis Files ("*Pueblo* Crisis") 1968, box 8, RG 59, NARA; 5AF FUCHU AS JAPAN 251012Z JAN 68, no subject, NSF Country Files, Asia and Pacific, box 257, LBJ.

13. HASC Report, 1673.

14. Ibid.

15. Memo from Gen. Earle Wheeler to LBJ, "Aircraft Support to *Pueblo,*" 30 January 1968, folder "Korea *Pueblo* Incident vol. 1, pt. B," NSF Country Files, Asia and Pacific, box 257, LBJ.

16. U.S. State Department, "Chronology of Diplomatic Activity in *Pueblo* Crisis," entry for 29 April 1968, Research Project 924, October 1968, doc. 2713, fiche 226, 1999, DDRS; hereinafter cited as "Chronology."

17. CINCPACFLT 240008Z January 1968, "USS *Pueblo* Incident," 24 January 1968, folder "Korea—*Pueblo* Incident—Military Cables, vol. 1," NSF Country Files, Korea, boxes 263, 264, LBJ; hereinafter cited as CINCPACFLT 240008Z January 1968, "USS *Pueblo* Incident," 24 January 1968.

18. Ibid. The ships were sent to 32 degrees, 30 minutes north latitude, 127 degrees, 30 minutes east longitude; ADMIN [i.e., commander not present] CINCPAC 230909Z January 1968, "USS *Pueblo* Incident," 23 January 1968, folder "Korea—*Pueblo* Incident, vol. 1, pt. A," NSF Country Files, Asia and Pacific, box 257, LBJ.

19. CINCPACFLT 231021Z January 1968, folder "Korea—*Pueblo* Incident, vol. 1, pt. A," NSF Country Files, Asia and Pacific, box 257, LBJ.

20. CINCPACFLT 240008Z January 1968, "USS *Pueblo* Incident."

21. Ibid.

22. COMSEVENTHFLT 231434Z January 1968, "*Pueblo* Incident," 23 January 1968, folder "Korea—*Pueblo* Incident, vol. 1, pt. A," NSF Country Files, Asia and Pacific, box 257, LBJ.

23. Commander Task Group 77.5 message 231520Z January 1968, as cited in CINC-PACFLT 240008Z January 1968 (a chronology of events). The operations were to take place near 35 degrees, 30 minutes north latitude, 131 degrees east longitude.

24. CINCPACFLT 231638Z January 1968, as cited in CINCPACFLT 240008Z January 1968, "USS *Pueblo* Incident."

25. Telephone conversations cited in CINCPACFLT 240008Z January 1968, "USS *Pueblo* Incident."

26. ADMIN CINCPAC 232227Z January 1968, "*Pueblo* Incident," 23 January 1968, folder "Korea—*Pueblo* Incident, vol. 1, pt. A," NSF Country Files, Asia and Pacific, box 257, LBJ.

27. National Military Command Center [NMCC], memo for the record, "Current Information Concerning USS *Pueblo* Incident," 23 January 1968, folder "Korea—*Pueblo* Incident, vol. 1A, pt. A," NSF Country Files, Asia and Pacific, box 257, LBJ.

28. ADMIN CINCPAC 240340Z, "Operating Instructions for *Pueblo* Incident," 24 January 1968, folder "Korea—*Pueblo* Incident, vol. 1, pt. A," NSF Country Files, Asia and Pacific, box 257, LBJ.

29. USFK/USAEIGHT Seoul Korea 230717Z January 1968, "U.S. Navy Hydrographic Ship," 23 January, folder "Korea Crisis (*Pueblo*) Files, 1968," Office of the Executive Secretariat, box 4, RG 59, NARA; Eighth Army Tactical Operations Center Log, entry for 231715I, January 1968, copy provided in response to FOIA request to U.S. Eighth Army.

30. ADMIN CINCPAC 231102Z January 1968, "USS *Pueblo*," 23 January 1968, LBJ.

31. NMCC, memo for the record and Commander in Chief, United Nations Command [i.e., in Korea; hereinafter CINCUNC] 070820Z February 1968, folder "Korea—*Pueblo* Incident—Military Cables, vol. 2, 2/68–3/68," NSF Country Files, Korea, boxes 263, 264, LBJ.

32. CINCUNC 241240Z January 1968, "North Korean Posture," 24 January 1968, as cited in *FRUS*, 313–15.

33. Ibid.; Eighth Army Tactical Operations Center Log, entries for 232115I, 240045I, and 261115I, January 1968, copies provided in response to FOIA request to U.S. Eighth Army.

34. Originator unknown, "Analysis of Communications/Command/Control Functions involved in USS *Pueblo* Capture," 30 January 1968, folder "*Pueblo* TS," McNamara Papers, RG 200, NARA.

35. Minutes prepared by Tom Johnson, "Notes of Meeting," 23 January 1968, as cited in *FRUS*, 461.

36. Memo, "Summary Minutes of *Pueblo* Group, 24 January 1968"; memo, "Notes of the President's Meeting with the National Security Council," 24 January 1968; memo, "Meeting on Korea Crisis without President," 24 January 1968; memo, "Notes of the President's Meeting, 24 January 1968"; all reproduced in *FRUS*, 468–95.

37. Minutes prepared by Tom Johnson, "Notes on the President's Breakfast Meeting," 25 January 1968, Tom Johnson Meeting Notes, box 2, LBJ.

38. Ibid.

39. Minutes prepared by Tom Johnson, "Notes on the President's Luncheon Meeting," 25 January 1968, Tom Johnson Meeting Notes, box 2, LBJ.

40. Memo from Russell Murray to Secretary of Defense, "Record of Meeting on January 25, 1968," folder "*Pueblo* Incident 1968," McNamara Papers, RG 200, NARA.

41. Ibid.; CNO Briefing Notes, 29 January 1968, CNO Operations Summaries, January 1968, NHC.

42. Ibid.

43. Ibid.

44. Minutes prepared by Tom Johnson, "Notes on the President's Thursday Night Meeting on the *Pueblo* Incident," 25 January 1968, Tom Johnson Meeting Notes, box 2, LBJ.

45. Minutes prepared by Tom Johnson, "Notes of Meeting," 26 January 1968, *FRUS*, 521–29.

46. Comment by Richard Helms in "Notes of President's Luncheon Meeting," 25 January 1968, *FRUS*, 506.

47. Memo, "Summary Minutes of *Pueblo* Group," 24 January 1968, *FRUS*, 475; memo, "Meeting on Korean Crisis without President," 24 January 1968, *FRUS*, 491; memo, "Notes on the President's Thursday Night Meeting on the *Pueblo* Incident," 25 January 1968, *FRUS*, 517; memo, "Notes of the President's Friday Morning Meeting on the *Pueblo* Incident," 26 January 1968, *FRUS*, 522. For Black Shield vulnerability, see discussion of the reconnaissance option in "North Korea—USS *Pueblo* Incident," box 17, Clark Clifford Papers, LBJ. For background on the A-12 Oxcart, see "The Oxcart Story," *Studies in Intelligence* 26, no. 2 (1992): 1–22; Paul Crickmore, *Lockheed SR-71: The Secret Missions Exposed* (London: Osprey Aerospace, 1993), 331.

48. Memo from Director of Korean Task Force to Secretary of State, "Sixth Closed Meeting at Panmunjom," 15 February 1968, *FRUS*, 625; memo from DDI to INR, "Comments on Draft Contingency Plan for Airborne Reconnaissance of North Korea," 19 February 1968, folder "*Pueblo* Crisis, vol. 7, Day-by-Day Documents, part 13, folder 1," NSF, NSC Historical Archives, *Pueblo* Crisis, box 30, LBJ.

49. The reconnaissance variants of the Ryan Firebee target drone were designated AQM-34Ns (Model 147 series). Variants could fly either photo or signals intelligence missions. Flying programmed tracks, such drones flew more than 130 missions against unfriendly countries between 1967 and 1971 and were heavily involved in the war in Vietnam. After the EC-121 shootdown in April 1969, the U.S. Air Force developed the AQM-34Q (147TE), a SIGINT version of the high-altitude reconnaissance drone designated the AQM-34P (model 147T). The 147TE drones started flying operational missions in October 1970 and were confined to the DMZ or offshore; they did not overfly DPRK territory; see www.vectorsite.net (as of September 2002); COMUSFK 281214Z January 1968, folder "091 Korea—*Pueblo* 23 January 1968–7 February 1968, vol. 1," Wheeler Records, box 29, RG 218, NARA.

50. Memo from Russell Murray to Secretary of Defense, "Record of Meeting on January 25, 1968," folder "*Pueblo* Incident 1968," McNamara Papers, RG 200, NARA.

51. CINCPAC 300708Z January 1968, folder "Korea—*Pueblo* Incident—Military Cables, vol. 1," NSF Country Files, Korea, boxes 263, 264, LBJ.

52. CIA, "*Pueblo* Sitrep [situation report]," 24 January 1968, NSF Country Files, Asia and Pacific, box 257, LBJ.

53. CIA Directorate for Intelligence, "Preliminary Assessment of Blackshield Mission 6847 over North Korea," 29 January 1968, folder "*Pueblo* Crisis 1968, vol. 4, Day-by-Day Documents, pt. 5, folder 5," NSF, NSC Historical Archives, *Pueblo* Crisis, box 28, LBJ.

54. Ibid.; memo, Director, DIA, "Requirement for a Second Black Shield Mission over North Korea," 29 January 1968, NSF, Intelligence File "NRO," box 9, LBJ.

55. CIA Intelligence Information Cable, "Implications of Reported Relocation of USS *Pueblo*," 12 February 1968, doc. 0651, fiche 56, 1999, DDRS.

56. DIA 292112Z April 1969, "*Pueblo* Crisis 1968, vol. 21, Military Messages," NSF, NSC Historical Archives, *Pueblo* Crisis, box 37, LBJ.

57. CIA memo, "North Korean Intentions," 23 January 1968, doc. 2488, fiche 220, DDRS; CIA/DIA/State memo, "Reactions to Certain U.S. Activities," 28 January 1968, doc. 2465, fiche 218, 1998, DDRS. See Hughes, "North Korea's Program for the Unification of Korea," for the best contemporary assessment of trends in North Korean behavior from 1966 to 1968.

58. See response to Senator William Fulbright's question no. 9, folder "*Pueblo* Crisis, 1968, vol. 10, Fulbright Letter," and appendix entitled "Representative North Korean Statements on Sea Incursions," *Pueblo* Crisis, 1968, vol. 11, Background Documents, NSC Historical Archives, *Pueblo* Crisis, boxes 31, 32, LBJ. The *New York Times* editorialized on 27 January 1968 that the official North Korean press commentary should have warned the United States that *Pueblo* was about to be seized. However, intelligence agencies had assessed such "spy boat" media treatment as not unusual.

59. CIA briefing package for high-level *Pueblo* advisory group chaired by former undersecretary of state George Ball, 5 February 1968, folder "*Pueblo* Crisis 1968, vol. 6, Day-by-Day Documents, part 10," NSC Historical Archives, *Pueblo* Crisis, boxes 29, 30, LBJ.

60. CIA memo, "Confrontation in Korea," 24 January 1968, doc. 2489, fiche 220, 1998, DDRS.

61. U.S. State Department memo, "Communist Reactions to Various Possible Courses of Action with Respect to North Korea," 26 January 1968, doc. 0906, 1999, DDRS.

62. CIA intelligence memo, "North Korea's Foreign Trade," 26 January 1968, 1998, DDRS.

63. "Status of Merchant Shipping in North Korea," 31 January 1968, NSF Country Files, Asia and Pacific, box 257, LBJ.

64. CIA memo, "North Korea's Foreign Trade," 26 January 1968, 1998, DDRS.

65. Portions from INR note 67, 24 January 1968, as cited in *FRUS*, 478.

66. CIA, "*Pueblo* Sitrep"; Memo, "Notes of the President's Luncheon Meeting," 25 January 1968, *FRUS*, 506.

67. U.S. State Department, "The USS *Pueblo* Incident," Research Project 939-C, October 1968, doc. 2712, fiche 226, 1999 DDRS.

68. The enclosures describing this and the other nine options are in the folder "North Korea—USS *Pueblo* Incident," box 17, Clark Clifford Papers, LBJ. Further observations are in "North Korean Aggression and the *Pueblo* Incident—Possible Strategies," 1 March 1968, doc. 3272, fiche 282, 1999, DDRS.

69. Memo from Adm. T. H. Moorer to Secretary of the Navy, "Draft Message OPLAN," 25 January 1968, file "Korea (*Pueblo*) 21 February 68—volume 3," Wheeler Records, box 29, RG 218, NARA.

70. "Action No. 1—Advising Soviets of Actual and Possible Military Moves," in folder "North Korea—USS *Pueblo* Incident," Clark Clifford Papers, box 17, LBJ.

71. W. Rostow, "Report on Meeting of Advisory Group, January 29, 1968," 1 February 1968, folder "Material regarding Vietnam and *Pueblo,* January–February 1968," NSF, Walt Rostow Files, box 10, LBJ.

72. Ibid.

73. Ibid.

74. "Notes of the President's Meeting with the Democratic Congressional Leadership," 6 February 1968, doc. 569, fiche 48, 1990, DDRS.

## *Chapter 5.* Stand Down

1. CINCPAC 030154Z February 1968, "Actions Related to the Korean Situation," 3 February 1968, box Korea Crisis "*Pueblo* Crisis Files, 1968," Office of the Executive Secretariat, box 4, RG 59, NARA.

2. Ibid.

3. Ibid.

4. Ibid.

5. JCS briefing paper, undated, "Order of Battle of United States and North Korean Forces," folder "091 Korea (BP) EC-121 Shootdown," Wheeler Records, box 31, RG 218, NARA.

6. CINCUNC 070820Z February 1968, "Status Report," 7 February 1968, folder "Korea—*Pueblo* Incident—Military Cables, vol. 2, 2/68–3/68," NSF Country Files, Korea, boxes 263, 264, LBJ; COMSEVENTHFLT 250332Z January 1968, "Operation Order: Formation Star," NSF Country Files, Asia and Pacific, box 257, LBJ.

7. U.S. State Department memo, "Actions by the United States and Republic of Korea," 10 April 1968, doc. 2704, fiche 225, 1999, DDRS; JCS 271735Z January 1968, "Deployment of Submarines to Vicinity of North Korea," 27 January 1968, folder "Korea—*Pueblo* Incident—Military Cables, vol. 1," NSF Country Files, Korea, boxes 263, 264, LBJ.

8. Commander in Chief, Pacific Fleet, "Pacific Area Naval Operations Review," February 1968, Records of CINCPACFLT 1941–1975, series 6, box 33 NHC.

9. CINCPAC 251817Z January 1968, no subject, 25 January 1968, and CINCPAC

300708Z January 1968, both in folder "Korea—*Pueblo* Incident—Military Cables, vol. 1," NSF Country Files, Korea, boxes 263, 264, LBJ.

10.  U.S. Seventh Fleet, "Monthly Historical Summary," January 1968, and U.S. Seventh Fleet, "Monthly Historical Summary," February 1968, both in box "Seventh Fleet Summaries January–December 1968," NHC; hereafter cited as U.S. Seventh Fleet, "Monthly Historical Summary."

11.  CINCPACFLT, "Pacific Naval Operations Review," February 1968, Records of CINCPACFLT 1941–1975, series 6, box 33, NHC.

12.  Ibid.; U.S. Seventh Fleet, "Monthly Historical Summary," January 1968, NHC.

13.  Secretary of State, untitled message, 7 February 1968, Central Foreign Policy Files, box 2267, RG 59, NARA; CINCPACFLT, "Pacific Naval Operations Review," February 1968.

14.  CTG Seven Zero Pt Six 071615Z FEB 68, "Formation Star Sitrep 89," 7 February 1968, folder "Korea—*Pueblo* Incident—Military Cables, vol. 2, 2/68–3/68," NSF Country Files, Korea, boxes 263, 264, LBJ; message from British defense attaché Seoul, 8 February 1968, FCO 23/345, PRO.

15.  Armbrister, *Accountability,* 266.

16.  U.S. Seventh Fleet, "Monthly Historical Summary," February 1968, NHC.

17.  CINCPACFLT 220102Z Feb 1968, "Harassment by Soviet Ships in the Sea of Japan," 22 February 1968, folder "Korean Crisis—Military Documents, vol. 7 of 8, 1 of 2," Office of Executive Secretariat Files, box 8, RG 59, NARA; CINCPAC 300708Z January 1968, "Korean Sitrep as of 300300Z JAN 68," folder "Korea—*Pueblo* Incident—Military Cables, vol. 1," NSF Country Files, Korea, boxes 263, 264, LBJ; CIA, "*Pueblo* Sitrep No. 13," 27 January 1968, fiche 2490, 1998, DDRS.

18.  SECDEF [Secretary of Defense] 021704Z February 1968, untitled, 2 February 1968, folder "Korea—*Pueblo* Incident—Military Cables, vol. 2, 2/68–3/68," NSF Country Files, Korea, boxes 263, 264, NHC.

19.  U.S. State Department, Korea Task Force, "Situation Report, 1700 Hours EST, January 26, 1968," LBJ.

20.  CSAF [Chief of Staff, U.S. Air Force] 270200Z January 1968, folder "Korea—*Pueblo* Incident—Military Cables, vol. 1," LBJ. A table by Walt Rostow entitled "Movement of Combat Aircraft to Korea Following *Pueblo* Incident," in a memo to the president dated 25–31 January 1968, contains details of these deployments.

21.  Department of Defense, "FY 1968 Supplemental Summary of Requirements," table A, undated, fiche number 1999-61, DDRS; CINCUNC 070820Z February 1968, "Status Report," 7 February 1968, folder "Korea—*Pueblo* Incident—Military Cables, vol. 2, 2/68–3/68," NSF Country Files, Korea, boxes 263, 264, LBJ.

22.  CINCPAC 030154Z February 1968, "Actions Related to the Korean Situation," 3 February 1968, in folder "Korea Crisis (*Pueblo* Crisis) Files, 1968," Office of the Executive Secretariat, box 4, RG 59, NARA.

23.  Message from British embassy, Seoul, to Foreign and Commonwealth Office, 30 January 1968, FCO 23/344, PRO.

24. CINCPAC 310706Z January 1968 ("personal for" from Sharp to Wheeler), untitled, 31 January 1968, folder "091 (Korea) *Pueblo* Incident," Wheeler Records, box 29, RG 218, NARA.

25. CINCPAC 300708Z January 1968, folder "Korea—*Pueblo* Incident—Military Cables, vol. 1," NSF Country Files, Korea, boxes 263, 264, LBJ.

26. COMUSKOREA Seoul Korea 200505Z March 1968, "Korea 1 May 1968–30 April 1969," folder "091 Korea," box 29, RG 218, NARA.

27. CINCUNC 270230Z January 1968, "Additional HAWK Battalions for Korea," 27 January 1968, folder "Korea Crisis—Military Documents, vol. 7 of 8," Office of the Executive Secretariat, box 8, RG 59, NARA; CINCPAC 300708Z January 1968, folder "Korea—*Pueblo* Incident—Military Cables, vol. 1," NSF Country Files, Korea, boxes 263, 264, LBJ; message, COMUSKOREA, "Korea Situation, Status of Actions," 19 February 1968, document provided in response to FOIA request to U.S. Eighth Army.

28. CINCUNC 070820Z February 1968, "Status Report," 7 February 1968, folder "Korea—*Pueblo* Incident—Military Cables, vol. 2, 2/68–3/68," NSF Country Files, Korea, boxes 263, 264, LBJ.

29. Memo from N. Katzenbach to LBJ, 7 March 1968, NSF Country Files, Asia and Pacific, box 256, LBJ. The South Koreans were concerned also about force protection. Cyrus Vance, who traveled to South Korea as a "presidential envoy," would recall, "We often heard them comment on their inability to contain North Korean infiltration teams. The South Koreans are fearful that a North Korean strike/reconnaissance team will destroy some major economic facility, e.g., a refinery or a dam." See Vance, memo to President, 20 February 1968, doc. 1511, fiche 121, 1996, DDRS.

30. Memo from Harold Brown to Secretary of Defense, "USAF Force Deployability," 24 January 1968, folder "*Pueblo* Incident 1968," McNamara Papers, RG 200, NARA.

31. CINCPAC 300708Z January 1968, folder "Korea—*Pueblo* Incident—Military Cables, vol. 1," NSF Country Files, Korea, boxes 263, 264, LBJ.

32. JCS 252347Z January 1968, "Ammunition Diversion," and JCS 252334Z January 1968, "Diversion of Air Munitions," both dated 25 January 1968, in folder "Korea—*Pueblo* Incident—Military Cables, vol. 1," NSF Country Files, Korea, boxes 263, 264, LBJ.

33. CINCUNC 291000Z January 1968, "Status Report," 29 January 1968, NSF Country Files, Asia and Pacific, box 263, LBJ.

34. COMUSKOREA 260820Z January 1968, "War Reserve Shortages," 26 January 1968, Korea Crisis *Pueblo* Files, 1968, Office of Executive Secretariat, box 4, NARA.

35. Korea Working Group, "North Korean Aggression and the *Pueblo* Incident: Possible Strategies," 13 March 1968, folder "*Pueblo* Crisis, vol. 7, Day-by-Day Documents, pt. 14, folder 2," NSF, NSC Historical Archives, *Pueblo* Crisis, box 30, LBJ.

36. CINCPAC 300708Z January 1968, folder "Korea—*Pueblo* Incident—Military Cables, vol. 1," NSF Country Files, Korea, boxes 263, 264, LBJ; memo, Chairman, JCS, to Secretary of Defense, "Ground Munitions Pre-positioned War Reserve Stocks in Support of Korean Contingencies," 10 February 1968, folder "Korea 1 August 1967–30 April 1968," Wheeler Records, box 28, NARA.

37. Ibid.; CINCUNC 291000Z January 1968, "Status Report," 29 January 1968, NSF Country Files, Asia and Pacific, box 263, LBJ.

38. CINCUSARPAC [Commander in Chief, U.S. Army Pacific] 062348Z February 1968, "Combat Readiness of USAEIGHT," 6 February 1968, folder "091 Korea (*Pueblo*) 23 January 68–7 February 68, vol. 1," Wheeler Records, box 29, RG 218, NARA.

39. Ibid.

40. CINCUNC/COMUSFK 100214Z February 1968, NSF Country Files, Asia and Pacific, box 263, LBJ.

41. Department of State Historical Office, "The USS *Pueblo* Incident" (Research Project no. 939-C), October 1968, 10, folder "*Pueblo* Crisis 1968 vol. 1, Basic Study and Presidential Decisions," 16 December 1968, NSF, NSC Historical Archives, *Pueblo* Crisis, 1968, box 27, LBJ.

42. CINCPAC Command History, 1968, 4:232–33, NHC; "Chronology," 7 February 1968.

43. Memo, British embassy to Foreign Office, 18 March 1968, FCO 21/345, PRO.

44. Memo, "Record of Meeting between Prime Minister and LBJ at White House on 9 February 1968," and message from Wilson to Kosygin, 14 February 1968, both in FCO 21/345, PRO.

45. Internal Foreign Office memo, 18 February 1968, FCO 21/345, PRO.

46. Message from State to U.S. embassy, Moscow, no subject, 24 February 1968, *FRUS*, 642–44.

47. Message from U.S. embassy, Seoul, to State, "Eleventh Senior MAC Members Meeting at Panmunjom, March 9, 1968," 9 March 1968, *FRUS*, 656.

48. Memo from Director, Korea Task Force, to Undersecretary of State, "Next Steps on *Pueblo*," 4 March 1968, *FRUS*, 652.

49. "Chronology," 13 March 1968.

50. Memo from Director, Korea Task Force, to Undersecretary of State, "Possible Actions in the Event the North Koreans Announce that They Intend to Try the *Pueblo* Crew," 15 March 1968, *FRUS*, 668–69.

51. Memo from Director, Korea Task Force, to Secretary of State, "*Pueblo*—Policy Issues Raised at Second Meeting of Senior Representatives," 4 February 1968, *FRUS*, 600–603.

52. Ibid.

53. "Chronology," 5–6 February 1968.

54. Memo from Deputy Director for Operations, NMCC, "Movement of *Enterprise* (CVAN-65)," 6 February 1968, and memo from Deputy Director for Operations, NMCC, "Current Summary of Korean Situation," 6 February 1968, both in folder "POL 33-6 KORN-US," Central Foreign Policy Files 1967–69, box 2268, RG 59, NARA; "Chronology," 5 February 1968, quoting SECSTATE [Secretary of State] 060003Z February 1968, and 6 February 1968, citing SECSTATE 062010Z February 1968.

55. "Chronology," 8 February 1968.

56. "Chronology," 15 February 1968 and 24 February 1968; message from General

Bonesteel to Admiral Sharp, "Assurances to ROK," 8 February 1968, folder "Korea 1 August 1967–30 April 1968," Wheeler Records, box 28, RG 218, NARA.

57. CINCPAC 030154Z February 1968, "Actions Related to the Korean Situation," 3 February 1968, Korea Crisis *Pueblo* Files, 1968, Office of the Executive Secretariat, box 4, RG 59, NARA.

58. CINCPACFLT, "Pacific Area Naval Operations Review," February 1968, "Records of CINCPACFLT 1941–1975, series 6," box 33, NHC.

59. U.S. embassy, Seoul, 260255Z February 1968, folder "POL 33.6 KORN-US," Central Foreign Policy Files, box 2266, RG 59, NARA.

60. SECSTATE message, "Aircraft Carriers in the Sea of Japan," 9 March 1968, file "*Pueblo* Crisis 1968, vol. 15," NSF, NSC Historical Archives, *Pueblo* 1968, box 34, LBJ; CINCPACFLT, "Pacific Area Naval Operations Review," February 1968, box "Records of CINCPACFLT 1941–1975, series 6," box 33, NHC.

61. Korea Working Group, "North Korean Aggression and the *Pueblo* Incident: Possible Strategies," 13 March 1968, folder "*Pueblo* Crisis, vol. 7, Day-by-Day Documents, pt. 14, folder no. 2," NSF, NSC Historical Archives, *Pueblo* Crisis, box 30, LBJ.

62. U.S. embassy, Seoul, 120243Z MAR 98, "Deployment of CVA's in Sea of Japan," 12 March 1968, folder "POL 33-6 KORN-US 3/668," box 2268, RG 59, NARA.

63. CINCPAC Command History, 1968, 4:250–51, NHC.

64. SECSTATE message transmitted 23 November 1968, untitled, folder "*Pueblo* Crisis, 1968, vol. 15 (2 of 2)," NSF, NSC Historical Archives *Pueblo* 1968, box 34, LBJ.

## *Chapter 6.* Denouement

1. For an early example of North Korea's demands, see memo from Director, Korea Task Force, to Secretary of State, "Sixth Closed Meeting at Panmunjom," 15 February 1968, *FRUS*, 624–25.

2. Ibid.; letter from K. M. Wilford, British embassy, Washington, to Foreign Office, "U.S.S. *Pueblo*," 18 March 1968, FCO 21/345, PRO.

3. Message from U.S. embassy, Seoul, to State, "Summary of Sixteenth Senior Members Meeting at Panmunjom," 8 May 1968, *FRUS*, 683–84.

4. Memo from Deputy Assistant Secretary of State for East Asian and Pacific Affairs to Secretary of State, "Status of *Pueblo* Talks at Panmunjom," 4 September 1968, *FRUS*, 697–700; message from U.S. embassy, Seoul, to State, "23rd Senior MAC Members Closed Meeting at Panmunjom," 10 October 1968, *FRUS*, 717–18.

5. Memo from R. J. Smith (Deputy Director for Intelligence, CIA) to William Trueheart (INR), "Comments on Draft Contingency Plan for Airborne Reconnaissance of North Korea," folder "*Pueblo* Crisis, vol. 7, Day-by-Day Documents, pt. 13, folder 1," NSF, NSC Historical Archives, *Pueblo* Crisis, box 30, LBJ; message from Director, National Security Agency, to White House, 14 February, as discussed in "Notes of the President's Luncheon Meeting," 13 February 1968, *FRUS*, 622.

6. CIA field report, "Militant Mood of Students in North Korea," 3 May 1968; CIA field report, "North Korean Intentions to Attack South Korea and Thus Divert American Attention from Vietnam," 3 May 1968; memo from Walt Rostow to LBJ, 4 May, 1968, all in folder "Korean Memos and Cables, 1 of 2, vol. 6, 4/68–12/68," NSF Country Files, Asia and Pacific, box 256, LBJ; DCI, Special National Intelligence Estimate, "The Likelihood of Major Hostilities in Korea," SNIE 14.2-68, 16 May 1968, *FRUS*, 428–29; hereinafter cited as SNIE 14.2-68.

7. State Department report, "Situation in North Korea," 14 August 1968, *FRUS*, 440.

8. Memo from Brown to Katzenbach, untitled, 14 May 1968, *FRUS*, 431.

9. For example, another Black Shield reconnaissance mission flew on 18 February.

10. SNIE 14.2-68, 429.

11. Ibid., 428.

12. Ibid.

13. CINCPAC 030154Z February 1968, "Actions Related to the Korean Situation," 3 February 1968, Korea Crisis *Pueblo* Files, 1968, Office of Executive Secretariat, box 4, RG 59, NARA.

14. CINCPAC Command History, 1969, 4:146–47, NHC.

15. Message from U.S. embassy, Seoul, to CINCPAC, 16 April 1968, *FRUS*, 418.

16. CINCPAC Command History, 1969, 4:254, NHC.

17. CINCPAC Command History, 1968, 4:248–50, NHC.

18. JCS, "Fact Book: EC-121"; DOD Document, "FY 1968 Supplemental Summary of Requests," 10 April 1968, DDRS CDROM 199030100705, microfiche 1999-61, DDRS.

19. DCI, annex to Special National Intelligence Estimate, "The Likelihood of Major Hostilities in Korea" (SNIE 14.2-68), 16 May 1968, *FRUS*, 432. Some units grew; for example, the headquarters element of USFK doubled in size!

20. CINCPAC Command History, 1968, 4:246, NHC.

21. DOD, Status Report, 11 November 1968, DDRS, CDROM ID 1995010100052, microfiche 1995-7, DDRS.

22. CINCPAC Command History, 1968, 4:222, NHC. Started in October 1967, the program was called the "Counterinfiltration-Counterguerilla Concept and Requirement Plan" (CIGOREP).

23. CINCPAC Command History, 1968, 4:212–13, NHC.

24. Message from U.S. embassy, Seoul, to CINCPAC, 16 April 1968, *FRUS*, 418.

25. CINCPAC Command History, 1968, 2:195, NHC.

26. Revenues and food gained from fishing had dropped substantially after the DPRK seized *Pueblo*. An August 1968 CIA field report stated that the North was no longer fishing in international waters because it feared the United States would seize the ships. The United States may have elected to play on these fears by hinting about its interest in the fish factory ships under construction. CIA field report, "North Korean Fears of Fishing in International Waters and Plans for Improving Fishing Industry," 10 August 1968, folder "Volume 12 CIA documents," NSF, NSC Historical Archives, *Pueblo*

Crisis, box 32, LBJ; message from State to U.S. embassy, The Hague, untitled, 11 September 1968, LBJ; memo from Jenkins to Rostow, 10 September 1968, footnote in *FRUS*, 719.

27. Message from State to U.S. embassy, Seoul, "Instructions for Twenty-fourth Meeting," 12 October 1968, *FRUS*, 719.

28. Message from State to U.S. embassy, The Hague, "NY Times Story on Verolme Factory Ships for North Korea," 26 November 1968, file "*Pueblo* Crisis, vol. 19, Telegrams to Posts Other than Seoul," NSF, NSC Historical Archives, *Pueblo* Crisis, boxes 36, 37, LBJ.

29. Mitchell Lerner, *The* Pueblo *Incident: A Spy Ship and the Failure of American Foreign Policy* (Kansas: University of Kansas Press, 2002), 210–13.

30. Memo from Undersecretary of State to LBJ, "Exercise Focus Retina," 23 October 1968, folder "*Pueblo* Crisis, vol. 8, Day-by-Day Documents, pt. 17, folder no. 5," NSF, NSC Historical Archives, *Pueblo* Crisis, box 30, LBJ.

31. Message from State to U.S. embassy, Seoul, untitled, 23 November 1968, NSF Histories, *Pueblo*—1968," box 34, LBJ; memo from Winthrop Brown (East Asia) to Secretary of State, "Naval Maneuvers in the Sea of Japan—Action Memo," 25 November 1968, folder "Military 1969 Military Operations," subject files of Office of Korean Affairs 1966–1974, Office of Executive Secretariat, box 3, RG 59, NARA. The U.S. Navy had not abandoned the Sea of Japan. A naval antisubmarine warfare group operated there between 2 and 9 June 1968, and USS *Hancock* operated there briefly in early December 1968.

32. Message from State to U.S. embassy, Seoul, "Instructions for Twenty-sixth Meeting," 11 December 1968, *FRUS*, 731–32.

33. Ibid.; CNO Briefing Notes for 21 November, 22 November, and 2 December 1968, CNO Flag Plot Operations Summaries/Briefing Notes, September–November 1968, box 28, NHC.

34. Memo from Undersecretary of State to LBJ, "USS *Pueblo*," 3 December 1968, *FRUS*, 726–27.

35. Message from State to U.S. embassy, Seoul, "Instructions for Twenty-sixth Meeting," 11 December 1968, *FRUS*, 731–34.

36. Memo from Undersecretary of State to LBJ, "USS *Pueblo*," 3 December 1968, *FRUS*, 726–27.

37. Message from State to U.S. embassy, Seoul, "Instructions for Twenty-sixth Meeting," 11 December 1968, *FRUS*, 731–34.

38. Editor's comments in *FRUS*, 740–41.

39. Armbrister, *Accountability*, 345.

40. Memo from Brown to Rusk, untitled, 23 December 1968, *FRUS*, 744.

41. CINCPAC Command History, 1969, 4:170–71, quoting J3 Brief, 46-69, HQ CINCPAC 8 March 1969, "Courses of Action concerning USS *Pueblo* JCSM-115-69," NHC; Ambassador Charles Bohlen to Secretary of State, "Military Operations off North Korea—Information Memo," 10 January 1969, folder "Military Operations 1969," subject files of Office of Korean Affairs, 1966–74, State Department, Office of Executive Secretariat, box 3, RG 59, NARA.

42. CNO Briefing Notes for 30 January, 5 February, 6 February, 11 February, and 12

February 1968, CNO Flag Plot Operations Summaries/Briefing Notes, January and February 1968, NHC.

43. Memo, "Ball Committee on the USS *Pueblo* Incident, Terms of Reference," undated, *FRUS*, 590–91.

44. Telephone conversation between LBJ and George Ball, 7 February 1968, *FRUS*, 613.

45. George W. Ball, *The Past Has Another Pattern: Memoirs* (New York: W. W. Norton, 1982), 436; memo for the record, "The Ball Report," 7 February 1968, *FRUS*, 614–15. The memo also mentioned that the President's Foreign Intelligence Advisory Board (PFIAB) was investigating certain aspects of the *Pueblo* incident. *Pueblo* was to be a "top priority" topic at the next PFIAB meeting, whose principal aim would be to determine the scope of any *Pueblo* incident reports that the intelligence community might undertake. The memo also mentioned that a group called the "Eaton Board" was studying the "many kinds of intelligence activities in which *Pueblo* was engaged."

46. U.S. House Armed Services Committee, *Hearings before the Special Subcommittee on the USS* Pueblo, HASC 91-101 (Washington, D.C.: U.S. Government Printing Office, 1969), 903; hereinafter cited as HASC Hearings.

47. Ibid.; memo from General Wheeler to Director, Joint Staff, "Possible Responses to North Korean Attack on the Republic of Korea," 19 April 1968, folder "Korea 1 August 1967–30 April 1968," Wheeler Records, box 28, RG 218, NARA.

48. Testimony prepared for use by Director, DIA, before HASC special subcommittee, March 1969, DIA Archives.

49. HASC Hearings, 903.

50. See draft response to Deputy Secretary of Defense attached to memo from EA and Naval Aide to Assistant Secretary of the Navy, "Response to Mr. Packard's Questions of 14 March on *Pueblo*," 18 April 1969, Double Zero Files, *Pueblo*, NHC.

51. Tab H, "Criteria and Procedures for Tasking Intelligence Collection Ships," as attached to ibid.

52. CINCPACFLT endorsement of report by Naval Court of Inquiry on *Pueblo*, 10 June 1969, DDRS. CINCPACFLT outlined several administrative changes in its endorsement of recommendation 4 (that procedures for risk assessment be improved at all levels of authority), 2. Theater guidance for mission approval and support was published in a CINCPAC letter signed on 23 December 1968 and in CINCPACFLT Instruction 003120.28. Memo from EA to Secretary of Navy, "Response to Mr. Packard's Questions of 14 March on *Pueblo*," 18 April 1969, Double Zero Files, *Pueblo*, NHC.

53. CINCPACFLT endorsement of report by Naval Court of Inquiry, 10 June 1969, DDRS. The endorsement notes that CINCPACLT operations order (OPORD) 304-69 contains this requirement.

54. Memo from Adm. B. Clarey to DCNO (Fleet Operations and Readiness), "*Pueblo* Follow-up," 21 May 1969, Double Zero Files, *Pueblo*, NHC.

55. Ibid.

56. HASC Hearings, 910–11.

57. James Ennes, *Assault on the* Liberty (New York: Ivy Books, 1979), 234–36.

58. HASC Report, 1677.

59. Letter from Political Adviser, CINCPAC, to Deputy Assistant Secretary of State, East Asian and Pacific Affairs, W. Brown, 7 August 1968, folder "Military 1968 ROE," subject files, Office of Korean Affairs 1966–74, Office of Executive Secretariat, box 1, RG 59, NARA.

60. Letter from Chargé d'Affaires, U.S. embassy, Seoul, to Country Director for Korea, 24 September 1969, folder "Military 1969 ROE," subject files, Office of Korean Affairs, Office of Executive Secretariat, box 3, RG 59, NARA.

61. Attachment to letter from Assistant Secretary of Defense for International Security Affairs to W. Brown, 28 August 1968, subject files, Office of Korean Affairs, Office of Executive Secretariat, box 3, RG 59, NARA.

62. Memo from Undersecretary of State to LBJ, "Review of United States Policy toward Korea: Status Report," 23 December 1968, *FRUS*, 455–57.

## *Chapter 7.* Round Two

1. Joint Staff reference aid, "Order of Battle of U.S. and North Korean Forces," folder "091 Korea (BP) EC-121 Shootdown," Wheeler Records, box 31, RG 218, NARA; Korean Central News Agency English-language broadcast, 18 April 1969, as monitored by British Broadcasting Corporation.

2. VQ-1 Command History, 1969, 8, NHC.

3. Robert Jackson, *High Cold War* (Somerset, England: Patrick Stephens, 1998), 96.

4. Testimony by General Wheeler and General Steakley, HASC Hearings, 907 and 923, respectively; Armbrister, *Accountability,* 118.

5. Untitled DIA background document prepared to support the director's testimony to the HASC subcommittee in March 1969, DIA Archives. In January 1967, three missions elicited reactions; in February 1967, two missions; and in March 1967, two missions. CINCPACFLT, "Fleet Operations Review, April 1969," Double Zero Files, NHC.

6. CIA Directorate of Intelligence, "Intelligence Memo: North Korea's Military Forces."

7. Testimony by General Steakley, HASC Hearings, 923.

8. Memo, "Summary Minutes of *Pueblo* Group," 24 January 1968, *FRUS*, 475.

9. DIA memo for the Joint Reconnaissance Center, "Possible North Korean Reactions to Daytime Peripheral Reconnaissance Flights," 26 December 1967, DIA Archives.

10. General Wheeler's testimony, HASC Hearings, 907, 919–20.

11. Ibid.

12. Testimony prepared for use by Director, DIA, before HASC subcommittee, March 1969, DIA Archives.

13. Memo of Conversation, "Korea," 20 November 1968, *FRUS*, 449–54. SNIE 14.2-69 is summarized as a footnote in *FRUS*, 452.

14. U.S. embassy, Seoul, 060908Z February 1969, "Internal Security: Continued Lull in North Korean Infiltration," folder "POL 23-7 1/1/69," Central Foreign Policy Files 1967–1969, box 2218, RG 59, NARA.

15. Memo from Assistant Director for Intelligence Production, untitled, forwarding sanitized version of General Carroll's statement, 20 March 1969, DIA Archives; DIA memo for the Joint Reconnaissance Center, "Possible North Korean Reactions to Daytime Peripheral Reconnaissance Flights," 26 December 1967, DIA Archives.

16. This paragraph estimates how the EC-121 mission was approved using the detailed discussion of reconnaissance validation contained in the sanitized version of General Carroll's statement before the HASC subcommittee, 20 March 1969, DIA Archives.

17. CINCPAC 220213Z April 1969, "Plan for Protection of Reconnaissance Aircraft in Korea Area," 22 April 1969, folder "091 Korea (BP) EC-121," Wheeler Records, box 31, RG 218, NARA.

18. Sanitized version of General Carroll's statement before the HASC subcommittee, 20 March 1969, DIA Archives.

19. JCS, "Fact Book: EC-121."

20. Ibid.; HASC Report, 1677.

21. JCS, "Fact Book: EC-121."

22. Ibid.

23. HASC Report, 1675.

24. VQ-1 Command History 1969, 28 February 1970, 8, NHC.

25. Draft version of HASC Report, 47c, NHC.

26. Armbrister, *Accountability,* 193.

27. Message from Mr. Freeman, British embassy, Washington, to Foreign Office, 23 April 1969, FCO 21/617, PRO.

28. Suh, *Kim Il Sung,* 231.

29. Ibid., 240–44.

30. Ibid., 239–44; Foreign Office Far Eastern Section, Research Department, "Changes in the North Korean Workers' Party Leadership since 1966," 30 September 1970, FCO 21/774, PRO. The State Department's Bureau of Intelligence and Research also cited the turbulence among the DPRK political elite. It pointed out that in November 1968, the defense minister was replaced and two other high-echelon party leaders with military and anti-ROK subversive responsibilities were removed. This purge was significant because it appeared to have occurred within Kim Il Sung's own faction as a result of policy differences and/or personal infighting. See INR, "North Korea: Party Purges Military Officials," 17 April 1969, Central Foreign Policy Files 1967–69, box 2281, RG 59, NARA.

31. Nixon, *RN,* 383.

32. CINCPAC Command History, 1969, 4:133, NHC.

33. Bonesteel oral history.

34. CINCPAC Command History, 1969, 4:133, NHC; U.S. Seventh Fleet, "Monthly Historical Summary," April 1969, 78, NHC.

35. HASC Report, 1675–79.

36. JCS, "Fact Book: EC-121"; FAIRECONRON One (VQ-1) 151416Z April 1969, "Navy Preliminary and Supplementary Message Report of Aircraft Accident," 15 April 1969, Double Zero Files 1969, NHC.

37. COMSEVENTHFLT 240151Z April 1969, "EC-121M Shootdown/SAR," 24 April 1969, folder "091 Korea (BP) EC-121 Shootdown," box 31, RG 218, NARA.

38. HASC Report, 1678–80; see also "Early Tests in Asia," in Kissinger, *White House Years.*

39. Ibid.

40. COMSEVENTHFLT 240151Z April 1969, "EC-121M Shootdown/SAR," 24 April 1969, folder "091 Korea (BP) EC-121 Shootdown," box 31, RG 218, NARA; HASC Report (draft); President Nixon, "The President's News Conference of April 18, 1969," *Public Papers of the Presidents, Richard Nixon, 1969* (Washington, D.C.: U.S. Government Printing Office, 1971), 155–56; ADMIN CINCPAC 151113Z April 1969, "Reconnaissance Plane Shootdown," 15 April 1969, Double Zero Files 1969, NHC.

41. Nixon, *RN,* 383. See also text of Richard Nixon press conference in *Weekly Compilation of Presidential Documents,* 21 April 1969, vol. 5, no. 16 (Washington, D.C.: Government Printing Office, 1969). See Kissinger, "Early Tests in Asia," in *White House Years;* DOD press release of 16 April 1969, as cited in State Department Historical Studies Division, "North Korean Downing of a U.S. Reconnaissance Plane: The EC-121 Incident, April 1969" (Research Project no. 964), October 1969, 2, folder "History Office Research Projects 1969–1974," Office of Executive Secretariat, box 6, RG 59, NARA; hereinafter cited as "The EC-121 Incident."

42. Seymour Hersh, *Kissinger: The Price of Power* (London: Faber and Faber, 1983), 69. In a Top Secret assessment produced four months after the shootdown, the CIA revealed no doubts that the attack was deliberate. It characterized the *Pueblo* seizure and the shootdown as "acts of political warfare" and judged that there was "little prospect" that Kim Il Sung would "abandon the political strategy" that produced the incidents. See CIA Intelligence Memo, "North Korean Political Strategy," 8 August 1969, available on the CIA's website as of 20 July 2003 (http://www.cia.gov).

43. See North Korean air order of battle chart dated 15 January 1969 in Joint Staff reference aid, "Order of Battle of U.S. and North Korean Forces," folder "091 Korea (BP) EC-121 Shootdown," Wheeler Records, box 31, RG 218, NARA.

44. See the Federation of Atomic Scientists' web page (www.fas.org as of September 2002) for additional MiG-21 specifications.

45. U.S. Seventh Fleet, "Monthly Historical Summary," April 1969, 62, NHC.

46. North Korean air order of battle chart dated 15 January 1969, in Joint Staff reference aid, "Order of Battle of U.S. and North Korean Forces," folder "091 Korea (BP) EC-121 Shootdown," Wheeler Records, box 31, RG 218, NARA.

47. CINCPAC 220213Z April 1969, "Plan for Protection of Reconnaissance Aircraft in Korea Area," 22 April 1969, in Wheeler Records, box 31, RG 218, NARA.

48. JCS, "Fact Book: EC-121."

49. For example, see KCNA 151000Z April 1969, as quoted by the BBC Monitoring Service.

50. Colonel Haig reported that USS *Tucker* had found two bodies and fuselage sections damaged by cannon and machine guns. Memo from Haig to Henry Kissinger, "Staff Meeting Items," 17 April 1969, Haig Chronological File, NSC Files, box 956, Nixon Collection, NARA; "The EC-121 Incident," 3. USS *Dale* 170750Z April 1969, Double Zero Files 1969, NHC reported that the search ships found two fuselage sections that had bullet holes.

51. CINCPACFLT, "Fleet Operations Review," April 1969, 20–21, NHC; COMSEVENTHFLT 151230Z April 1969, "PARPRO," 15 April 1969, Double Zero Files 1969, NHC, re PARPRO cancellation; CTF Nine Six 150915Z April 1969, "Tactical Surveillance Ops," 15 April 1969, Double Zero Files 1969, NHC.

52. Testimony by General Wheeler, HASC Hearings, 904. A memo from James Murray for the British secretary of state ("Notes for Cabinet Meeting," 23 April 1969, FCO 21/617, PRO; hereinafter Murray memo) also mentioned there was no evidence that North Korea planned additional provocations.

53. Murray memo.

54. U.S. Information Service, London press release, "U.S. Statement at Panmunjom, 18 April 1969," 21 April 1969, FCO 21/617, PRO.

55. Pyongyang Home Service 150655Z April 1969, and KCNA at 151000Z April 1969. These and all subsequent translations are in the BBC Monitoring Service *Daily Reports*, April 1969.

56. Pyongyang Home Service 172200Z April 1969, and KCNA 190433Z April 1969.

57. Pyongyang Home Service 162103Z April 1969.

58. KCNA 151000Z April 1969.

59. Pyongyang Home Service 172200Z April 1969.

60. KCNA 231035Z April 1969, and Pyongyang Home Service 231000Z April 1969.

61. KCNA 230114Z April 1969.

62. Messages from British embassy, Seoul, to Foreign and Commonwealth Office dated 17–18 April 1969, FCO 21/617, PRO. Text of North Korean MAC statement contained in message from British embassy, Seoul, to Foreign and Commonwealth Office, 30 April 1969, FCO 21/617, PRO.

## *Chapter 8.* A Tentative Response

1. Several sources discuss the national-level decision-making process after the EC-121 shootdown. See H. R. Haldeman, *The Haldeman Diaries* (New York: Berkeley Books, 1995); Haldeman, *Ends of Power* (New York: Times Books, 1978); Nixon, *RN;* Kissinger, *White House Years;* Alexander Haig, *Inner Circles: How America Changed the World* (New York: Warner Books, 1992); and Hersh, *Price of Power.*

2. JCS 151702Z April 1969, as cited in JCS 160210Z April 1969, "Movement of CVA

Task Forces," Wheeler Records, box 31, RG 218, NARA; hereinafter cited as JCS 160210Z April 1969, "Movement of CVA Task Forces."

3. CINCPAC, Command History, 1969, 4:140, NHC.

4. JCS 160210Z April 1969, "Movement of CVA Task Forces."

5. Report, U.S. Seventh Fleet, "Monthly Historical Summary," April 1969, 1, 53, NHC; CINCPAC Command History, 1969, 4:141, NHC.

6. CINCPACFLT, "Fleet Operations Review," April 1969, 21, NHC; USS *New Jersey* 172140Z April 1969, "Weekly Narrative 11–17 Apr 1969," 17 April 1969, Double Zero Files 1969, NHC. The navy operations staff seemed skeptical about the need for naval gunfire support. N33 (a subordinate of the vice CNO) sent a memo to the CNO noting that "intel" had not found lucrative targets any closer than Wonsan. Operating off Wonsan, *New Jersey* would be vulnerable to antishipping missiles and more likely to come under air attack. Handwritten note from N33 to 00, 15 April 1969, Double Zero Files 1969, NHC.

7. U.S. Seventh Fleet, "Monthly Historical Summary," April 1969, 59, NHC; COM-SEVENTHFLT 190442Z April 1969, "Contingency Ops," 19 April 1969, Double Zero Files 1969, NHC.

8. U.S. Seventh Fleet, "Monthly Historical Summary," April 1969, 54, NHC.

9. Memo for the record from Haig to Kissinger, untitled, 21 April 1969, Haig Chronological File, NSC Files, box 956, Nixon Collection, NARA.

10. CINCPAC Command History, 1969, 4:140, NHC.

11. Joint Staff Point Paper, "EC-121M Incident in Sea of Japan," 15 April 1969, Wheeler Records, box 31, RG 218, NARA.

12. JCS 191348Z April 1969, "Improved Posture of PACOM Air Forces," 19 April 1969, folder "Chairman's Messages 1 January 1969–30 April 1969," Wheeler Records, box 161, RG 218, NARA.

13. Ibid.; CINCPAC 200710Z April 1969, "Force Posture," 20 April 1969; JCS 201803Z April 1969, "Force Posture," 20 April 1969; and JCS 200035Z April 1969, "Preparatory Actions," 20 April 1969, all in folder "Chairman's Messages 1 January 1969–30 April 1969," Wheeler Records, box 161, RG 218, NARA.

14. CINCUNC 150851Z April 1969, Double Zero Files 1969, NHC; CINCPAC 200036Z April 1969, "Force Posture," 20 April 1969, Double Zero Files 1969, NHC.

15. CINCPAC 200447Z April 1969, "Operational Readiness," 20 April 1969, folder "Chairman's Messages 1 January 1969–30 April 1969," Wheeler Records, box 161, RG 218, NARA.

16. CINCPAC Command History, 1969, 4:134–35, NHC.

17. Information paper entitled "Aircraft Shelter Program for Korea," in JCS, "Fact Book: EC-121."

18. CINCPAC 200036Z April 1969, "Force Posture," 20 April 1969, folder "Chairman's Messages 1 January 1969–30 April 1969," Wheeler Records, box 161, RG 218, NARA.

19. Message from British embassy, Seoul, to Foreign and Commonwealth Office, 17 April 1969, FCO 21/617, PRO; "The EC-121 Incident," 4.

20. JCS 192355Z April 1969, "Preparatory Actions," 19 April 1969, and JCS 210035Z April 1969, "Preparatory Actions," both in folder "Chairman's Messages 1 January 1969–30

April 1969," Wheeler Records, box 161, RG 218, NARA; CNO Briefing Notes/Operations Summary for 21 May 1969, CNO Briefing Notes, May 1969, NHC.

21. See Kissinger, *White House Years,* 315–16. The minutes of the NSC's deliberations after the EC-121 was shot down remain classified, although much of the resulting NSC message traffic is in the public domain. Consequently, much of this section is based on memoirs and secondary sources.

22. Ibid., 320.

23. Ibid., 315.

24. Memo from Col. R. Pursely to Henry Kissinger, untitled, 15 April 1969, file "091 Korea (BP) EC-121 Shootdown," box 31, RG 218, NARA.

25. Memo from R. Robinson to General Wheeler, untitled, 15 April 1969, folder "091 Korea (BP) EC-121 Shootdown," box 31, RG 218, NARA.

26. "The EC-121 Incident," 5–6.

27. Kissinger, *White House Years,* 317.

28. Ibid.

29. "The EC-121 Incident," 7.

30. Ibid.

31. Ibid., 7–9. State's history concluded, however, that in this meeting U.S. decision makers ruled out retaliation: "It was implicit from the discussion that no military action would be taken." See Kissinger, *White House Years,* 317.

32. Nixon, *RN,* 474.

33. Hersh, *Price of Power,* 731.

34. Haig, *Inner Circles,* 207.

35. Haldeman, *Haldeman Diaries,* 63; probable State Department chronology of crisis, "EC-121 Shootdown: A Chronology," undated, Office of Executive Secretariat, History Office Research Projects, 1967–79, box 6, RG 59, NARA; memo from Haig to Kissinger, "Wrap-up of Latest Data on Korean Incident," 16 April 1969, Haig Chronological File, NSC Files, box 956, Nixon Collection, NARA.

36. Haldeman, *Haldeman Diaries,* 64.

37. Kissinger, *White House Years,* 319.

38. Memo from Haig to Kissinger, "Status Report of Actions Taken to Provide to the President," 17 April 1969, Haig Chronological File, NSC Files, box 956, Nixon Collection, NARA.

39. Memo (originator unknown), "Question of Legal Justification for United States Forcible Action against North Korean Military Establishment," 17 April 1969, Office of Executive Secretariat, History Office Research Projects, 1967–79, box 6, RG 59, NARA.

40. CINCPAC 160840Z April 1969, "Movement of CVA Task Forces," 16 April 1969, folder "091 Korea (BP) EC-121 Shootdown," Wheeler Records, box 31, RG 218, NARA.

41. Ibid.

42. Hersh, *Price of Power,* 72.

43. JCS, "Fact Book: EC-121."

44. Ibid.

45. U.S. Seventh Fleet, "Monthly Historical Summary," April 1969, 62, NHC.

46. CINCPAC 170223Z April 79 ("personal for" message from CINCPAC to CJCS), no subject, 17 April 1969, folder "091 Korea (BP) EC-121 Shootdown," Wheeler Records, box 31, RG 218, NARA.

47. CINCPAC Command History, 1969, 4:143, NHC.

48. U.S. Seventh Fleet, "Monthly Historical Summary," April 1969, 63, NHC; JCS 212304Z April 1969, "Reconnaissance of North Korea," 21 April 1969, Double Zero Files 1969, NHC.

49. JCS 171415Z April 1969, "Retaliatory Plan," 17 April 1969, folder "Chairman's Messages 1 January 1969–30 April 1969," Wheeler Records, box 161, RG 218, NARA.

50. JCS 182047Z April 1969, "Retaliatory Plan," 18 April 1969, folder "Chairman's Messages 1 January 1969–30 April 1969," Wheeler Records, box 161, RG 218, NARA.

51. U.S. Seventh Fleet, "Monthly Historical Summary," April 1969, 63, NHC.

52. CINCPAC Command History, 1969, 4:143, NHC; memo, "Alternative Responses, EC-121 Shootdown," 17 April 1969, folder "EC-121 Shootdown," Wheeler Records, box 31, RG 218, NARA.

53. JCS 032255Z June 1969, and JCS 041630Z June 1969, both in Wheeler Records, box 31, RG 218, NARA.

54. CINCPAC Command History, 1969, 4:44, NHC; CINCPAC 170745Z April 1969, "Talos Shoot," 17 April 1969, folder "Chairman's Messages 1 January 1969–30 April 1969," Wheeler Records, box 161, RG 218, NARA.

55. CINCPAC 170745Z April 1969, "Talos Shoot," 17 April 1969, Wheeler Records, RG 218, NARA; U.S. Seventh Fleet, "Monthly Historical Summary," April 1969, 75–76, NHC; JCS 191535Z April 1969, "Use of Talos Ship," 19 April 1969, folder "Chairman's Messages 1 January 1969–30 April 1969," Wheeler Records, box 161, RG 218, NARA.

56. CINCPAC 190114Z April 1969, "Seizure of Korean Fish Factory Ship," 19 April 1969, folder "Chairman's Messages 1 January 1969–30 April 1969," Wheeler Records, box 161, RG 218, NARA.

57. Memo from Director, Joint Staff, to CJCS, "Seizure of North Korean Fish Factory Ships," 25 April 1969, folder "EC-121 Shootdown," Wheeler Records, box 31, RG 218, NARA; JCS 262010Z April 1969, "Seizure of [redacted]," 26 April 1969, folder "Chairman's Messages 1 January 1969–30 April 1969," Wheeler Records, box 161, RG 218, NARA.

58. Probable State Department chronology of crisis, "EC-121 Shootdown: A Chronology," undated, Office of Executive Secretariat, History Office Research Projects, 1967–79, box 6, RG 59, NARA.

59. "The EC-121 Incident," 11–13, 19–20.

60. Ibid., 14–15.

61. Ibid., 15.

62. Ibid., 17; see also memo from Haig to Kissinger, "Reconnaissance Flights Targeted on North Korea," 30 April 1969, Haig Chronological File, NSC Files, box 956, Nixon Collection, NARA.

63. "The EC-121 Incident," 17–18.

64. Document labeled "Option II, B" attached to "The EC-121 Incident" and contained in "History Office Research Projects 1969–1974," box 6, RG 59, NARA.

65. Untitled memo addressing U.S. statements to be made in Panmunjom after notional retaliation, 17 April 1969, and memo entitled "Possible Security Council Action in Event of Armed Reconnaissance Mission against North Korea," 17 April 1969, both attached to "The EC-121 Incident."

66. Nixon, *RN*, 475; Haldeman, *Haldeman Diaries*, 65.

67. U.S. Seventh Fleet, "Monthly Historical Summary," April 1969, 54, NHC.

68. Ibid., 54, 67. Once the United States withdrew its carriers from the Sea of Japan, Soviet aerial reconnaissance became more problematic. The Seventh Fleet retained a GCI-capable picket ship in the Sea of Japan to help protect PARPRO missions; however, Soviet aircraft made several high-speed, low-altitude runs against it. Secretary of Defense Laird warned that such flights were "significantly more dangerous in view of heightened tensions in the Sea of Japan" and because North Korea used similar aircraft, and asked for a démarche calling for Moscow to desist. Letter from Secretary of Defense to Secretary of State, 26 August 1969, folder "POL 33-6 US-USSR 1/1/67," Central Foreign Policy Files, box 2668, RG 59, NARA.

69. CINCPACFLT, "Fleet Operations Review," April 1969, 108, NHC.

70. JCS 210225Z April 1969, "Task Force Operations," 21 April 1969, folder "Chairman's Messages 1 January 1969–30 April 1969," Wheeler Records, box 161, RG 218, NARA; U.S. Seventh Fleet, "Monthly Historical Summary," April 1969, 57, NHC.

71. U.S. Seventh Fleet, "Monthly Historical Summary," April 1969, 58–59, NHC.

72. "The EC-121 Incident," 20.

73. CINCPAC Command History, 1969, 4:141, NHC; U.S. Seventh Fleet, "Monthly Historical Summary," April 1969, 57, NHC.

74. CINCPAC 282130Z April 1969, "Seventh Fleet Operations," 28 April 1969, RG 218, NARA.

75. JCS 172324Z June 1969, "Seventh Fleet Operations," RG 218, and JCS 052225Z May 1969, both in folder "Chairman's Messages 1 August 1969–30 September 1969," Wheeler Records, box 161, RG 218, NARA. Secretary of Defense Laird advised that one attack carrier with A-6s should be kept within twenty-six hours' steaming time of the Sea of Japan until 25 May. After that, another carrier (not necessarily A-6 equipped) would be in Sasebo, Japan, or at least in a position to respond quickly, twenty to thirty days of every month. Memo from Haig to Kissinger, 2 May, "Haig Chronology May, 2 of 2," Haig Chronological File, NSC Files, box 956, Nixon Collection, NARA.

76. CINCPAC 010542Z May 1969, "Seventh Fleet Operations," folder "Chairman's Messages 1 January 1969–30 April 1969," Wheeler Records, box 161, RG 218, NARA.

77. JCS 172324Z June 1969, "Seventh Fleet Operations," folder "Chairman's Messages 1 January 1969–30 April 1969," Wheeler Records, box 161, RG 218, NARA.

78. JCS 181808Z April 1969, "Resumption of Reconnaissance in the Sea of Japan," folder "Chairman's Messages 1 January 1969–30 April 1969," Wheeler Records, box 161, RG 218, NARA.

79. JCS 182051Z April 1969, "Resumption of Reconnaissance in the Sea of Japan," 18 April 1969, folder "Chairman's Messages 1 January 1969–30 April 1969," Wheeler Records, box 161, RG 218, NARA.

80. CTF Seven One 232326Z April 1969, "SOJ Recce Ops," 23 April 1969, Double Zero Files 1969, NHC. Severe weather led to the cancellation of the over-water portion of the Commando Royal track. See CTU 240200Z April 1969, "Commando Royal," 24 April 1969, Double Zero Files 1969, NHC.

81. Nixon, *RN*, 476; 556 RECONSQ [Reconnaissance Squadron] YOKOTA 210530Z April 1969, Double Zero Files 1969, NHC; JCS 231747Z April 1969, "Reconnaissance Missions," 23 April 1969, and JCS 291856Z April 1969, "Reconnaissance Missions," 29 April 1969, both in folder "Chairman's Messages 1 January 1969–30 April 1969," Wheeler Records, box 161, RG 218, NARA.

82. White House memo for Secretary of State, Secretary of Defense, and DCI, "U.S. Fighter Aircraft Operating as Combat Air Patrol in Support of Reconnaissance Missions Targeted on North Korea," 30 April 1969, as cited in "The EC-121 Incident," 16; CNO Briefing Notes, 1 May 1969, CNO Notes/Operations Summary, May 1969, NHC.

83. CINCPAC 281230Z April 1969, "Seventh Fleet Operations," JCS 292233Z April 1969, "Task Force Operations," 29 April 1969, and CINCPAC 292233Z April 1969, all in folder "Chairman's Messages 1 January 1969–30 April 1969," Wheeler Records, box 161, RG 218, NARA.

84. CINCPAC, "Plan for Protection of Reconnaissance Aircraft in Korean Area," 22 April 1969, and Joint Staff, "Point Paper for the Chairman, JCS, for a meeting with the SecDef on 24 April 1969—Resumption of Reconnaissance," undated, both in folder "091 Korea (BP) EC-121 Shootdown," Wheeler Records, box 31, RG 218, NARA.

85. Ibid.; and memo from Kissinger to Secretary of State, Secretary of Defense, DCI, and CJCS, "Seventh Fleet Operations and Resumption of Reconnaissance in the Korean Area," 26 April 1969, folder "091 Korea (BP) EC-121 Shootdown," Wheeler Records, box 31, RG 218, NARA.

86. Joint Staff, "Point Paper for the Chairman, JCS, for a Meeting with the SecDef on 24 April 1969—Resumption of Reconnaissance," undated, Wheeler Records, box 31, RG 218, NARA.

87. VQ-1 Command History, 28 February 1970, 8, NHC; memo, POL/PW "ROE," 10 September 1969, folder "Military 1969 ROE," lot files, Office of Korean Affairs 1966–74, box 3, RG 59, NARA.

88. Nixon, *RN*, 385.

89. Kissinger, *White House Years*, 321.

90. Memo from Haig to Kissinger, untitled, 28 April 1969, folder "Haig Chronology April 1969, 1 of 2," Haig Chronological File, NSC Files, box 956, Nixon Collection, NARA; emphasis added.

91. Haig, *Inner Circles*, 206.

92. Kissinger, *White House Years*, 321.

93. Message from British embassy, Washington, to FCO, 23 April 1969, FCO 21/617, PRO.

94. Nixon press conference, 18 April 1969, in *Weekly Compendium of Presidential*

*Documents,* 21 April 1969; telegram from British embassy, Washington, to FCO, 29 April 1969, and speaking notes from James Murray for Secretary of State, 30 April 1969, FCO 21/617, PRO.

95. Memo from James Murray, "U.S. Reaction to Further Military Provocations by North Korea," 4 July 1969, FCO 21/617, FCO.

## *Chapter 9.* Lessons Learned

1. Memo from General Wheeler to Director, Joint Staff, "EC-121 Shootdown," 17 April 1969, file "EC-121 Shootdown," Wheeler Records, box 31, RG 218, NARA.

2. JCS 191517Z April 1969, as cited as reference in CINCPAC 220213Z April 1969, "Plan for Protection of Reconnaissance Aircraft in Korean Area," 22 April 1969, folder "091 Korea (BP) EC-121 Shootdown," Wheeler Records, box 31, RG 218, NARA; COM-SEVENTHFLT 200204Z April 1969, "Court of Investigation for Loss of EC-121 in Sea of Japan," 20 April 1969, Double Zero Files 1969, NHC.

3. Letter, Vice Adm. N. C. Johnson to Dr. Kissinger, 21 April 1969, file "EC-121 Shootdown," box 31, RG 218, NARA.

4. Memo from Acting Chairman, JCS, to Vice Director, Joint Staff, "JCS Ad Hoc Fact Finding Body," 5 May 1969, folder "EC-121 Shootdown," box "Wheeler Files 091 Korea," box 31, RG 218, NARA.

5. Memo from Deputy Secretary of Defense, "Review of Vulnerable Intelligence Collection," 29 May 1969, folder "Review of Vulnerable Intelligence Collection," NSC Files, subject files, box 332, Nixon Collection, NARA.

6. Ibid.

7. Seymour Hersh, *The Target Is Destroyed* (New York: Random House, 1986), 221.

8. Some of the ships were decommissioned in 1969. This would suggest that the decision to scrap them probably occurred before the shootdown—perhaps as an outgrowth of the *Pueblo* and *Liberty* incidents.

9. Memo from P. Henze (NSC) to Zbigniew Brzezinski, "March Reconnaissance Schedule," 24 February 1979, Digital National Security Archive, George Washington University, Washington, D.C. Of the March 1979 missions, 150 were in response to national tasking, 231 resulted from theater tasking, and 49 were for fleet support.

10. Memo from Director, Joint Staff, to CJCS, "Spread Sheet—EC-121 Incident," 28 June 1969, file "EC-121 Shootdown," box 31, RG 218, NARA.

11. Hersh, *The Target Is Destroyed,* 221.

12. Oral history, Adm. John Hyland Jr., interview designated "Hyland #6-355," 31 May 1984, U.S. Naval Institute.

13. CINCPAC 220334Z June 1969, "Information and Communications Procedures in Emergencies," 22 June 1969, folder "Chairman's Messages 1 May 1969–30 July 1969," Wheeler Records, box 161, RG 218, NARA.

14. CINCPAC 150534Z July 1969, "Information and Communications Procedures in Emergencies," folder "Chairman's Messages 1 May 1969–30 July 1969," Wheeler Records, box 161, RG 218, NARA.

15. Report of the C3 subcommittee of the House Armed Services Committee, "Review of Department of Defense Worldwide Communications Phase I," 10 May 1971.

16. Haldeman, *Haldeman Diaries*, 65.

17. Memo from Henry Kissinger, "Contingency Planning for Korea," National Security Study Memo 34, 21 March 1969, Digital National Security Archive, George Washington University; message, JCS ("personal for" from General Wheeler), "Retaliatory Strike against the Changjin Power Plant in North Korea," 3 June 1969, and message, JCS (J-3), "Retaliatory Strike against the Changjin Power Plant in North Korea," 4 June 1969, both in folder "Korea 1 May 1969–31 August 1969," Wheeler Records, box 30, RG 218, NARA.

18. CINCPAC Command History 1969, 4:147, NHC.

19. British Foreign Office Far Eastern Section, "Changes in the North Korean Workers' Party Leadership since 1966," 30 September 1970, FCO 23/774, PRO.

20. Suh, *Kim Il Sung*, 248.

21. U.S. embassy, Seoul, 280030Z September 1969, "Internal Security: Status of NK Infiltration," 28 September 1969, folder, "POL 23-7 1/1/69," Central Foreign Policy Files 1967–1969, box 2281, RG 59, NARA.

22. Memo from W. Brown to Ambassador Johnson, "Basing of U.S. Strip Alert Planes at Tainan Airfield on Taiwan—Action Memo," 29 May 1969, Digital National Security Archive, George Washington University.

23. CINCPAC Command History 1969, 1:135, NHC.

24. Ibid. The JCS requirement for continued airborne fighter protection is not surprising because the intelligence community had finally released an assessment warning that the North might attempt additional attacks on U.S. naval and air assets. In mid-1969 the CIA wrote that Pyongyang might attempt provocations against U.S. personnel and installations in the South as well as "further attacks" on U.S. ships or aircraft that may offer targets of opportunity. CIA Intelligence Memo, "North Korean Political Strategy," 8 August 1969, available on the CIA's website as of 20 July 2003 (http://www.cia.gov).

25. CINCPAC Command History, 1970, 2:383, NHC.

26. John Singlaub, "Army Regroups 1973–1976," in *Hazardous Duty* (New York: Summit Books, 1991); hereinafter cited as Singlaub, "Army Regroups."

27. See ibid. for a detailed theater perspective of the tree-trimming incident. My discussion borrows heavily from that text.

28. Ibid.; see also Federation of Atomic Scientists web page article, "Operation Paul Bunyan 'Tree/Hatchet Incident' 18 August 1976" (www.fas.org/man/dod-101/ops/paul bunyan.htm as of July 2002).

29. National Security Council, "Minutes," 18 August 1976, DDRS digital document 1996010100431, fiche 1996-33, DDRS.

30. State Department, Korea Working Group Action Spreadsheet, 19 August 1976, DDRS digital document 199601010234, fiche 1996-20, DDRS.

31. The Wild Weasels carried missiles designed to destroy North Korean radar sites, particularly those associated with the high-threat SA-2 surface-to-air missiles.

32. Singlaub ("Army Regroups") noted that as the United States refined its targeting solution on North Korean radar sites as a result of these flights, U.S. Forces Korea ordered that Nike Hercules surface-to-air missiles be put in the surface-to-surface mode. Had the North fired on the SR-71, U.S. Forces Korea could have launched the Nike Hercules missiles against the offending SAM radar sites within minutes.

33. Quote from *1976 Annual History Report, United Nations Command/United States Forces, Korea/Eighth Army,* as cited in Singlaub, "Army Regroups."

34. Singlaub, "Army Regroups."

35. Ibid.

36. Kissinger, *White House Years,* 317.

37. Singlaub ("Army Regroups") felt that there was a fifty-fifty chance of war breaking out when the UN Command forces cut down the tree.

38. *New York Times,* 28 August 1981, 1; Foreign Broadcast Information Service, *FBIS Trends,* 1 September 1982, 17, DDRS; U.S. Eighth Army, Annual Report, 1981, 27, Oberdorfer Collection, National Security Archive, George Washington University.

39. Korean Central News Agency, 30 December 1999, 30 June 2003.

40. Pyongyang Korean Central Broadcasting Station 312200Z May 2000.


## *Chapter 10.* Conclusions

1. Henry Kissinger advised President Nixon that twenty-four aircraft had been attacked or damaged worldwide between 1949 and 1969, and another seventeen had been downed. Memo, Kissinger to Nixon, "Incidents since 1949," 17 April 1969, folder "Incidents since 1949," NSC Files, box 332, Nixon Collection, NARA; DOD chart provided for HASC Hearings, 922.

2. Richard Betts, *Surprise Attack* (Washington, D.C.: Brookings Institute, 1982), 119; emphasis added.

3. Ibid., 122.

4. Source is Reuters report summarized on USS *Pueblo* Association website (www.usspueblo.org).

5. Betts, *Surprise Attack,* 128.

6. Ibid., 96.

7. Korean Central News Agency, 30 December 2002; Bradley Graham, "North Korea Trails U.S. Spy Plane," *Washington Post,* 4 March 2003; E. Schmitt, "North Korean Fliers Said to Have Sought Hostages," *New York Times,* 8 March 2003.

8. Ibid.

9. In open session, General Wheeler told the HASC subcommittee that in executive session he would provide them a list of steps taken since *Pueblo.* The list may have included proposed changes within NSA or DIA, but I did not find it in my research. See HASC Hearings, 919.

# BIBLIOGRAPHY

## Archival and Special Collections

Declassified Documents Reference System

Lyndon B. Johnson Library, Austin, Texas

    Audiovisual Archives (still photo collection)

    National Security Files

        Country Files, Korea, boxes 255–64

        Files of Walt Rostow, boxes 1, 10

        National Security Council History, *Pueblo Crisis,* 1968, boxes 27–37

    Papers of Clark Clifford, box 17

    Tom Johnson Meeting Notes, boxes 2–4

National Archives and Records Administration, College Park, Maryland

    Central Files, Korea, 1967–69, boxes 2254–61, Record Group 59

    National Security Council Report on the *Pueblo* Incident, Donated Papers of Robert McNamara, Record Group 200

    National Security Files, Richard M. Nixon Collection

    Office of Executive Secretariat, lot files, Record Group 59

    Records of U.S. Joint Chiefs of Staff, Records of Chairman (Gen.) Earle Wheeler, 1964–70, boxes 160–61; and folder "091 Korea," boxes 29–30, Record Group 218

    U.S. Naval History Still Photographs, Record Group 428

National Security Archive, George Washington University, Washington, D.C.

    Digitized National Security Archive

    Donald Oberdorfer Korea Material Collection

Naval Historical Center, Washington, D.C.

    Naval Aviation History Branch

    Command Histories

    Operational Archives Branch

        CINCPAC Command Histories 1968–69

        CNO Double Zero Files

        Seventh Fleet Summaries

UK Public Records Office, Kew Gardens, United Kingdom

    Records of Foreign and Commonwealth Office Records and Its Predecessors (FCO)

    Records of Ministry of Defence (DEFE)

## Nonarchival Primary Sources

BBC Monitoring Service. *Daily Reports.* April 1969. London: Her Majesty's Stationary Office, 1969.

Nixon, R. *Public Papers of the Presidents, Richard Nixon, 1969.* Washington, D.C.: U.S. Government Printing Office, 1971.

U.S. Congress. House Armed Services Committee. *Hearings before the Special Subcommittee on the USS* Pueblo. HASC 91-101. Washington, D.C.: U.S. Government Printing Office, 1969.

———. *Review of Department of Defense Worldwide Communications. Phase I, 10 May 1971.* Washington, D.C.: U.S. Government Printing Office, 1971.

———. Special Subcommittee on the USS *Pueblo. Inquiry into the USS* Pueblo *and EC-121 Plane Incidents.* HASC 91-12. Washington, D.C.: U.S. Government Printing Office, 1969.

U.S. Department of State. *Foreign Relations of the United States 1964–1968.* Volume 29, part 1: *Korea.* Washington, D.C.: U.S. Government Printing Office, 2000.

## Oral Histories

Lyndon B. Johnson Library, Austin, Texas
Oral History of Paul Warnke, 1971
U.S. Army Military History Institute, Carlisle Barracks, Pennsylvania
General Charles Bonesteel III Oral History, 1972
U.S. Naval Institute, Annapolis, Maryland
Oral Histories of Adm. John Hyland, 1984; Adm. U. S. Grant Sharp, 1970; Adm. Thomas Moorer, 1976

## Secondary Sources

Armbrister, Trevor. *A Matter of Accountability: The True Story of the* Pueblo *Affair.* New York: Coward-McCann, 1969.

Ball, George W. *The Past Has Another Pattern: Memoirs.* New York: W. W. Norton, 1982.

Bamford, James. *Body of Secrets.* New York: Doubleday, 2001.

Bucher, Lloyd. *Bucher: My Story.* Garden City, N.Y.: Doubleday, 1970.

Downs, Chuck. *Over the Line: North Korea's Negotiating Strategy.* Washington, D.C.: American Enterprise Institute Press, 1999.

Ennis, James. *Assault on the* Liberty. New York: Ivy Books, 1979.

Haig, Alexander. *Inner Circles: How America Changed the World.* New York: Warner Books, 1991.

Haldeman, H. R. *Ends of Power.* New York: Times Books, 1978.

———. *The Haldeman Diaries.* New York: Berkeley Books, 1995.

Hersh, Seymour. *Price of Power: Kissinger in the Nixon White House.* New York: Summit Books, 1983.

Isaacson, Walter. *Kissinger: A Biography.* New York: Simon and Schuster, 1992.

Jackson, Robert. *High Cold War.* Somerset, England: Patrick Stephens, 1998.

Johnson, Lyndon. *The Vantage Point.* New York: Holt, Rinehart and Winston, 1971.

Kissinger, Henry. *The White House Years.* Boston: Little, Brown, 1979.

Koh, B. C. "The *Pueblo* Incident in Perspective." *Asian Survey* 91 (January–June 1969): 264–80.

Lee, Hy-Sang. *North Korea: A Strange Socialist Fortress.* Westport, Conn.: Praeger, 2001.

Lerner, Mitchell. *The* Pueblo *Incident: A Spy Ship and the Failure of American Foreign Policy.* Kansas: University Press of Kansas, 2002.

Mobley, R. "EC-121 Down!" *Naval Institute Proceedings* 127 (August 2001): 62–66.

———. "Pueblo: A Retrospective." *Naval War College Review* 54 (Spring 2001): 98–118.

Nixon, Richard. *RN: Memoirs of Richard Nixon.* New York: Grosset and Dunlap, 1978.

RAND Corporation. *The Operational Assessment of Risk: A Case Study of the* Pueblo *Mission.* Santa Monica, Calif.: RAND Corporation, 1971.

Sarantakes, Nicholas. "The Quiet War: Combat Operations along the Korean Demilitarized Zone." *Military History* 64 (April 2000): 439–58.

Scalapino, Robert, and Chong-Sik Lee. *Communism in Korea.* 2 vols. Berkeley: University of California Press, 1972.

Singlaub, John. *Hazardous Duty.* New York: Summit Books, 1991.

Suh, Dae-Sook. *Kim Il Sung: The North Korean Leader.* New York: Columbia University Press, 1988.

Tart, Larry, and Robert Keefe. *The Price of Vigilance: Attacks on American Surveillance Flights.* New York: Ballantine Books, 2001.

# INDEX

A-12 Oxcarts: as difficult targets, 105; flight over North Korea, 54
A-6s: availability of, 135–36; strike plans and, 128
advisory system, 145
aerial reconnaissance, 157–58. *See also* reconnaissance missions
AGER (auxiliary general environmental research vessel): contingency planning for, 94; elimination of, 145; paradox of collection and, 22; relevance of, 97; support needed for, 90; tasking of, 93
AGIs: freedom of the seas and, 159; monitoring of task force and, 134
AGTR (auxiliary general technical research vessel), 23; contingency planning for, 94; elimination of, 145
airborne protection, 117
aircraft: disposition of, 43–44; in the theatre, 65–66. *See also* specific aircraft
airfields: possible attacks on, 126. *See also* specific airfields
Air Force, North Korean (NKAF): aircraft of, 65–66; air superiority of, 5, 18–19; EC-121 shootdown and, 1, 105, 106; naval support and, 33; reactions to reconnaissance aircraft, 99–103, 163; sensitivity about Wonsan, 27
Air Force, ROK: disposition of aircraft, 43–44; growth of, 154
Air Force, U.S.: disposition of aircraft, 43–44; force buildup of, 69–70, 119; increasing air defense readiness, 49; recommendations of, 52; vulnerability of aircraft in ROK, 83–84; war preparations, 1
air munitions, 72
Air National Guard, 150
air strikes: elimination of, 62; possibility of, 59, 123–24
air-to-air missiles, 99–100

ammunition, possible shortfalls of, 52, 72
antiballistic missile systems, 124
antisubmarine warfare support, 67
apology to North Korea, 88–89
armada, 134
Armbrister, Trevor, 4, 33
armistice violations, 131–32
Army, ROK, 17
Army, U.S.: attempts to increase manpower, 71; divisions in ROK, 9
assassination, 5, 15. *See also* Blue House raid
*Assault on the Liberty,* 95
Atsugi Air Station: as base for VQ-1, 106; board of investigation at, 143–44

B-52s, 129, 151
Badger bombers, 134
Ball, George, 91–92
Ball Report, 157–58
*Banner,* USS: decommission of, 145; missions of, 23–25, 67; possible positioning on North Korean coast, 60, 62; Soviet encounter with, 69
Bar Locks radar, 99, 111
barrier combat air patrols, 138
Bear bombers, 134
behavior, of North Korea, 5–6, 20–21, 103
Berger, Samuel, 75
Betts, Richard, 158–60
Black Shield aircraft: A-12 Oxcarts as, 54, 105; disapproval of missions over North Korea, 27; possible resumption of missions, 63; results of mission over North Korea, 55, 82; SR-71s as, 105, 152, 154
blockades: as economic pressure, 62; possibility of, 59–60
Blue House raid: events of, 15; influence on U.S. intelligence collection, 39; influence on U.S.–ROK relations, 76; Pyongyang's state of alertness and, 41

Collett (DD-730), 47
combat air patrol (CAP), C-130 flights and, 137
command and control: changes to, 155; flawed communication within, 140; lessons-learned topics and, 93; need to consult and, 38; of North Korea, 110; orders to tighten, 120; PARPRO and, 142; response to *Pueblo* incident and, 40; reviews of, 144
Commando Clinch, 161
communications systems: mishandling of message traffic, 3–4; security of, 49; shortfalls of, 146–47, 163–64
communism, 123
Communist Party's Liaison Bureau, 17–18
COMNAVFORJAPAN (Commander, Naval Forces Japan): plans for *Pueblo* patrols, 24–25; request for assistance, 42–43; risk assessment for USS *Pueblo* and, 28–29, 38
COMSEVENTHFLEET (Commander, Seventh Fleet), 9, 127. *See also* Seventh Fleet
COMUSFK (Commander in Chief, U.S. Forces Korea): concerns about war, 6; hats of, 9–10; initial responses to seizure, 45–49; manpower shortages and, 73; need for intelligence collection, 26–27; need for SNIE on North Korea, 100–101; on North Korean behavior prior to shootdown, 106; preparations for war and, 71–73; preparing the ROK for war, 84–85; reservations about USS *Pueblo* patrol, 29, 38; ROK's desire for retaliation, 76–77; ROK relations and, 24, 43; role in incidents, 2. *See also* EC-121 incident; USFK
Congress, U.S.: communications shortfalls and, 146–47; hearings of, 142; search for scapegoats, 26
contingency planning: for AGER/AGTRs, 94; CINCPAC and, 65–66; for EC-121 incident, 125–31; historical record and, 7; lack of prepared plans, 147, 164–65; during *Pueblo* negotiations, 80–82; review of, 142; for tree-trimming incident, 153; Wheeler's criticisms of, 92
Coral Sea, USS, 78
counterair capability, 118–19

crew: of the EC-121, 106, 121; negotiations and, 73; Pyongyang's attitude towards, 56–57; release of, 89; reports from, 41–42; threats to put on trial, 73–74, 75; treatment of, 1
crisis management: EC-121 incident and, 121, 124; upgraded command posts and, 146. *See also* contingency planning
Critical Collection Problems Committee, 27
cryptographic material, 62
CTF 69 (Commander, Task Force 69), 23
Cuba, 95
CVA (attack aircraft carrier): need for in Sea of Japan, 136; positioning of, 125; withdrawal from theatre, 77–78

Dae-Sook Suh: conclusions about partisan generals, 149; explanation of North Korea's buildup, 13
*Dale*, USS (DLG-19), 112
DCI (director of Central Intelligence): advice to Johnson, 81; approval of mission schedules, 32; Korea Working Group options and, 62–63; North Korean media and, 35; opposition to military retaliation, 123, 134; role in incidents, 9
decision makers, U.S.: after seizure, 49–53; after shootdown, 117; distrust of North Korea and, 8; frustration over lack of contingency plans, 164–65; options considered, 4; pattern analysis and, 160; range of concerns, 21; Vietnam War and, 77. *See also* lessons-learned; specific decision makers
DEFCON (Defense Readiness Condition), 45, 47–48, 151
Defender Station, 118, 135
defensive patrols, 31
Democratic People's Republic of Korea (DPRK): air and air defense forces of, 18–19, 126; anomalous behavior of, 5–6; attitude of, 20–21, 101; balance of power, 16; demands of, 79–80; desire for unification and, 56; economic and political vulnerabilities of, 12, 16, 57–58, 62–63; First Army of, 71–72; ground forces of, 17–18; inappropriate technology of, 104; infiltration by, 49, 71; intentions of, 8, 55; motivations for EC-121 shootdown, 103–6; naval forces of, 19;

Korean Worker's Party, 36, 148
Korea Task Force: EC-121 incident and, 122; information gaps and, 82; military action and, 74; repositioning of *Enterprise* and, 75
Korea Working Group: EC-121 incident and, 122; options studied by, 74–75; range of actions developed by, 151; "think papers" summaries, 59–63
Kosygin, Aleksei, 74, 75–76
Kotlin destroyer, 68, 134
KPA (Korean People's Army): ground forces of, 17–18; heightened alert of military, 55; Kim's criticisms of, 104; understanding of capabilities, 4
Krupynyy destroyer, 68, 134
Kunsan Air Base, 69, 72
Kuter, Laurence, 91–92
Kwanju, 69
Kynda-class cruisers, 68

Laird, Melvin: freedom of the seas and, 89; Nixon on retaliation and, 124; opposition to military retaliation, 123, 134; safety of recce sorties and, 139. *See also* NCA
land-based aircraft, advantages of, 126–27
leadership. *See* decision makers
Leonard, James: role in incidents, 2; summary of shootdown episode, 140–41. *See also* Department of State, U.S.
Lerner, Mitch, 86–87
lessons-learned: about intelligence collection, 90–92, 143–48; changes to operations, 154–55; command and control topics, 93; process after incidents, 6; risk assessment and, 36–39, 93–94; rules of engagement and, 96–97; support of missions and, 96–96. *See also* tree-trimming incident
Liaison Bureau, 104
*Logic of Craziness, The,* 159–60

*Mahan,* USS (DLG-11), 112
manpower shortages: of the KPA, 17; of USFK, 52, 73
Marine Corps, U.S., readiness preparations of, 119
maritime blockades, 57
Maritime Self-Defense Force, 89
Marocchi, John, 29–30

*Matter of Accountability, A* 4
McCain, John: contingency options and, 147–48; desire for retaliation and, 125–26, 127–28; force buildup and, 166; response to shootdown and, 116–17; role in incidents, 2. *See also* CINCPAC
McConnell, John, 144
McDonald, David, 91–92
McKee, Seth, 24, 44
McNamara, Robert, 50, 53, 91
MDL (Military Demarcation Line), 27
media: North Korean, 5, 35–36, 112–13, 159, 162–63; United States, 35
*Midway,* USS, 152
MiG-17s, 99
MiG-21 Fishbeds: inventory of North Korea, 18; role in shootdown, 104–5, 110–12
Military Armistice Commission, 73, 114–15, 131–32
military intelligence. *See* intelligence collection
Military Sea Transportation Service, 72
mining, of harbors, 60, 65, 126
mirror imaging, 159
missile control radar, 99
Mitchell, John, 144
monitoring, of EC-121, 109
Moorer, Thomas, 52, 61
Mountain Home Air Force Base, 152

Najin, 56
National Military Command Center, 95–96
national security, intelligence community's contributions to, 2–4
National Security Council, 7
naval blockades: as economic pressure, 62; possibility of, 59–60
Naval Court of Inquiry: mission approval and, 28, 34–35; review of *Pueblo* incident, 92–93
Naval Forces Europe, 90
Navy, DPRK, sensitivity of, 33
Navy, ROK, operation preparations, 66
Navy, Soviet, 23
Navy, U.S.: failure to respond to *Pueblo* incident, 3; force buildup of, 66–71, 117–18; release of buildup ships, 77–78; response to shootdown, 135; restricted resources of, 140; restriction on North Korea's coast and, 89; review of *Pueblo* incident, 92–93; war preparations of, 1

# ABOUT THE AUTHOR

**Richard A. Mobley** is a retired naval intelligence officer. He served as Chief of Indications and Warning at U.S. Forces Korea headquarters. He also was concerned with North Korea as chief of the research department at the former Fleet Ocean Surveillance Information Facility in Kami Seya, Japan, and during two western Pacific deployments aboard USS *Enterprise*. He is currently an intelligence analyst for the U.S. government.